W9-CPB-266

WOMEN'S STUDIES QUARTERLY

VOLUME 42   NUMBERS 1 & 2   SPRING/SUMMER 2014

An educational project of the Feminist Press at the City University of New York and the
Center for the Study of Women and Society at The Graduate Center, City University of New York

EDITORS
Amy Herzog, Queens College and The Graduate Center, City University of New York
Joe Rollins, Queens College and The Graduate Center, City University of New York

GUEST EDITORS
Rosalind Petchesky, Hunter College and The Graduate Center, CUNY
Meena Alexander, Hunter College and The Graduate Center, CUNY

ART EDITOR
Margot Bouman

FICTION/NONFICTION/PROSE EDITOR
Nicole Cooley

POETRY EDITOR
Kathleen Ossip

EDITORIAL ASSISTANTS
Elena Cohen
Lindsey Eckenroth

EDITORS EMERITAE
Victoria Pitts-Taylor 2008–2011 ▪ Talia Schaffer 2008–2011
Cindi Katz 2004–2008 ▪ Nancy K. Miller 2004–2008
Diane Hope 2000–2004 ▪ Janet Zandy 1995–2000
Nancy Porter 1982–1992 ▪ Florence Howe 1972–1982; 1993–1994

The Feminist Press at the City University of New York
EXECUTIVE DIRECTOR
Jennifer Baumgardner

EDITORIAL DIRECTOR
Amy Scholder

SENIOR EDITOR
Jeanann Pannasch

EDITORIAL ASSISTANT
Julia Berner-Tobin

ART DIRECTOR
Drew Stevens

WSQ: Women's Studies Quarterly, a peer-reviewed, theme-based journal, is published in the summer and winter by the Feminist Press at the City University of New York, The Graduate Center, 365 Fifth Avenue, Suite 5406, New York, NY 10016.

COVER ART
"... whatever she saw go on in that barn," by Nell Painter. Digital collage on paper. © 2013 Nell Painter. For more information, see page 183.

WEBSITE
feministpress.org/wsq

EDITORIAL CORRESPONDENCE
WSQ: Women's Studies Quarterly, The Feminist Press at the City University of New York, The Graduate Center, 365 Fifth Avenue, Suite 5406, New York, NY 10016; wsqeditorial@gmail.com.

PRINT SUBSCRIPTIONS
Subscribers in the United States: Individuals—$40 for 1 year; $90 for 3 years. Students—$28 for 1 year. (Student subscribers must provide a photocopy of current student identification.) Institutions—$75 for 1 year; $180 for 3 years. Subscribers outside the United States: Add $25 per year for delivery; add $50 per year for expedited delivery. To subscribe or change an address, contact WSQ Customer Service, The Feminist Press at the City University of New York, The Graduate Center, 365 Fifth Avenue, Suite 5406, New York, NY 10016; 212-817-7915; info@feministpress.org.

FORTHCOMING ISSUES
Solidarities, Shefali Chandra, Washington University in St. Louis, and Saadia Toor, College of Staten Island, City University of New York
Child, Sarah Chinn, Hunter College, City University of New York, and Anna Mae Duane, University of Connecticut

RIGHTS & PERMISSIONS
Fred Courtright, The Permissions Company, 570-839-7477; permdude@eclipse.net.

SUBMISSION INFORMATION
For the most up-to-date guidelines, calls for papers, and information concerning forthcoming issues, write to WSQ: Women's Studies Quarterly at the Feminist Press at the City University of New York, wsqeditorial@gmail.com, or visit feministpress.org/wsq.

ADVERTISING
For information on display-ad sizes, rates, exchanges, and schedules, please write to WSQ Marketing, the Feminist Press at the City University of New York, The Graduate Center, 365 Fifth Avenue, Suite 5406, New York, NY 10016; 212-817-7915; marketing@feministpress.org.

ELECTRONIC ACCESS AND SUBSCRIPTIONS
Access to electronic databases containing backlist issues of WSQ may be purchased through JSTOR at www.jstor.org. Access to electronic databases containing current issues of WSQ may be purchased through Project Muse at muse.jhu.edu, muse@muse.jhu.edu; and ProQuest at www.il.proquest.com, info@il.proquest.com. Individual electronic subscriptions for WSQ may also be purchased through Project MUSE.

ISSN: 0732-1562   ISBN: 978-155861-854-1 $25.00

Contents

Editors' Note: The Teaching Poor

To admit to one's own poverty and debt, as an academic, is to step into a minefield of shame and self-doubt, even within feminist circles. To be sure, many feminist scholars have labored intensely to document structural economic injustice around the globe, and a large number of academics productively extend their research into practices of advocacy and activism. Most of us have been trained to recognize that the personal is the political. That does not necessarily make it easier to disclose that one is in debt or struggling to pay one's bills, particularly to colleagues or advisors. Poverty is something that happens to someone else, or that one can proudly claim to have overcome in the historical past (neoliberal-bootstrap stories abound, but they can also function as a moral reproach to those currently in debt, a status that still smacks of a personal failure). Poverty is something we research, not something we experience or are complicit in, certainly not within our own departments.

And yet many of us are in debt and struggling with poverty. Contingent faculty comprise the majority of the academic workforce, and fewer and fewer PhDs entering the field can expect to find fulltime employment. Most students in the United States graduate in debt, and they owe significantly more than in previous years.[1] The economic crisis in academia disproportionately impacts women, who are paid less than their male colleagues (based both on rank and overrepresentation at lower-paying institutions), are less likely to receive tenure, are more likely to head single-parent households, and are more likely to work as contingent faculty, particularly in the humanities (Schell 1998; Mason and Goulden 2004; Finley 2009). Even those who secure coveted tenure-track positions are

WSQ: Women's Studies Quarterly 42: 1 & 2 (Spring/Summer 2014)

not immune from the economic crisis, particularly when teaching at public institutions where research and travel funds are limited and workloads are heavy. The line between contingent and fulltime faculty blurs, too, when one considers that many tenure track faculty began their careers as adjuncts, accruing increased debt along the way.

With so much at stake, it is critical for feminist scholarship to address the economic crisis within academia head-on. As evidenced by the heated exchanges that have recently erupted via social media, the process will be a painful one (Potter 2013; Schuman 2013). Yet those among us who have the privilege of job security bear a responsibility—to the students we are training and the contingent faculty who support our positions—to advocate for more equitable working conditions and a sustainable field. To do so, however, requires confronting a seemingly insurmountable and deeply entrenched system, one in which we are all insidiously imbricated. We are in dire need of a frank conversation about the nature of debt, about its history and temporal nuances, about the ways in which it binds and severs ties between various actants, about its psychological machinations, and our own participation within its cycles.

Rosalind Petchesky and Meena Alexander's intervention into these waters could not be more timely. *Debt* offers an inspired and often startling take on the multifaceted nature of indebtedness. These range from Monica Johnson's graphic novel depicting the struggles of a loan-burdened graduate, to Nell Painter's meditation on *Beloved*, to a roster of chapters grappling with questions of reparations, refusals, credit, "feminist indebtedness," gratitude, and the fraught economies of care-based labor. The global focus of these interdisciplinary efforts, which include significant feminist and queer critiques of prevailing discourses on debt, dovetail into both activist and artistic proposals for upending paradigms of obligation. It is a collection that significantly advances our understanding of the gendered nature of debt.

Given the deep-seated ways in which the shame of debt can be internalized (and ignored), we are particularly pleased to feature Janet Yoon's haunting portrait of "The Formerly Middle Class" for this issue's Alerts and Provocations. Yoon, an architect and design researcher, takes a spatial approach to the slow economic decline experienced by many U.S. households. As people shift into decreasingly stable and often nomadic domiciles, their experience of urban space is transformed. The formerly middle class are not typically "visible" as homeless; taking advantage of mobile technologies and resources accrued from their former lives, they operate within "slack" spaces in their communities (libraries, gyms, universities, and parking lots), exerting huge amounts of labor to maintain some semblance of normalcy and routine. We are struck by the resonances between Yoon's project and Ira Steward's 1873 commentary on middle-class poverty (reprinted in this issue courtesy of Stuart Ewen). The burden of keeping up appearances continues to shape the culture of poverty in complex and counterintuitive ways.

As we reach the end of our term as the general editors of *WSQ*, the subject of debt proves especially poignant. We owe an enormous amount of gratitude to Meena Alexander and Ros Petchesky for assembling such a rich and challenging volume of work. Our editorial assistants, Elena Cohen, Meredith Benjamin, Zoë Meleo-Erwin, and Lindsey Eckenroth, have worked tirelessly to bring each issue to press, and we have continued to enjoy the support, provocation, and friendship of our esteemed editorial board. Kathy Ossip, Nicole Cooley, and Margot Bouman, our poetry, prose, and art editors, have, as always, pushed the boundaries of our themes in rewarding new directions. And the Feminist Press, particularly Jeanann Pannasch, Drew Stevens, Cary Webb, and Gloria Jacobs, gave us the expertise, support, and latitude to test our ideas (even when it meant more work for themselves). We also owe thanks to each of the guest editors we've worked with over the past three years; the experience of collaborating with you has enriched our own thinking enormously. Finally, we are thrilled to welcome a talented new team of editors to this post, Cynthia Chris and Matt Brim, both of the City University of New York, as well as Jennifer Baumgardner, the incoming executive director of the Feminist Press. Their collective commitments to innovative scholarship, interdisciplinary thinking, and new modes of activism suggest a dynamic future for the journal.

Amy Herzog
Associate Professor of Media Studies
Queens College
PhD Program in Theater
The Graduate Center
City University of New York

Joe Rollins
Associate Professor and Executive
Officer of Political Science
Queens College and
The Graduate Center
City University of New York

Note

1. See statistics at www.projectonstudentdebt.org.

Works Cited

Finley, Ashley. 2009. "Women as Contingent Faculty: The Glass Wall." *On Campus With Women* 37(3). http://www.aacu.org/ocww/volume37_3/feature.cfm?section=1.

Mason, Mary Ann and Marc Goulden. 2004. "Do Babies Matter (Part II)? Closing the Baby Gap." *Academe* 90(6):10–15.

Potter, Claire. 2013. "Job Market Rage Redux." *The Tenured Radical*, December 23. http://chronicle.com/blognetwork/tenuredradical/2013/12/job-market-rage-redux/.

Schell, Eileen E. 1998. *Gypsy Academics and Mother-Teachers: Gender, Contingent Labor, and Writing Instruction*. Portsmouth, NH: Heinemann-Boynton/Cook.

Schuman, Rebecca. 2013. "A Radical Defense of the Status Quo." *Pan kisses kafka*, December 23. http://pankisseskafka.com/2013/12/23/a-radical-defense-of-the-status-quo/.

Introduction: Life and Debt

Rosalind Petchesky and Meena Alexander

Give back the life I gave
you pay me my money down
so there's no question
I did it for love for anything
but desire
put a tarnished nickel in my dish
so the guard will know
when he comes
with a bleeding chicken
tied to his wrist
with a bitter promise
that we are not kin
uncommitted forever.
    —*Audre Lorde, "Generation III"*

What, precisely, does it mean to say that our sense of morality and justice is reduced to the language of a business deal? What does it mean when we reduce moral obligations to debts? What changes when the one turns into the other? And how do we speak about them when our language has been so shaped by the market? . . . . A debt is the obligation to pay a certain sum of money. As a result, a debt, unlike any other form of obligation, can be precisely quantified. . . . One does not need to calculate the human effects; one need only calculate principal, balances, penalties, and rates of interest. . . .
    —*Graeber,* Debt: The First 5,000 Years

WSQ: Women's Studies Quarterly 42: 1 & 2 (Spring/Summer 2014) © 2014 by Rosalind Petchesky and Meena Alexander. All rights reserved.

As editors, we share a personal debt—and a professional lifetime of giving and receiving—to the City University of New York, Hunter College, and the PhD programs in Political Science (Ros) and English (Meena) at the CUNY Graduate Center. These have been the academic homes whose students and colleagues have nurtured our thinking for so many years but also the incubator of some troubling thoughts about the meaning, in everyday life terms, of debt. The question of a whole generation of young people bound by student debt is something that we see close at hand. It forms part of a whole chain of injustices that affect them not only as students but also as recent immigrants (or children of immigrants), working-class people, and victims of racism and gender inequality—imminent castaways in a precarious job market, in addition perhaps to their being foot soldiers in the armies of the medically uninsured and credit-deficient.

So our decision to devote an issue of *WSQ* to the theme of "Debt" was initially driven by the outrage we shared with the Occupy Movement, the Occupy Student Debt Campaign, and their many allies across the globe at the ways in which higher education—our work world—has become "a profit engine for financiers, asset speculators, and real estate developers" (Occupy Student Debt Campaign 2013). As our CUNY colleague, sociologist Jack Hammond, has written concerning "the student debt bubble," "At more than one trillion dollars, student loans have grown to exceed total credit card debt. Debt has become a standard part of the college experience. Students take it on because they expect it to pay off in better jobs and higher salaries. But many will be disappointed" (Hammond 2012). Monica Johnson's marvelous graphic novel, *The Adventures of Dorrit Little*, one chapter of which is printed in this issue, illustrates the dire experience and limited choices of a typical student slaving away at a low-paying, food service job while contemplating the lifetime of debt that grad school is likely to entail. Moreover, as Dorrit's wan expressions only hint at, new findings by medical researchers at Northwestern University show that the stresses of having to pay off massive loans are hitting young people with health as well as financial costs—in the form of higher blood pressure, hypertension, and depression (Von Hoffman 2013). Is student debt becoming an apparatus for training and disciplining bodies, an apprenticeship in debt enfranchisement? Has debt become the newly normal way of performing citizenship?

Debt is thus not only a bleak reality that corrodes our institutions, families, and communities; it also raises larger political, philosophical, and historical questions that resonate globally. In contemplating an issue of *WSQ* that would capture this landscape, we asked, what does it mean to live in a world of debt—whether you are a college student in the United States, a struggling farmer in India, a homeowner, or a country? What does it mean to forgive a debt? How have these meanings shifted over time? Do ancestral debt, ritual sacrifices to the gods, tribal and national vendettas, debts to parents and children, colonial debt, slavery and indenture hover as foreshadowings of the late capitalist turn, when *debt becomes a way of life*? With the dizzying rise of globalization in the so-called developing world, debt has invaded the structures of personal and communal meaning making. Farmers in India have found themselves victims of spiraling debt, something brought out powerfully in A. R. Vasavi' s essay, "Debt and Its Social Entrapments." In Jodi Kim's eloquent reflections, through a reading of Manjula Padmanabhan's play, *Harvest*, on the transnational sale of body parts; and in Mahasveta Devi's now classic text, "Douloti the Bountiful," rendered here in an extract from Gayatri Chakravorty Spivak's taut, elegant translation, we see the degradation of life-worlds and the human pain it exacts.

Whether seeking justice or imposing injustice, debt has its own temporality, compressing and bringing forward pasts, reconfiguring and elongating futures. Under conditions of neoliberal globalization, green card holders and naturalized citizens find themselves beholden to the nation-state; indeed this expectation of gratitude becomes an unwritten part of admission into America. Those without debt (mortgages, loans, credit cards) by definition have no credit—are discredited, literally disenfranchised, and placed in a kind of moral and political state of exception at the extreme end of which reside undocumented migrants and refugees. What are the racialized, gendered, sexual, and generational effects, and affects, of these contemporary realities?

The submissions to *WSQ* published here address many of these complicated aspects of debt. Annie Spencer's review essay guides us deftly through Graeber's monumental and widely read historical overview of debt as it predates and intertwines with capitalism. But Spencer also brings a critical feminist, intersectional reading to this work, showing how both Graeber and Strike Debt (see "An Ode to the Debt Resistor") fail to sufficiently incorporate differences of gender, race, and ethnicity into their analyses of debt's power relations. A corrective to this omission comes from southern Europe and Josep Maria Antente and Esther Vivas's astute analysis of the harsh austerity policies adopted to address the sovereign debt crises in Mediterranean countries (Greece, Portugal, Spain). Particularly attentive to the gender impacts of these policies, Antentas and Vivas also highlight a theme that echoes repeatedly in this issue of *WSQ*: the popular movements of resistance and refusal ("We owe nothing, we'll sell nothing, we'll pay nothing!") that have arisen in the region, as they did in previous years in Latin America, to protest failed austerity policies. As we know from the *Indignado* and Occupy movements of recent times, resonances across these regionally based movements mark the dynamic, transformative side of globalization.

Furthering the theme of debt's global dimensions as well as the urgent need for strategies of refusal, Nora Kenworthy's analysis, based on her fieldwork in Southern Africa, of global public health as a system that exacts "debts of gratitude" and new forms of neocolonial entrapment helps us to think more critically about the double-sidedness of aid and so-called humanitarian relief. Does Fanon's perspective of reparations, which Kenworthy reprises for this moment, assert a reversal in roles between debtor and beneficiary, South and North? Similarly, Claire McKinney's review of four books on global reproductive health resituates population and reproductive health policies as forms of neoliberal exchange that create what she calls "feminist indebtedness." It is incumbent on "feminist technoscience," she urges, rather than colluding with mainstream reproductive health policies, to develop a more radical vision and response.

Several of the contributors to this volume rethink issues of debt from the standpoint of women's productive and reproductive labor, both historically and in the present. Ira Steward was a labor organizer in 19th century America who filed a searing report on poverty and the conditions of low-income working people, including women, for the Massachusetts Bureau of Labor Statistics in 1873. We are grateful to our CUNY colleague Professor Stuart Ewen for sharing this important historical document with us and providing an eloquent introduction that highlights Steward's attention to the gendered realities of working-class poverty. Clearly, Steward's commentary on middle-class people's striving to "keep up appearances" despite meager earnings and the condition of being "without credit and without resources" could apply to millions of supposedly middle-class people—encumbered by debt—in North American and European societies today.

Lana Swartz also brings a social historian's perspective to bear on matters of debt, gender, and class. Swartz documents the shift from charge cards to credit cards and finally payment regimes in 20th century America, arguing that forms of payment actually double as vehicles for transacting and realizing identity, especially identity based on gender, race, class, and marital status. It is illuminating to consider Steward's and Swartz's histories alongside Rebecca Colesworthy's critique of Facebook COO Sheryl Sandberg's current bestseller, *Lean In*. Reading Sandberg's highly privileged messages through Virginia Woolf's wisdom about creative women's societally constrained condition, Colesworthy raises the question of how differences of class and political understanding may shed quite a different light on the social debts working women are expected to pay. Finally, Heather Berg brings us back to strategies of refusal in her highly original article reassessing the Marxist feminist literature on reproductive labor. Berg's provocative argument aims a frontal challenge at what she calls the "social necessity debt"—the tendency of social service workers (teachers, child and elderly care workers, nurses and other hospital workers) to submit to super-exploitation because of the "caring" nature of our work. She urges instead a radical strategy of resistance, like the *indignados*, that holds capital rather than care workers accountable for social needs.

Turning debt on its head means, as Fanon recognized a half-century ago, demanding payment on the debts of empire as well as the debts of capital. The global atrocities of slavery, colonialism, occupation, and forced migration urge us to understand debt as a moral as well as a material imperative. In her moving account of the recent political campaigns by the Canadian indigenous feminist movement, Idle No More, Amanda Morris reminds us of the profound moral debt owed to indigenous peoples everywhere, but especially in North America. Her essay, as well as the vivid photograph by Kevin Konnyu of an Idle No More drum dance protest, points to the amazing leadership asserted by women in their role as "debt collectors" in tribal claims and collective struggles for land restoration, environmental justice, and sovereignty rights. Nicholas Gamso's review essay focuses on two new books, by Mimi Thi Nguyen and Lisa Marie Cacho respectively, that expose the persistent imperial debts and deficits that continue to haunt the lives of immigrants from post-colonial and post-conflict societies, whether Mexico or Vietnam. Gamso highlights the shared view of these authors—informed by critical theories of Derrida, Foucault, Agamben, Patterson, and others—that, despite attempts at "immigration reform," an "elaborate system" of border patrol, fences, deportations, stigma, joblessness, and multiple forms of exclusion signifies "the workings of permanent moral debt." Like Gamso, Kenworthy, and others in this volume, Saffo Papantonopoulou also exposes the underside of "debts of gratitude" in her remarkable article, "'Even a Freak Like You Would Be Safe in Tel Aviv'" (originally a paper in CUNY's "Homonationalism and Pinkwashing" conference in April 2013). Along with a stringent critique of "pinkwashing" in the contradictory Israeli policies toward gay, lesbian, and transgender subjects as contrasted with the harsh treatment of Palestinians in the West Bank and Gaza, Papantonopoulou offers us a splendid example of transgender auto-ethnography in the context of Palestinian solidarity work. And she helps us to think about debt queerly.

We agreed on Toni Morrison's *Beloved* as this issue's "Classic Revisited" because it seemed epically yet precisely to foreground this question of moral debt, central to many of our contributors. Whether focusing on slavery (Clough), memory (Perez), pedagogy (Webb), or citizenship and inclusion (Zamalin), the four prose reflections on this great novel collected here all signal ways in which, in Richard Perez's words, *Beloved* "initiates conversations surrounding what was lost, established, and still owed." *Beloved* is a text that reminds us that, beyond its obvious burdens, debt makes powerful ethical and historical claims on us that contain seeds of feminist, antiracist, and progressive transformation. Demands for reparations or redress for the descendants of slavery and victims of apartheid or occupation are based on an assumption that, as Stephen Best and Saidiya Hartman write, "assessing debt and calculating injury [may] itself [be] a formula for justice." But is the language of debt ("You owe me!") sufficient to encompass ethical bonds and social justice? And what happens when debt overwhelms moral obligations, de-moralizing both debtor and creditor? These questions have profoundly personal, bodily resonances. Meena wrote to Ros:

> When you asked me to be your co-editor, I immediately said yes, both because I had seen it close at hand and because right from childhood the idea of debt had lodged in my head. When I was a child I saw a note in my grandfather's hand, on his study table, with the letters IOU writ large, in ink. I had no idea what it meant. He said he had lent money to his friend who lived across the road had a printing press and had run short of money and this was a reminder. Somehow those letters kept returning to me in dreams. Years later I wrote a poem called "House of a Thousand Doors" evoking a woman, a bride who kneels in all her life-

time, at each of the thousand doors of her ancestral house: "her debt is endless". The idea of a grievous debt, something one owes due to who one is—a debt ontological almost, from which there is no respite, took hold of my imagination. Later I made a poem called "Raw Meditations on Money." At the heart of it is the image based on a true story of three sisters in South India who killed themselves, strung themselves up on the ceiling fan, so their father, who was struggling so hard, would not have to pay dowries for them. Vasavi's work on the rising number of farmers who have committed suicides, driven by debt, is another telling of this all too harrowing story.

Debts owed and paid through the body find expression through art, literature and poetry. We asked Nell Painter, the distinguished historian and biographer of Sojourner Truth, now turned artist, to focus her artistic vision on *Beloved*. Nell graciously took time in the summer, and made the piece for us, based on a poetic fragment of Morrison's text (". . . whatever she saw go on in that barn"), that we are proud to feature both on the cover and in the inner pages. T. L. Cowan and Jasmine Rault add to Papantonopoulou's project of queering debt, here by reflecting on the complexities of constructing a lesbian art exhibition. Through compelling reviews of Cheryl Dunye's film *The Watermelon Woman* and the Fae Richards Photo Archive, Cowan and Rault describe painful issues of "foreclosure," credit, "bad debt," and racial exclusion in the contemporary New York gay and lesbian art and performance scene. In so doing, they challenge us to think of "debt as a cultural condition and a mode of inquiry, rather than . . . an individualized economic problem." Along with work by five remarkable poets featured in this volume and a short story by Jayanti Tamm, they also illustrate that debt exists at a profoundly affective and interpersonal as well as cultural and socioeconomic level. We see this most poignantly in Larisa Jasarevic's fascinating portrayal of another precarious landscape "sustained by debt"—the informal lending and borrowing among intimates, kin, clients, and local banks in contemporary Bosnia. Jasarevic's analysis of these relations shows how financial arrangements and affective relations of love, desire, passion, and envy are intricately intertwined. While the tradition of reading the future—and risk—in coffee grinds may be culturally specific, this connection between debt, divination, desire, betrayal, and repair surely has much larger reverberations, circling back perhaps to *Beloved*.

Rosalind Pollack Petchesky is a Distinguished Professor of Political Science (Emerita) at Hunter College and the Graduate Center, CUNY, and the recipient of a MacArthur "genius" fellowship. Her numerous books and articles on sexual and reproductive rights in relation to globalization, militarism, and social justice have derived from decades of transnational feminist activism and been translated into many languages. Petchesky's most recent article, "Owning and Disowning the Body," will appear in the *Oxford Handbook of Transnational Feminist Movements* in 2014.

Meena Alexander is a Distinguished Professor of English at Hunter College and the Graduate Center, CUNY, and an internationally acclaimed poet whose works have been translated and set to music. Her seventh book of poetry, *Birthplace with Buried Stones*, has just been published. Her writings, including the memoir *Fault Lines*, are considered important for the evolving understanding of postcoloniality. Alexander's numerous awards include those from the Guggenheim, Fulbright, and Rockefeller Foundations, the American Council for Learned Societies, and the Arts Council of England. Alexander's edited volume *Indian Writers on Writing* will appear as part of the Writers World Series in 2015 with Trinity University Press. *www.meenaalexander.com*

Works Cited

Alexander, Meena. 1988. *House of a Thousand Doors: Poems and Prose Pieces.* Washington, DC: Three Continents Press.

———. 2008. "Raw Meditations on Money." In *Quickly Changing River* edited by Meena Alexander. Evanston, IL: Triquarterly Books/Northwestern University Press.

Best, Stephen and Saidiya Hartman. 2005. "Fugitive Justice." *Representations* 92 (1):1–15.

Fanon, Frantz. 1963. *The Wretched of the Earth.* New York: Grove Press.

Graeber, David. 2012. *Debt: The First 5,000 Years.* Brooklyn & London: Melville House.

Hammond, Jack. 2012. "What's Driving the Student Debt Bubble?" *The Boston Occupier.* Boston: Free Press.

Lorde, Audre. 1986. "Generation III." In *Our Dead Behind Us*, 66–67. New York: Norton.

Occupy Student Debt Campaign. 2013. "A Statement from the Occupy Student Debt Campaign Initiatives." http://www.occupystudentdebtcampaign.org/click-to-read-our-statement-on-student-debt-reform-initiatives/.

Von Hoffman, Constantine. "Heavy debt wrecking health of young Americans." *CBS Money Watch*, Aug 23, 2013, http://www.cbsnews.com/news/heavy-debt-wrecking-health-of-young-americans/.

PART I. **GLOBAL FLOWS**

Debt and Its Social Entrapments

A. R. Vasavi

Between 1997 and 2012, nearly two hundred thousand agriculturists committed suicide in India.[1] Most official reports, studies, and testimonials considered indebtedness and the burdens of debt defaulting to be the key reasons for such distress.[2] Yet indebtedness is not just an economic factor but also a social condition that marks the life-worlds of victims and their families. Debt, as part of the capitalization of agriculture and rural economies, is a signal aspect of the circuits of capital and is promoted as an inevitable process of economic growth and productivity. Even as debt forges new relationships between creditors and debtors, it generates a cultural grammar in which "repayment," "interest," "mortgage," "deferment," "reclaim," "seizure," and so on become part of the lexicon of the everyday life of debtors. In the telling words of Margaret Atwood, debt as a "human construct mirrors and magnifies both voracious human desire and ferocious human fear" (2008, 2). And in the life-worlds of marginal agriculturists, whose already tenuous economic position is made more vulnerable by debt, the entrapments of indebtedness become the final straw that destroys their very reason for living.

The increasing integration of agriculturists into the market economy has led to reordering the cultural basis of Indian agriculture.[3] Although it is well known and an established fact that the agrarian system has long been hierarchical, with caste-based allocation of rights over land and its resources, regional agricultural practices were conducted on a pattern of collectively shared knowledge forms and rhythms. Such agricultural patterns were also marked by shared agricultural knowledge and linked to local cultural patterns.[4] Regional or agro-ecology-specific agriculture was

WSQ: Women's Studies Quarterly 42: 1 & 2 (Spring/Summer 2014)

based on a society-nature relationship in which society relied on a corpus of collective knowledge to appropriate nature within a range of hierarchical social and economic structures and relationships. While the structure of social activities was itself linked to the ecological and agricultural cycles, the key idioms and terms of cultural life were drawn from and linked to agricultural activities.[5] Even as agriculture was based on differential rights and status, it provided a larger collective identity to a range of people who performed different functions in its processes. In addition, as studies (Amin 1982; Breman 2007) have elaborated, agriculture in India drew on a network of relationships in which cooperation and extension of assistance for a range of activities formed part of the production processes themselves.

But the changes induced by the capitalization of agriculture and the retained caste-based social bases of production have altered this collective orientation and exacerbated the multiple risks that most agriculturists face.[6] This is particularly so for marginal agriculturists whose precarious economic position is worsened by the risks of the new capitalist order. As marginal cultivators, their position in the local and macro economy is one of marginality, not merely from their ownership or cultivation of limited plots and sizes of land (with an average of only 1.33 hectares per cultivating household) but also from the marginal political and social position they occupy in the immediate and larger political economies of the nation. What Sanyal (2007) and Akhram-Lodhi and Kay (2009) identify as markers of marginality is valid for all the households that experienced suicides. These markers include not only access to or ownership of limited landholding, but marginal cultivators also suffer from insecurity of ownership and tenancy, produce for both consumption and sale, are structurally situated in conditions where the surplus production is often transferred to dominant classes, and are subject to processes of semi-proletarianization and pauperization. Additionally, most marginal cultivators are also from the lower-ranked *jatis* and hence lack the social and cultural capital to emerge as successful or entrepreneurial agriculturists.

Agricultural Individualization

Induced and enticed into the capitalist agricultural economy, marginal cultivators face multiple challenges. As individual players, they must seek knowledge and credit and access the market on a personal basis, thereby individually bearing a larger burden of the web of risks than they would have in the context of agriculture as embedded in the local cultural world. Plans and strategies that are afforded by or are available to dominant castes, the primarily landowning or cultivating castes, are not within reach for the low-ranked or new agricultural players. Independent decisions, made especially in the context of recently nucleated families, place enormous burdens on individuals who are operating individually and are not part of collective decisions. Each agriculturist faces the burden of large debts, loss of crops, and loss of face. All of these—the separation of agriculturists from each other, the loss of a shared body of knowledge and practices, the onerous burden of risks borne by heads of households and enterprising individuals, and the precarious position of new agriculturists—can be identified as leading to the individualization of agriculture.[7]

In the individualization of agriculture lies the disembedding of the shared social and cultural basis of agriculture and the insertion of the individual agriculturist as an "independent" player into the market economy. In being constituted as an individual agriculturist, the average marginal agriculturist lacks any substantial support or wherewithal to be a fully prepared and competitive economic player. For one, most members of the household and family are also, in most cases, in conditions of vulnerability. Any new demand on the marginal household and family economy, without adequate replenishment from additional sources, triggers within it mechanisms of fission and places special burdens on the already fragile households that become vulnerable.

Capitalization of agriculture within an unaltered agrarian social fabric results in the working of two differing sets of cultural logics, that of privileging or pressing the individual to act for his or her own economic benefit under the new economic regime and the continued pressures of having to subscribe to collective social activities.[8] The individual, though permitted to be an independent economic actor, is also expected to subscribe to and adhere to the cultural pressures of the social world. As a result, the average marginal agriculturist bears two contradictory and loaded burdens: being individualized at the economic level and shouldering the multiple risks associated with commercial agriculture and at the same time playing out the roles and responsibilities associated with being an obedient and active social player. What Julie Livingston highlights for Botswana, which has also recorded high levels of suicide during a time of economic boom, is relevant here: "It is not that social life has atrophied or constricted so much as the relations between self and others have shifted in disorienting ways as consumption and sociality stoke one another" (2009, 675). These pressures are in turn enhanced by conditions of declining capability at the household level and a further erosion of possible support structures.

Bearing the burden of repeated and multiple loans from varied sources, juggling creditors, and seeking support and numerous forms of financial assistance become the game plan of the desperate. What in standard economic analyses seem like poor decisions and excessive risks are really desperate measures of the marginal and the vulnerable to tide themselves over in times of distress. The loss of crops from either pests or diseases or the lack of remunerative prices and the inability to repay the debts compound the conditions of desperation. Indebtedness produces among the victims and their families multiple forms of entrapments that lead to the loss of their sense of honor and the erosion of self-worth.

Debt and Its Cultural Load

Indebtedness is not a new cultural or economic phenomenon in the lives of most Indians. Hindu scriptural and cultural injunctions see debt, or *rna*, as constitutive of the personhood of Hindus (Malamoud 1996). Economically, a long history of agricultural indebtedness (Stokes 1978) has marked the lives of most agricultural families and households. Indebtedness is also a significant social act, entering into which involves the negotiations of power, identities, and selfhood. Personalized loans from friends, relatives, neighbors, and members of the local elite entail entering into relationships of obligations and pressures. If indebtedness itself is a multiple burden, borne only with the hopes and expectations of crafting a new life, then the failure to repay becomes additionally burdensome. Each reminder and pressure placed on the debtor becomes an infringement on her or his sense of self and honor. Failure to repay debts and the onerous pressures placed on defaulters, especially the forms of taunts, threats, and public notices, constitute instances of humiliation.

Such forms of humiliation also become intense when social relations are in flux and subalterns are attempting to overcome entrenched forms of discrimination or disadvantage (Palshikar 2010). And in many cases the humiliation in front of others that occurs when individuals are unable to repay loans is the last straw that leads to the act of suicide. Various reports provide poignant portrayals of such conditions. For the Punjab, Iyer and

Manick (2000) describe how Balwinder Singh, a Jat Singh, had borrowed money from agricultural commission agents and a cloth merchant to purchase and set up a tube well and fix a pump set in his land of three and a half acres. He had failed to repay on time, as the market price has not been remunerative, and he had been humiliated in front of others. After a period of restlessness and anxiety, he consumed pesticides and died. Similarly, in the village of Muddenahally, in the Hassan district of Karnataka, I recorded the suicide of an agriculturist Thammaiah, at the age of fifty-five.[9] Known as an enterprising agriculturist, Thammaiah had given up his caste occupation of toddy tapping and had taken to agriculture. He had worked hard to purchase three hectares of land and in recent years had worked even harder to take to commercial agriculture. The declining water table and the drought in 2003 had laid his fields bare and the one hundred and forty thousand rupees that he had borrowed the previous year at an interest rate of 36 percent, to sink a well, had grown in compound rates. He had taken out more loans for the weddings of his son and daughter and was worried about his fields' lack of production. He had desperately tried to increase his income through sale of *neera*, a liquor made from coconut trees, but this was not as lucrative as he had expected. As his debts piled up and he failed to make repayments, the creditors started to visit his village and his home. Unable to bear these periodic visits, Thammaiah often stayed out in the fields and refused to come home regularly. On the morning of September 9, 2003, a neighbor and fellow agriculturist found him hanging from a tree in his field.

New Desires and Desperation

The burdens of commercial agriculture and its multiple risks are not the only pressures on most agriculturists. A combination of the capability decline of households and the increasing burdens on families and households compounds the pressures faced by many families and has led to a serious imbalance in the economic capabilities of managing land and also catering to the needs of the family.[10] New aspirations toward educating children and growing pressures from socially prescribed consumption, especially in the spheres of rituals and marriage, create serious conflicts in the use of scarce economic resources. Under such conditions, perhaps what is more burdensome is the fact that individualization in agriculture is not matched by individualization in social and cultural life or by a concomitant individualization in the social sphere. The larger aspiration to achieve upward social mobility, with additional pressures coming from the expansion of the market and the intrusion of the media and its dissemination of consumer desires, has often meant that new lifestyles are marked by consumer goods (Rutten 1995; Breman 2007). Along with these trends comes the commercialization of rituals whereby new goods are added to the list of ritual transactions and new rituals are adapted for the life cycles of individuals and families. These obligations and pressures leave many an agriculturist with multiple burdens. As most of the cases from the suicide reports highlight, each person, in the context of this dual burden of new economic pressures and risks, bears the social burdens of subscribing to both preexisting and new collective social obligations. The celebration of life cycle rituals such as those in the puberty rituals of girls and the annual *satyanarayan vrats* (religious rites invoking blessings for the year) that have become part of the symbolic capital of families have added to the pressures and indebtedness. Consumerism-related requirements such as possessing a television or a motorcycle or having the desire for a new house, make demands on the family budget and induce many agriculturists to seek out loans. Weddings, for long the single biggest source of indebtedness and misery for Indian agriculturists, remains the largest single financial burden on families, and the spread of dowry practices and the increase in the amounts and the types of goods involved in the celebration of weddings contribute to the new financial burdens. Hence many of the suicides committed by active, entrepreneurial agriculturists were linked to the expenses they had incurred in getting their children, especially daughters, married. Three of the six cases of suicides by agriculturists that I reviewed were directly related to onerous debts that fathers had incurred in providing dowries for their daughters, in arranging for the wedding ceremonies, or in funding the building of better houses prior to the wedding. In each case, debts had increased beyond anticipated levels when crops failed or the prices of produce had collapsed.

These diverse and multiple social forms of life, in which subscription to cultural demands combines with an increasing individualization within the economic domain that subordinates agriculturists to the market and to social entrapment, mark the lives of many marginal cultivators. Berking's observation of this contradiction, wherein there is "the individualization of life conduct and the pluralization of life-forms" (1996, 191) has resonance here. In the larger cultural frame in which economic modernization is absorbed along with an intensification of traditionalization, the individual bears the burdens of both worlds: risk and isolation at the economic level, social pressure to prescribe to common desires and expectations, and stigma at the violation of these social norms and standards at the social level. The result is intense stress, which is manifested in several ways.

Biographies of Risk

The disengagement and distantiation of individuals from collective networks and the burden on individuals has been elaborated by Beck and Beck-Gernsheim (2002) for the West. They note the increasing individualization of individuals, the separation of individuals from group and collective moorings, and the placing of additional burdens of risk on individuals. This, the process of the disengagement of individuals from collective networks and the stress on the "do-it-yourself biography" is also relevant in the context of growing individualization in agriculture. Compounding established cultural norms of responsibility is the need to handle and resolve problems and challenges on one's own, especially those that are linked to the external world of commercial transactions and to the world of capital.

Richard Swift's description of one of these victims, Bravin Vijay, age twenty-six, of Sunna village in Vidarbha, highlights how these risks and burdens were borne at an individual level:

> On 25 November 2006 [Bravin Vijay] . . . got up early and rode his new (but unpaid-for) motorbike out into the fields and hanged himself from an electrical pole. Bravin was deep in debt to both moneylenders and the co-operative bank. A loan for a well had come up dry. Cotton prices were what they were. He was responsible not only for his new wife but also for his parents and siblings. He was caught between the obligations of old rural India and the desires of shiny new consumer India, as represented by his new motorbike. He must have felt that he could satisfy neither. His father referred to Bravin as a sensitive son who felt that "all the responsibilities fell on him." (2007, 6)

What surfaces here about the indebted agriculturist (marginal in economic and social position and seeking to engage with capital and high technology) are characteristics of what Beck and Beck-Gernsheim describe as being aspects of risk societies, where a narrative becomes a "do-it-yourself biography" that is "always a risk biography, indeed a tightrope biography, a state of permanent (partly overt, partly concealed) endangerment" (2001, 3). And, as they elucidate, the do-it-yourself biography does often become a "breakdown biography." Much of this is relevant for understanding how the world of new agriculture (with new commercialized inputs, fluctuating markets, and unstable weather conditions) for individualized agriculturists brings with it a higher risk of this imminent breakdown. Withdrawn into their individualized households and families, agriculturists are often unable to gauge the risks involved in engaging with an unpredictable market; varying and unreliable climatic conditions; an unreliable quality of seeds, fertilizers, and pesticides; and untested forms of new agricultural practices.

Although all the reports recognize the extent to which such widespread and high indebtedness among agriculturists was considered by most of the families to be the key reason for the distress experienced by the victims and that led to their suicide, the social impact of such indebtedness and its implications have not been acknowledged. Since the key sources of non-institutional credit have been agribusiness agencies, which provide both inputs at deferred credit to agriculturists and loans, and new moneylenders and government employees, including relatives and friends, who draw on their urban salaries, they pose a double burden on agriculturists. For one, interest rates have been exorbitant (ranging from 24 to 45 percent per annum) and, in addition, they are linked to the agriculturists' personal and social networks. Inability to pay is often met with ridicule, ostracism, or public humiliation. As several reports and case studies highlight, many of those who committed suicide did so after experiencing such humiliation or facing threats of dispossession of their assets.

Subjectivities of Humiliation

Threatening and humiliating encounters between creditors and the indebted create a deep sense of shame among the indebted. Within the framework of a culture that privileges honor and relegates its loss to that of subjectivities of shame and loss of self are narratives that indicate what triggered the drastic resort to suicide. The narratives primarily document the deep sense of shame that the victims experienced. Shame here is a result of a loss of public esteem, honor, and self-worth. All these are relational identities and subjectivities that mark individuals in their self-constitution. Shame, either constructed by oneself or experienced in front of others becomes a diminishment of the self (Taylor 1985). Most of the victims, who were in their own ways entrepreneurs and initiators, had faced a deep sense of disappointment, a social fall in their standing and in their potential to have grown economically and socially. A loss of crops and subsequent conditions of penury or a loss of face in being accosted or exposed as a defaulting debtor added to the victims' distress. Relatives, mostly widows and older children, narrate the state of mind, social relations, and orientation of the victims just before the latter committed suicide. While the term "depressed" or "being depressed" was typically not used, family members and neighbors commonly describe the victim as spending long hours alone, being preoccupied or upset, or crying when looking at the crops. Although most of the suicide victims have been men, given that it is mostly men who hold decision-making positions and are considered heads of households, there are cases of women who have also committed suicide. In Mandya district (Karnataka), Savitramma described to me how her friend Chanamma, a woman past her sixties who had hanged herself at home, had, during the previous two weeks, appeared to be desolate and was not communicating with others.[11] Chanamma had received a second notice from the bank to repay her outstanding loans. To repay her debts she had sold one acre of the family's land and had only another acre left. As a widow who had sought to make a better life for her family and who had struggled alone to undertake new cultivation on her land, she was completely distraught by the new notice from the bank. Her childhood friend and cousin reported, "She used to sit near the field and not do anything," and, "She had stopped talking to us and did not join us for lunch in the fields."

Aparna Pallavi's description of her interaction and interview with Chandrakala Meshram, widow of Gangaram, a Gond who had committed suicide in a village in Yawatmal district, Maharashtra, captures the deep sense of loss, shame, and desperation that the victim must have experienced. As the widow describes it, Gangaram had "stopped telling me anything. Where money was coming from, who he was borrowing from, what the crop was like. He was not like that earlier." Further, "He used to look tired more often. He was brooding. I had never seen him that way before" (Pallavi 2007, 43–44).

Raised expectations, hopes pinned on crops that would have high market value, that would make possible a better life and the fulfillment of aspirations—and the inverse of all this, failure of the crops, the inability to get adequate market prices, the inability to repay debts—lead to deeply felt forms of both disappointment and diminishment.[12]

In their commentaries on the life of the victims, many village residents noted the prevailing conditions and empathized with the loss of social standing of the victims: "He felt small"; "He was concerned about the loans"; "He felt that he had wasted his labor"; "She did not have the stomach for such dishonor"; "[She was] a hardworking woman who only wanted the best for her family and was always very upright."

Shame as the social emotion that arises from the monitoring of one's own actions by viewing oneself from the standpoint of others (Fullagar 2003) places heavy burdens on those who have ventured to enhance the well-being of families, only to leave them worse off or to expose them to degradation that they had not known. Here shame emanates not from a simple reproduction of a "culture of shame" or a "culture of honor" with its strict codes of conduct and principles of adherence to norms and rules. Rather, shame here is a result of the excessive burden that each victim had borne in the new "competitive individualism" that has resulted from the entrenchment of the new commercial and capitalist agriculture. As Kathryn Dudley has elucidated for the United States, expanding capital and the ethos associated with it generate a competitive individualism in which agriculturists compete with each other: "When economic dislocation erodes the institutional infrastructure that organizes a particular way of life, a cultural system can be stretched to the limits of coherence and its underlying contradictions revealed" (2002, 187). In the context of large swathes of rural India, where customary norms of highly skewed and differentiating gender differences continue to hold, the erosion of the sense of masculinity—derived from and driven by a largely patriarchal culture in which the man is solely responsible for personal and familial success—exacerbates the social and psychological wounds of these cultivators. Encapsulated by caste, capital, and gendered cultures that reinforce masculine privilege but also burden men, men who consider themselves to have failed in their duties, in their ability to sustain their families, and who see their economic failure as a personal failure become easy victims of stress. These forms of social entrapments that debts induce mark not only men but also female members of society, who as widows and dependent daughters of suicide victims continue to experience the onerous burdens of being indebted. Stranded without male heads of households, denied rights to land and decision making, lacking familial and community support, and often overlooked by the state, women left behind by male victims of suicide become further subjected to intense forms of distress. As Padhi describes for the Punjab, women who because of traditional norms were expected to be immured residents of households are suddenly thrust into a hostile world. As a result, "the so-called dependents are made to become providers; the disenfranchised called upon to play the role of decision-makers" (2012, 137).

Conclusion

If debt is increasingly a near-universal condition and indebtedness is "the very substance of all human relations" (Graeber 2011, 260), then its cultural contours speak in varied languages of emotional and social distress. And, in the "imagined economies of globalization" (Cameron and Palan 2004), among marginal cultivators who seek desperately to engage with this new economy, debts are the new nightmares that they are rarely able to forget or overcome. Spreading from individual to individual, household to household, group to group, debts are being promoted as inevitable strategies in the new economic game. Debt may be the "new fat" (Atwood 2008, 41) and the ways to attain it and defray it have led to both industries and strategies that mark the new pathways of growing capitalization of production and life. Debt and indebtedness generate entrapments that not only scar individual lives but also mark the human condition as one of imbalance: between aspiration and realization, between creditor and debtor, between desire and desperation, and between life and death.

Acknowledgments

Thanks to Professor Peter van der Veer and the Max Planck Institute for Religious and Ethnic Diversity, Göttingen, for the three-month fellowship during which this essay was finalized.

A. R. Vasavi, a social anthropologist, is currently a senior fellow at the Nehru Memorial Museum and Library, New Delhi. Her most recent book is *Shadow Space: Suicides and the Predicament of Rural India* (2012), from which this essay has been redeveloped. Her research interests are in the areas of agrarian studies, sociology of education, and sociology of India.

Notes

1. Data are from the National Crime Records Bureau (2008), supplemented with updates from various regions.
2. Analyses of narratives about the suicides and the conditions of families have been collated from various official reports and studies. These include Citizens' Report 1998; Commission on Farmers' Welfare 2005; Christian Aid 2005; Farmers' Commission of Experts and Vyavasayaranga Parikakshana 2002; NABARD 2008; and a range of government reports.
3. By emphasizing the cultural and not the social structural changes in rural, agrarian structures I do not overlook the extent to which the social structural basis, drawn on the caste-based allocation of resources, is largely intact. Cultural changes are primarily in the arena of forms of practices of agriculture and in the meaning and significance of agricultural activities, gender relations and status, and the new consumer culture and neotraditionalization, linked primarily to Sanskritization.
4. In many cases, agriculture was a combination of performance (Richards 1993) that draws on cultural idioms and symbols and the social network and was also planned, as agriculturists sought to integrate the new knowledge system disseminated and the new networks that were emerging with the market.
5. See my work on agricultural land use and the classification system (Vasavi 1999).
6. The sociological and, recently, even the economic literature has stressed that there have been a retention of agrarian structures that lead to a coinciding of caste and class structures in rural India (see Harriss-White and Janakarajan 2004)
7. I first used the phrase *individualization of agriculture* in 1999 after a review of suicides by agriculturists in Bidar (see Vasavi 1999). As I elaborated in other essays that followed (Vasavi 2009), I was unaware of the specific usage of the term *individualization* by Ulrich Beck and Elizabeth Beck-Gernsheim (2001) and now note that it was used in 2001 (in German, and in 2002 in the English edition). In an interview in the same book, Ulrich Beck qualifies the meaning of individualization by noting that it refers to "the transformation of work; the decline of public authority and increasing personal isolation; a greater emphasis on individuality and self-reliance" (202). He goes on to note that individualization encapsulates "the sociological transformation of social institutions and the relationship of the individual to society" (202). While much of this refers to the West and its second phase of modernity, I note the relevance of some of this in the context of the commercialization of agriculture and the entry of the neoliberal market in rural India.

8. I draw on the term "cultural logics" as used by Aihwa Ong (1999) to describe the cultural factors or reasons invoked by actors in both economic and political contexts.

9. From a field study conducted in 2004 in Hassan and Mandya districts of Karnataka.

10. For details on how capability decline at the household level accounts for the further impoverishment of families, see Elson 1998.

11. Field notes, 2004.

12. There is an extant body of literature in psychology that explores the concept of "diminishment." I have not drawn on this concept or its related literature and have instead focused on rendering the local expressions of "being made small," "feeling small," and so on as imparting the general cultural and social meaning of diminishment, closer to the idea of loss of honor.

Works Cited

Akram-Lodhi, A. Haroon, and Christobal Kay. 2009. *Peasants and Globalisation: Political Economy, Rural Transformation and the Agrarian Question.* London: Routledge.

Amin, Shahid. 1982. "Small Peasant Commodity Production and Rural Indebtedness: The Culture of Sugarcane in Eastern U.P., c.1880–1920." In *Subaltern Studies Vol I: Writings on South Asian History and Society.* Ed. Ranajit Guha. 39–87. New Delhi: Oxford University Press.

Atwood, Margaret. 2008. *Payback: Debt and the Shadow Side of Wealth.* London: Bloomsbury.

Beck, Ulrich, and Elizabeth Beck-Gernsheim. 2002. *Individualization: Institutionalized Individualism and Its Social and Political Consequences.* London: Sage.

Berking, Helmuth. 1996. "Solidary Individualism: The Moral Impact of Cultural Modernisation in Late Modernity." In *Risk, Environment, and Modernity: Towards a New Ecology,* ed. Scott Lash and Bronislaw Szerszynski, 190–201. London: Sage.

Breman, Jan. 2007. *The Poverty Regime in Village India.* New Delhi: Oxford University Press.

Cameron, Angus, and Ronen Palan. 2004. *The Imagined Economies of Globalisation.* London: Sage.

Christian Aid. 2005. *The Damage Done: Aid, Death, and Dogma.* http://www.christianaid.org.uk/indeth/505caweek.

Citizens' Report. 1998. *Gathering Agrarian Crisis: Farmers' Suicides in Warangal (AP).* MS. Hyderabad: Citizens Committee.

Commission on Farmers' Welfare. 2005. Report of the Commission on Farmers' Welfare. Hyderabad: Commission for Farmers' Welfare.

Dudley, Kathryn Marie. 2002. "The Entrepreneurial Self: Identity and Morality in a Midwestern Farming Community." In *Fighting for the Farm: America Transformed*, ed. Jane Adams, 175–91. Philadelphia: University of Pennsylvania.

Elson, Diane. 1998. "The Economic, the Political, and the Domestic: Businesses, States, and Households in the Organisation of Production." *New Political Economy* 3(2):1–18.

Farmers' Commission of Experts and Vyavasayaranga Parikakshana. 2002. *Report of the Farmers' Commission of Experts on Agriculture in Andhra Pradesh*. Hyderabad: Navya.

Fullagar, Simone. 2003. "Wasted Lives: The Social Dynamics of Shame and Youth Suicide." *Journal of Sociology* 39(3): 48–60.

Graeber, David. 2011. *Debt: The First 5,000 Years*. Brooklyn, New York: Melville House.

Harriss-White, Barbara, and S. Janakarajan. 2004. *Rural India Facing the Twenty-First Century: Essays on Long Term Village Change and Recent Development Policy*. London: Anthem Press.

Iyer, Gopal, and M. S. Manick. 2000. *Indebtedness, Impoverishment, and Suicides in Rural Punjab*. Delhi: Indian.

Livingston, Julie. 2009. "Suicide, Risk, and Investment in the Heart of the African Miracle." *Cultural Anthropology* 24(4): 652–80.

Malamoud, Charles. 1996. *Cooking the World: Ritual and Thought in Ancient India*. Translated from the French by David White. New Delhi: Oxford University Press.

NABARD. 2008. *Action Plan to Address Agrarian Distress in India*. New Delhi: NABARD.

National Crime Records Bureau (NCRB). 2008. *Accidental Deaths and Suicides in India: 1997–2006*. New Delhi: Ministry of Home Affairs.

Ong, Aihwa. 1999. *Flexible Citizenship: The Cultural Logics of Transnationality*. Durham: Duke University Press.

Padhi, Ranjana. 2012. *Those Who Did Not Die: Impact of the Agrarian Crisis on Women in Punjab*. New Delhi: Sage.

Pallavi, Aparna. 2007. "Land Titles Don't Come Easy for Farm Widows." http://www.womenenvironment.org/detail.php?pageId=806.

Palshikar, Sanjay. 2010. "Understanding Humiliation." In *Humiliation: Claims and Context*, ed. Gopal Guru, 79–92. New Delhi: Oxford University Press.

Richards, Paul. 1993. "Knowledge or Performance ?" In *An Anthropological Critique of Development: The Growth of Ignorance*, ed. M. Hobart, 61–78. London: Routledge.

Rutten, Mario. 1995. *Farms and Factories. Social Profile of Large Farmers and Rural Industrialists in West India.* New Delhi: Oxford University Press.

Sanyal, Kalyan. 2007. *Rethinking Capitalist Development: Primitive Accumulation, Governmentality, and Post-colonial Capitalism.* New Delhi: Routledge.

Stokes, Eric. 1978. *The Peasant and the Raj: Studies in Agrarian Society and Peasant Rebellion in Colonial India.* Delhi: Vikas.

Swift, Richard. 2007. "Death by Cotton." *New Internationalist* 399. http://newint.org/features/2007/04/01/farmersuicide.

Taylor, Gabriele. 1985. *Pride, Shame, and Guilt: Emotions of Self-Assessment.* Oxford: Clarendon Press.

Vasavi, A. R. 1999. *Harbingers of Rain: Land and Life in South India.* New Delhi: Oxford University Press.

Vasavi, A.R. 2009. "Suicides and the Making of India's Agrarian Distress." *South African Review of Sociology.* 40(1): 94–108.

Woman Is an Object Without History
(and Other Reflections upon Reading David Graeber's
Debt: The First 5,000 Years)

Graeber, David. *Debt: The First 5,000 Years.* Brooklyn, New York, Melville House, 2011.

Annie Spencer

David Graeber's *Debt: The First 5,000 Years* offers a *longue durée*, longer than most, through the lens of debt. Debt is an institution older than money, Graeber reminds us, and excavating the historical and anthropological record of the emergence and workings of debt rather than that of capital, the commodity form, or the wage-labor relation, allows for an inquiry into social relations and modes of domination that predate capitalism and are central to its configuration and reproduction. In making this inquiry, Graeber adds his voice to the chorus of public scholarship seeking to more comprehensively gauge the totality of all that must be transformed or destroyed in order for the full liberation of all people to occur. Graeber's contribution to the creation of a "useable past"(Robinson [1983] 2000; Quan 2005) has three parts: (1) the central role of violence and domination in the creation of quantifiable equivalences and markets; (2) the nature of the modern state and the need to reexamine taken-for-granted notions of states and markets as discrete entities; and (3) the role of ideological infrastructures of control and attendant, legitimizing narratives of morality, justice, and deserving. Further still, through Graeber's debt goggles emerges a depiction of the modern state that has at its existential core the capacity and compulsion to create both markets and money, the latter guaranteed ultimately by "the value of the power to turn others [human beings] into money" (171). This insight offers a pointed intervention into a number of dominant historiographies on the origins of capitalism. Put succinctly, Graeber tells us that "the story of the origins of capitalism, then, is . . . the story of how an economy of credit was converted into an economy

 WSQ: Women's Studies Quarterly 42: 1 & 2 (Spring/Summer 2014)

of interest; of the gradual transformation of moral networks by the intrusion of the impersonal—and often vindictive—power of the state" (332).

The Emergence of Something New—Debt in the Post-Keynesian Era

According to Graeber, periods of credit money have alternated with periods of bullion (coinage) over the past five thousand years of human history with coinage predominating in periods of "generalized violence" and credit money predominating in periods of relative calm, or within sociogeographical networks governed by trust and mutual accountability. Shifts between the two cycles are characterized by a high degree of social upheaval and crisis. Excavating these patterns renders legible the material tethers connecting the production of money (and its double, debt) with warfare and violence in the name of state making and market making.

Graeber's proposed "shape to the past" (381) allows for a political imaginary of the present moment as one on the precipice of something— potentially—wholly new. He frames the 1971 decision by Richard Nixon to abandon the dollar-gold peg, the final remnant of the international gold standard, as the beginning of a new era of credit money, wherein the capacity to create money (through the issuance of debts that must be repaid, and nearly always with interest) proliferates into more and more hands.[1] The recession that followed the untying and subsequent devaluing of the dollar engulfed much of the 1970s, a period that saw massive restructuring at every scale attributable to, "the movement of dollars away from gold and capital away from production" (Gilmore 1999, 178).

The General Condition of Debt

In its increasingly boom-bust manner, the global economic growth that followed in the period since the unpegging of the dollar has been predicated on debt. And, it follows, debt has become an increasingly prominent theme in national and international political discourse—from debt crises and jubilee movements in countries with low GDP per capita, to the subprime mortgage crisis, the looming student debt crisis, and the constant and vapid mainstream political debate over the national debt in the United States. In the past thirty-plus years in the United States, increasing numbers of people from an increasingly diverse spectrum of lived experience have found themselves increasingly indebted. The rhetoric of the post-

1971 financial turn promised that a democratization of capital, or rather the extension of debts to more people for more things, would be a springboard for opportunity and economic growth. Microfinanciers; payday loan sharks; and darlings Sallie, Fannie, and Freddie cloaked themselves as public servants and spoke of the emancipatory potential of access to credit.

As the privilege to become indebted was extended to more people for the fulfillment of increasingly basic needs, the state did its part by revising debtor laws to favor creditors, simultaneously repealing usury laws while drastically curtailing the legal circumstances under which borrowers could be exempted from debt contracts, no matter how predatory. These efforts included the exemption of federally guaranteed student loans from bankruptcy protections in 1978, extended to education loans issued by private banks in 2005. This process occurred in tandem with the ballooning of the for-profit education sector, which has been enormously successful in extracting debt-financed tuition and fees in exchange for the promise of an opportunity at a better life from students who are overwhelmingly people of color and from low-income backgrounds. It also bears mentioning that the tightening of protections for lenders of student loans coincided with a 900 percent increase in the rate of tuition over the same period—a phenomenon that was only possible because of the ubiquitous and well-oiled student lending machine on college campuses everywhere, and legitimized by the myth of student loan debt as "productive debt" (see Harris 2011).

It is by now common knowledge that the ballooning of household debt levels over the period since the mid-1970s in the United States coincided with stagnant wage growth over the same period. The extension of credit had a dual ameliorative effect for an economy in crisis: (1) it allowed for the standard of living, among those deemed creditworthy, to remain more or less unchanged, thus limiting the likelihood that declining real wages would result in political unrest and, crucially, (2) it offered a short-term solution to the problem of effective demand, an inherent crisis within capitalism as the profit motive inevitably squeezes wages and limits the extent to which individuals can buy things. This strategy worked well for many years, which is to say, those who suffered did so alone, invisibly, and were successfully cast as "failures" when they did become visible. Graeber explores the moralism tied to the institution of debt, the ideological anchoring of the debt relation to religious notions of sin and virtue. And indeed, this ephemeral but nonetheless material condition accounts for the effectiveness of debt as a tool of coercive power. Debt is an instrument of control that is individualizing and largely invisible unless and until the number of debtors unable or unwilling to service their debts reaches levels that signal a threat to the continual flow of capital and to the legitimacy of the state-enforced system of private debt peonage.

Occupy and the Limits to a Future Without a Past

The sense of the emergence of something new was palpable in the fall of 2011 in Zuccotti Park. Wide variation in protestors' intellectual and experiential understanding of the nature of the problem complicated attempts to move beyond the suspension of a time and space for generalized protest and prefigurative practice. With the history of radical, antiracist, and anti-imperialist organizing efforts successfully written out of the dominant narratives of American social movements of the past, difficult conversations about the nature of gendered and racialized systems of oppression were at times volatile and often resulted in a splintering off of discussion of these issues and of those committed to their relevance into siloed working groups. This lack of a shared understanding of how the present came to be through the past stifled "the movement's" attempts to move forward. In its broadest sense, Occupy Wall Street (OWS) was constrained by the narrow substance of its common political analysis that "shit is fucked up and bullshit."[2]

Graeber had finished writing *Debt* by the time he was participating in the planning of what would become OWS. Yet when protestors gathered in Zuccotti Park, debt emerged organically as a theme around which many began to organize, first under discrete issues such as student debt, health care costs and coverage, and predatory lending and foreclosure, and later under the umbrella Strike Debt, which sought to highlight the sameness of these seemingly disparate issues and to spur a wide-ranging debt refusal movement.[3] Strike Debt, through its Rolling Jubilee campaign to purchase and abolish defaulted medical debt, and its publication of *The Debt Resistors' Operations Manual* (2012), achieved moderate success in building public recognition of the pervasiveness of debt as an instrument of exploitation and control and introduced into the public debate the language of refusal, a withdrawal of consent from the status quo of borrowing to live.[4]

The Limits to a Debt-Centered Analysis

Graeber, in his book, and OWS, in its iteration as Strike Debt, share a conviction that pulling the thread of debt unravels and demystifies the present world order. Yet debt, as pervasive and nefarious as it is, is not a catchall diagnostic of the present moment. It is one among several punitive institutions of the crisis-ridden, racial capitalist state, whose purpose is to individuate and pathologize the rampant social disorder of a society organized around the relentless pursuit of compound growth (cf. Gilmore 1999).[5] Attempts to distill the complex webs of power, violence, and exploitation that constitute *the nature of the problem* to a single, linchpin instrument run the risk of minimizing or erasing significant parts of the story. Such oversimplification invalidates individuals' experiential knowledge of other forms of violence and control and reinforces a perceived naturalness or givenness to what Stuart Hall calls "fatal couplings of power and difference" (quoted in Gilmore 2004) whose existence cannot be explained by debt and whose abolition will not be secured through mobilizing around debt alone.

Gender, Extraction, and Uneven Development

Racialization (and its attendant ideological construct, white supremacy) and genderization (and its attendant ideological construct, cis-heteropatriarchy) are the bedrock upon which the capitalist world system sits.[6] Recognition of this fundamental reality is lacking in Graeber's analysis, though his inquiry is rife with examples of gendered and racialized oppression. Again and again throughout *Debt*, we see examples of women reduced to objects, as symbols of men, as prizes to be adorned or commons to be expropriated, and yet Graeber never turns over the stone of the gender distinction—the process by which female-sexed bodies are produced as Woman. In his own accounts, the degradation of women is a preexisting given. Rather than elucidating the work the gender distinction does in structuring the division of labor and power relations (including debt) (Gonzalez 2012; Valentine 2012), Graeber settles for a baseline condition of women in ancient Sumer. There he argues, "One cannot speak of full gender equality. . . . Still, one gets the sense of a society not so different than that which prevails in much of the developed world today"

(178). In his contentment with the good-enough standard of present-day Western gender inequality, Graeber falls into precisely the trap identified by Marxist feminist scholars more than three decades ago, perpetuating the violent myth of a natural givenness to the hierarchical gender distinction. This oversight muddles the centrality of group-differentiated social hierarchies to the continued viability of capital accumulation (Robinson [1983] 2000; Smith 1984; Katz 2001; Gilmore 1999).

Specificities of Difference Production—Debt Among Other Forms of "Unfreedom"

Graeber's history of debt insufficiently accounts for the conditions under which human beings, at the scale of the living body, are divided, marked, and produced as less-than-human. In addressing the "curious puzzle of the *cumal*, the slave-girl currency of medieval Ireland" (171), or exploring the LeLe practice of village wives, who were kept in common and did not have the right to refuse sex, or informing us of Sumerian priestesses who, like Hindu *devadasis*, sometimes had "the responsibility to make themselves sexually available to worshippers on certain ritual occasions" (181), Graeber remains committed to his Great Answer: "Still, the really critical factor here was debt" (180).[7] The role debt plays in the above examples is that of a legitimizing narrative. Debt is central to the ideological infrastructure that explains, in these examples, why these human beings could be reduced to a subhuman condition with their apparent social consent. Graeber commits a critical error in conflating the legitimizing institution with the condition itself, an oversight that allows him to barely scratch the surface of his own questions regarding the *cumal*. [8]

Toward New Theories for Action

Cedric Robinson, in the closing chapter of his *Black Marxism*, states, "For the realization of new theory we require new history" ([1983] 2000, 307). In one sense, Graeber's book provides a new history on which to base new theory and practice toward emancipatory social change. He observes that, in order to be treated as currency, human beings must be reduced to the state of money; that is, they must be ripped from their contexts and presented as objects "valuable precisely for their lack of history" (386). He reminds us that we must contend with the very nature of the modern state, that money and debt are two sides of the same coin, and that they arise out of violent efforts to quantify precisely that which is owed in relations of hierarchal power between individuals or groups. Uncovering the violence of the institution of debt and its historical role in legitimizing exploitative relations of extraction and appropriation is central to the political project of reconstructing a useable history. Yet, in conflating the institution of debt with the nature of the problem, both Graeber and the Strike Debt movement construct a theory of political action that does not place adequate emphasis on the role of difference, as it pertains to the legitimation of who can be indebted and why and as it relates to other modes of domination and control that produce the essential unevenness required for continued capital accumulation.

Annie Spencer is a doctoral candidate in geography at the City University of New York Graduate Center and a teaching fellow at Hunter College. Spencer's work examines state improvement schemes, the quest for growth, and everyday wageless life in the post-American century.

Notes

1. While surely debt arrangements exist during periods in which bullion predominates, the dollar-gold peg was governed by a seemingly natural limit that constrained the ability and consolidated the power to produce money into far fewer hands, and mainly the hands of the Federal Reserve Bank (364).
2. As read the placard of one protester in the park whose image and words were widely reproduced.
3. The author organized with the Occupy Student Debt Campaign and Strike Debt through the Fall of 2012.
4. "To the financial establishment of the world, we have only one thing to say: We owe you nothing," reads the back cover of the manual, echoing a Strike Debt protest banner. (See "An Ode to the Debt Resistor," this issue.)
5. In addition to the end of gold convertibility, 1971 also marks the fateful year that Nixon uttered the wretched phrase "War on Drugs" for the first time, propelling into existence another punitive ideological state apparatus and the rationale needed to mobilize state resources against the over-accumulation of idled land, labor, capital, and state capacity. (Gilmore 2007)
6. I define *genderization* as the set of practices and social processes, inherently violent, that produce and reproduce female-bodied human beings as Woman. Following Valentine (2012) I hold that we cannot take up the ques-

tion of gender without addressing the central role of sexual violence in its production and maintenance.

7. "For a very long time, the intellectual consensus has been that we can no longer ask Great Questions. Increasingly, it's looking like we have no other choice" (25).

8. His questions being, "How did that happen?" (128) and "Why women?" (172).

Works Cited

Federici, Silvia. 2004. *Caliban and the Witch*. New York: Autonomedia.

Gilmore, Ruth Wilson. 1999. "Globalization and U.S. Prison Growth: From Military Keynesianism to Post-Keynesian Militarism." *Race and Class* 40(2/3):171–88.

———. 2004. "Fatal Couplings of Power and Difference: Notes on Racism and Geography." *Professional Geography* 54(1):15–24.

———. 2007. *Golden Gulag: Prisons, Surplus, Crisis, and Opposition in Globalizing California*. 1st ed. Berkeley and Los Angeles: University of California Press.

Gonzalez, Maya Andrea. 2012. "Communization and the Abolition of Gender." In *Communization and Its Discontents: Contestation, Critique, and Contemporary Struggles*, ed. Benjamin Noys, 219–236. New York: Autonomedia.

Hall, Stuart. 1992. "Race, Culture, and Communications: Looking Backward and Forward at Cultural Studies." *Rethinking MARXISM*. 5(1):10–18.

Harris, Malcolm. 2011. "Bad Education." *n + 1*, April 25. http://nplusonemag. com/bad-education.

Katz, Cindi. 2001. "On the Grounds of Globalization: A Topography for Feminist Political Engagement." *Signs* 26(4):1213–34.

Mies, Maria. (1983) 2000. *Patriarchy and Accumulation on a World Scale: Women in the International Division of Labour*. London: Zed Books.

Quan, H. L. T. 2005. "Geniuses of Resistance: Feminist Consciousness and the Black Radical Tradition." *Race and Class* 47(2): 39–53.

Robinson, Cedric J. (1983) 2000. *Black Marxism: The Making of the Black Radical Tradition*. Chapel Hill: University of North Carolina Press.

Smith, Neil. 1984. *Uneven Development: Nature, Capital, and the Reproduction of Space*. Oxford, UK: Blackwell.

Strike Debt. 2012. *The Debt Resistors' Operations Manual*. New York: Strike Debt. http://strikedebt.org/The-Debt-Resistors-Operations-Manual.pdf.

Valentine, P. 2012. "The Gender Distinction in Communization Theory." *LIES: A Journal of Materialist Feminism* 1. http://liesjournal.net/download/.

An Ode to the Debt Resistor
From *The Debt Resistors' Operations Manual*

Strike Debt/Occupy Wall Street

Everyone is affected by debt, from recent graduates paying hundreds of dollars in interest on their students loans every month, to working families bankrupted by medical bills, to elders living in "underwater" homes, to those taking out payday loans at 400% interest to cover basic living costs, to the teachers and firefighters forced to take pay cuts because their cities are broke, to countries pushed into austerity and poverty by structural adjustment programs.

Everyone seems to owe something, and most of us (including our cities) are in so deep it'll be years before we have any chance of getting out—if we have any chance at all. . . . We are told all of this is our own fault, that we got ourselves into this and that we should feel guilty or ashamed. But think about the numbers: 76% of Americans are debtors. How is it possible that three-quarters of us could all have just somehow failed to figure out how to properly manage our money, all at the same time? And why is it no one is asking, "Who do we all owe this money to, anyway?" and "Where did they get the money they lent?"

At the same time, we keep hearing about financial capitalism: the fact that most of the profits on Wall Street no longer have much to do with producing or even selling anything, but are simply the fruits of speculation. This is supposed to be very complicated—"Somehow they have just figured out a way to make money out of thin air; no, don't even try to understand how they do it." . . .

In fact, bankers *are* allowed to make money out of thin air—but only if they lend it to someone. That's the real reason everyone is in debt: it's a

 WSQ: Women's Studies Quarterly 42: 1 & 2 (Spring/Summer 2014)

shakedown system. The financial establishment colludes with the government to create rules designed to put everyone in debt . . . with the entire apparatus of government, police and prisons providing enforcement and surveillance. Instead of taxing the rich to generate money to build and maintain things like schools and roads, our government actually borrows money from the banks, and the public pays the interest on these loans. As we've learned through scandal after scandal, this process is riddled with fraud, rigged from the start to steal money that should be going to social necessities. Financial capitalism is mafia capitalism.

. . . We are under no moral obligation to keep our promises to liars and thieves. In fact, we are morally obligated to find a way to stop this system rather than continuing to perpetuate it. This collective act of resistance may be the only way of salvaging democracy because the campaign to plunge the world into debt is a calculated attack on the very possibility of democracy. It is an assault on our homes, our families, our communities and on the planet's fragile ecosystems—all of which are being destroyed by endless production to pay back creditors who have done nothing to earn the wealth they demand we make for them.

To the financial establishment of the world, we have only one thing to say: We owe you nothing. To our friends, our families, our communities, to humanity and to the natural world that makes our lives possible, we owe you everything. Every dollar we take from a fraudulent subprime mortgage speculator, every dollar we withhold from the collection agency is a tiny piece of our own lives and freedom that we can give back to our communities, to those we love and respect. These are acts of debt resistance, which come in many other forms as well: fighting for free education and healthcare, defending a foreclosed home, demanding higher wages and providing mutual aid.

. . . Literally millions of people . . . cannot pay the enormous sums that the financial elites claim they owe. They are the Invisible Army of Defaulters. Instead of a personal failure, refusing to pay under our current system is an act of profound moral courage. We see our situation as connected, and we can look for ways to step out of the shadows together. . . .

This operations manual—written by an anonymous collective of resistors, defaulters, and allies from **Strike Debt and Occupy Wall Street**—is for all those being crushed under the weight of debt. It aims to provide specific tactics for understanding and fighting against the debt system so that we can all reclaim our lives and our communities. It contains practical information, resouces, and insider tips for individuals dealing with the dilemma of indebtedness in the United States today and also introduces ideas for those who have made the decision to take collective action.

The Scissors of Debt: Comments from Southern Europe

Josep Maria Antentas and Esther Vivas

The debt crisis and austerity policies are hitting the societies of Europe's Mediterranean periphery, particularly Portugal, Greece, and Spain, hard. With the onset of the economic crisis, a whole growth and development model based on low wages and property speculation has come crashing to the ground. But in addition, as a result of the adjustment measures implemented, the entire social model and the system of social rights won in previous decades have entered into crisis. The austerity measures affect welfare states that are particularly fragile compared with the European Union average. The Mediterranean countries, especially Portugal, Greece, and Spain, developed weak welfare states in comparison with the European Union as a whole. These countries established their welfare regimes later, in the 1970s, in an international context in which neoliberal policies were already gaining the upper hand as Keynesian policies were being abandoned (Rodríguez Cabrero 2004; Adelantado 2000). This does not mean, of course, that on a world-comparative scale the workers in Mediterranean Europe did not achieve a standard of social rights unheard of on other continents. But the future of these rights is now under threat from the austerity bulldozer.

Debt Crisis and Political Crisis

If during the 1980s, 1990s, and 2000s we saw the impact of foreign debt crisis on the people of the South through the systematic application of programs of structural adjustment and social cuts that were claimed to be necessary in order to deal with the payment of the debt, today it is the

Mediterranean periphery of Europe that is caught up in the whirlwind of the debt crisis.

As part of the socialization of banking debts, in the European Union (EU) as a whole, 1.7 trillion euros were allocated to rescuing private banking during the early period of the crisis (CADTM 2010). This aggravated the situation of public accounts, placing the countries of the European periphery in the eye of the hurricane and intensifying attacks on social rights and their reduction to a subaltern status within the EU. The very nature of the EU has made it particularly vulnerable to the crisis. First, monetary union and the creation of the eurozone were affected on the basis of heterogeneous economies with uneven productivity levels and no intention of correcting these divergences. Even before the outbreak of the crisis, these imbalances were clearly visible as the disparities between the growth rates of the different member states increased still further (Husson 2010). Prior to the onset of the crisis, the differences between the EU countries in terms of productive structure and position in the international economy led to a marked contrast between, on the one hand, a core of competitive countries, such as Germany, the Netherlands, and Austria, that built up balance of trade surpluses and, on the other, a group of less competitive countries with balance of trade deficits, such as the so-called PIGS (Portugal, Italy, Greece, and Spain) (Medialdea 2010). The euro has acted as an instrument limiting wages and public expenditure, depriving the countries with lower productivity levels of the room for maneuver allowed by currency devaluation. It has been used by Germany, with its strength in technology and productivity, to become the eurozone's leading export power.

Second, the EU lacks the democratic mechanisms for making decisions on a continental scale. Its institutional architecture is a combination of an interstate logic, through unequal negotiations between its member states, and a suprastate logic, through the operation of the European institutions headed by the European Commission, control of which depends, in the last instance, on negotiations between the member states. The only European institution elected on the basis of representative-democratic mechanisms, the European Parliament, lacks any real power and is not at the center of the EU's policy deliberation and policy-making process. This institutional architecture has proved to be extremely functional as far as the interests of the big business organizations and their pressure groups are concerned, as they have generally found the corridors of Brussels, far removed from public scrutiny, highly conducive to their lobbying (Balanyá et al. 2002).

The combination of what is generally called Europe's "democratic deficit" and neoliberal and monetarist policies led in the 1990s and 2000s to a gradual crisis of legitimacy of the European integration project (Pedrol and Pisarello 2005). The foremost expression of this was the failure of what was commonly referred to as the "European Constitution" (whose official title was Treaty Establishing a Constitution for Europe) following the "no" result in the French referendum on May 29, 2005, with 55 percent of voters rejecting the treaty, thus leaving its future on hold. Strangely enough, the EU project's legitimacy crisis was less pronounced in the Mediterranean periphery, in countries such as Portugal, Greece, and Spain, where, until the outbreak of the current economic crisis, the ruling classes succeeded in associating the EU with "modernity" and "progress" as opposed to the international isolation and backwardness these countries had experienced during the military dictatorships in the second half of the twentieth century.

With the explosion of the current crisis the imbalances at the root of the neoliberal European project have intensified, exacerbating tensions within this project and reinforcing the hierarchical center-periphery relationships. The unstable equilibrium prior to the crisis exploded. The "financial coups" in Greece and Italy at the end of 2011, with the appointment, following pressure from international financial institutions and European authorities, of the governments led by, respectively, Papademos and Monti—both figures coming from the financial world and linked to Brussels—are the clearest example of a logic in which the core states and commanding bodies of the European Union act de facto as a "neocolonial power" with its own periphery. This way the EU "appears as what it is: a deadly menace to the most elementary democratic rules, even the liberal parliamentary system" (Kouvelakis 2011).

Since the onset of the crisis, political life in the periphery of Europe has become increasingly and ever more clearly dependent on and subordinate to the Troika—the European Commission, the European Central Bank and the International Monetary Fund (IMF)—and the policy of the German government. Greece and Portugal have endured official "bailouts" with extremely strict economic strings attached. Delegations of the Troika, popularly known as the Men in Black, regularly visit both countries to oversee compliance with these conditions (Camargo 2013)—a scenario reminiscent, albeit in a different institutional context, of the structural adjustment plans implemented in Latin America in the 1980s and 1990s under the aegis of the IMF. In Spain, the central government's entire policy since 2010, first under Rodríguez Zapatero and then Rajoy, has been geared toward complying with the Troika's and Germany's "suggestions." Although the country has not received a formal bailout and so has not been subjected to such direct oversight by the Troika, but rather a more indirect and less visible process, a one-hundred-billion euro rescue package restricted to the banking system was put in place in June 2013 following the collapse of Bankia. The risk premium has been used throughout this period as a tool of permanent blackmail to justify the need for a never-ending adjustment policy.

The economic crisis becomes a political crisis in which democratic-institutional mechanisms and traditional party systems implode, within the framework of an oligarchic and de-democratizing involution of liberal parliamentary systems. The direct takeover of command by the financial powers since the crisis broke out, putting leading figures (mostly men) from the finance and banking sector at the head of governments and key ministries, is a very clear sign of this. The proliferation of former directors of Goldman Sachs in central political positions in various EU countries exemplifies this tendency. Nor should it be forgotten that Spain's current minister for the economy and competitiveness, Luis de Guindos, is a former president of Lehman Brothers for Spain and Portugal. It is possible to say, following Jacques Rancière (2006), that parliamentary democracies have become "oligarchic rule-of-law states." A professionalized minority subordinate to the economic power elites monopolizes political representation and excludes the majority de facto from real decision making, although it continues to draw its formal legitimacy from the majority via universal suffrage and electoral victories.

We are moving toward a model of "isonomic oligarchy," that is, a type of regime in which there is no absolute suppression of rights and freedoms but rather a marginalization and reduction of them, preserving "mixed regimes in which oligarchic and democratic elements coexist, but in which the latter occupy a marginal role" (Pisarello 2011a, 185). A concrete example of de-democratization in action is the amendment to the Spanish Constitution rushed through parliament by the two main political parties, the Spanish Socialist Workers Party and the Popular Party, in August and September 2011. The amendment to Article 135 introduced the concept of a balanced budget and established payment of the debt and interest as the absolute priority. This amendment, put forward on August 23 at the height of the summer holiday season, was fast-tracked through a few weeks later by the two major parties in the Spanish parliament, the Congress of Deputies, without even putting the proposed amendment to the constitution to a referendum. In this way one of the precepts of neoliberalism and austerity policies was built into the constitution following a scheme "aiming to enshrine in rules of the highest juridical rank—treaties, constitutions, organic laws—an ideological model that is so closed that it excludes alternative models, thereby distorting the scope of the democratic principle" (Pisarello 2011b).

Austerity and the Gender Debt

The sovereign debt crisis and the rising public debt are used by creditors, as well as by governments and institutions, as an argument for applying measures of adjustment: the reduction of public expenditure, privatization, cuts in social services, the erosion of labor rights, and so on, with the consequent transfer of the cost of the crisis to the ordinary people (Toussaint 2012). Austerity affects the working and middle classes and implies a loss of social and labor rights for a large part of society. The economic crisis and adjustment policies affect in particular ways some specific social groups based on gender, age, or ethnicity. For example, one of the most striking and often analyzed effects of the crisis is the rise in mass unemployment among youth (Juventud Sin Futuro 2011).

Here we will use the case of Spain to provide some analysis of the specific effects of austerity, which is not gender neutral, for women. There is a specific gender dimension to the loss of rights and increasing inequality brought about by austerity policies. Cuts to social benefits and the privatization of public services hit women directly and specifically as a result of the specific role women play in society, in the family, and inside the labor market because of the sexual division of labor.

First, cuts specifically affect policies on equality. In Spain, for example, budgets affecting equality have been cut by 42 percent since the onset of the crisis, resulting in the shutting down of equal opportunity programs and a reduction by 28.5 percent in services providing aid and assistance to women experiencing domestic violence. That means, for example, that agents for equal opportunities (in charge of implementing equality policies) were fired; specific aid services to women affected by domestic violence such as local information services, emergency centers, and shelters were closed down; and programs to promote equality at work were removed. These measures not only do away with policies necessary for equality between men and women but also, as the Gender Committee of the Citizen Debt Audit Platform points out, convey the idea that policies on equality are "superfluous policies that can only be afforded in times of economic prosperity"(*Comisión de género de la PACD* 2013a).

Second, the cuts in social expenditure, which mostly take the form of eliminating jobs and lowering wages, are concentrated in highly feminized sectors such as health and education. For instance, in 2012 women were 54.3 percent of the public sector workforce, while they represent only 45.3 percent of the total workforce (Ezquerra, 2012a). But between the second quarter of 2012 and the same period in 2013, 67 percent of jobs lost in the public sector affected women, that is, 133,400 out of 197,900 (CCOO 2013). At the same time, steps such as freezing pensions and lengthening the contribution period on which pension entitlement is based also have negative consequences for women, for the following reasons: (1) women's greater presence in the informal economy, which is estimated to represent around 20 percent of Spanish GDP (Jiménez Fernández and Martínez-Pardo del Valle 2013); (2) their greater presence in part-time work, as 75 percent of part-time workers are women; and (3) their generally intermittent employment record as a result of caring for others, so that in turn they face more objective difficulties in building up the minimum contributions required (Ezquerra 2011).

Third, cuts in basic social services such as for health care, education, and child care centers, lead to their provision, cost, and responsibilities being transferred to unpaid care work. Studies show that care and domestic labor is distributed unevenly among women and men: according to the 2009–10 Survey of Time Uses, by the Spanish National Statistics Institute (INE in its Spanish acronym), women spend an average of two and a quarter hours daily more than men in domestic and care work, although the historical tendency is a progressive reduction of this gap (INE 2011). Social cuts in this scenario mean that whatever the state's social services stop doing is passed directly mostly on to women as wives, mothers, and daughters. Unremunerated work tends to adapt to the economic situation in a countercyclical fashion: the more stable the economy, the more formerly unpaid work becomes waged work, whereas in a crisis, it is squeezed out of the labor market and reverts to being unpaid. This means that even if income decreases because of unemployment, family welfare deteriorates to a lesser extent at the expense of an increase in the unremunerated housework and care work performed by women (Larrañaga 2009). The response to the crisis consists, therefore, in transferring a large part of the workload to the family sphere, which means basically women. A quite visible and widely observed example of this dynamic has been cuts in the budget allocation for implementing the Dependency Law (which funds services required by dependent people). The National Reforms Plan 2013, announced in May 2013, included a trimming of 1.1 billion euros, which in practice represents the near derogation of this law, reduced to an empty shell with paltry funding. The reduction in state-provided allowances for those looking after dependent people has a threefold consequence: job losses in the highly feminized care sector; deterioration of everyday life for dependent people; and workload transfer mostly to women, in their roles as mothers and wives, to take care of dependent relatives.

Odious Debt, Illegitimate Debt, Audits, and "Debtocracy"

The repudiation of debt by those who suffer its consequences has been a constant throughout history.[1] The doctrine of odious debt, which under international law is used to demand the nonpayment of a debt contracted by a government and used against its people, has been put forward and applied for the nonpayment of debts incurred throughout the nineteenth, twentieth, and twenty-first centuries (Toussaint and Millet 2010).

As the main proponent of the doctrine, the legal theorist Alexander Sack defined "odious debt" in 1927: "When a despotic power contracts a debt, not for the needs or in the interests of the state, but rather to strengthen its despotic regime, to suppress a popular insurrection, etc, this debt is odious for the people of the entire state. . . . This debt does not bind the nation; it is a debt of the regime, a personal debt contracted by the ruler, and consequently it falls with the demise of the regime" (CADTM 2008). This doctrine has been applied or invoked at different moments in history. In 1898, the United States used it to avoid paying the debt that the Spanish state claimed from it over Cuba, one of Spain's former colonies, which then became a U.S. protectorate. At the Paris Peace Conference, the United States argued that the Cuban debt was odious because it had been used to suppress popular uprisings, the people had not consented, and the creditors were aware of this and therefore of the risk of nonpayment. The argument was accepted and the debt was canceled. In 1919, the Treaty of Versailles cleared Poland from paying part of the debt contracted by the German and Prussian governments for their colonization and its use against its people. And we could cite other examples (Toussaint and Millet 2010).

More recently, the United States wielded this doctrine to avoid accepting responsibility for debts acquired by the government of Iraq when that country came under U.S. administration in 2003. However, the United States finally renounced the odious debt argument, aware as it was of the precedent that could be established, and the debt relief was finally carried out citing reasons of "sustainability" (CADTM 2008).

Organizations that have mobilized against foreign debt, such as the Jubilee South network and the Belgium-based international network, the Committee for the Abolition of Third World Debt (CADTM in its French acronym), have led campaigns and initiatives to expose the illegality, usury, and illegitimacy of the debt and consequently to encourage its nonpayment. Audits have been one of the main instruments used for this purpose. Carrying out an audit of debts makes it possible to investigate why the debts were contracted, what they were used for, and who benefited, and to expose irregularities in their contracting, to reveal the complicity of their creditors and to obtain the legal foundations for their repudiation.

By the middle and end of the 2000s, these initiatives became widespread in the countries of the South, especially in Latin America, impelled by organizations, social movements, and some others with the involvement of their governments. In part they were the culmination of a long process of social mobilization throughout the previous decade in favor of canceling the foreign debt of the countries of the South, both in the affected countries and in the countries of the North, under the impulse of the Jubilee 2000 and Jubilee South campaigns (Vivas 2007).

Perhaps the best-known case is that of Ecuador. The debt audit carried out in this country was the most important experience of this kind, as it included the active involvement of the government, academics, and local and international social organizations and led to the political decision not to pay part of the debt. In 2007 the Public Credit Integral Audit Commission, comprising representatives of the Ecuadorian government and social organizations from Ecuador and other countries, was set up to identify Ecuador's illegitimate debt by means of an exhaustive examination of the debt incurred with multilateral creditors, though also including commercial loans, bilateral loans, and bonds. The audit's final report, presented in September 2008, concluded that a large part of the debt was illegitimate. As a result, the government declared a moratorium on the payment of part of the private debt and made a counteroffer to pay 30 percent of its value. In this way the Ecuadorian government saved some 2.2 billion dollars, plus 6 billion dollars of interest, which it allocated to social resources (Piñero, Chantry, and Fresnillo 2011).

Now, in the context of the foreign debt crisis and the use of debt as a justification for policies of structural adjustment, the question of the yoke of debt has become a central aspect of the movement against the policies of austerity imposed in Mediterranean Europe. The debt issue has been incorporated in two ways by the movement against austerity, and these feed back on each other. On the one hand, it appears as a cross-issue in specific struggles against cuts (in health, education, etc.) and the impositions of the Troika. In terms of the movement, the debt then becomes the keystone and the unifying element for explaining the mechanism for transferring the costs of the crisis to the bulk of the population and its export to the European periphery. The repudiation of the debt thus becomes a unifying thread, a reference framework, for the rejection of each specific and concrete austerity measure. This refusal is expressed, for example, by the slogan "We Owe Nothing, We'll Sell Nothing, We'll Pay Nothing" used in Greece by the Squares movement (as the indignant and occupier movement was dubbed in that country) in June 2011.

On the other hand, as well as including the rejection of debt in the demonstrations against cuts, specific campaigns have emerged against debt itself. These campaigns have launched initiatives based on public auditing, following the Latin American example of the previous decade. As has already been noted, the audit is conceived as a pedagogical tool allowing ordinary people to understand the functioning of the state, the economy, and institutional relationships in order to equip them with arguments and reasons for combating austerity. As well as referring to the previously mentioned odious debt doctrine, the citizen debt audit movement has introduced another key idea: illegitimate debt. In other words, the audit is conceived as an instrument to distinguish the portion of the debt that may be regarded as legitimate from that which is not.

The concept of illegitimate debt goes beyond that of odious debt, which is recognized in international law, and serves to denote, for example, debts contracted as a result of bank bailouts, the construction of unnecessarily huge and environmentally destructive infrastructures, subsidies to private companies that mistreat their workers, and so on. The concepts of "legitimate" and "illegitimate" debt are not static or formally defined, however. They are politically constructed and in dispute. What is eventually going to be considered an illegitimate debt that shouldn't be paid, as the result of an audit, will depend on the balance of forces between the political and social actors of a given country.

Debt audit processes can have a dynamic that is, as pointed out by some authors, somewhat analogous to the classic claim made by the labor movement for workers' control, but with important differences resulting from the change in context and the phase that neoliberal capitalism is currently in. The ultimate goal of workers' control was based on control in the workplace (the factory, the company, and so on) with the expectation of extending it to the whole of society and the state, in a bottom-up dynamic. In the case of the audit, the reverse is true. It begins by controlling the practices of the state and of its debt so as to extend this experience, from the top downward, to all work centers in production and in all the places where there is exploitation and oppression, including the service and public sectors (Mitralias 2011).

The first campaign in Mediterranean Europe to promote a public debt audit was launched in Greece, the European country most affected by the sovereign debt crisis. In late 2010 and early 2011, faced with the impasse in which the country found itself, the Greek Auditing Commission of the Public Debt, made up of social organizations, political parties, trade unions, and academics, was established with the aim of promoting a public debate and popular participation in the decisions made about the debt. The aim was to question the stance adopted by the government and the international community with regard to this debt. The commission sought to bring the debt contracts (some of which were made with the mediation of global investment bankers such as Goldman Sachs, and others earmarked for financing the purchase of arms, and so on) into the open and to put an end to the opacity of their management. An additional aim was to spread the idea that the need for repayment of the debt is not something so self-evident, but will rather depend on its nature and on whether or not it is considered odious or illegal (Lapavitsas 2010).

The Citizens' Campaign for Auditing the Debt in Spain sprang from the "Living in a Debtocracy" ("Viviendo en Deudocracia" in Spanish) conference, held in Madrid in October 2011, which brought together some thirty groups and members of social movements interested in promoting this initiative. Months later, in March 2012, the Platform for Auditing the Public Debt: We Don't Owe, We Won't Pay was formally constituted, devoted to raising awareness of the debt and its central importance in understanding the present crisis. It works not as a mass movement but rather as an education and awareness platform that spreads a critical view about debt and its payment.

Resistance to Austerity from a Gender Perspective

The citizen audit movement has also gradually incorporated a feminist perspective that points out the gender dimension of the crisis and the austerity policies justified by the need to pay off the debt. This gender perspective is the result of the intersection between the women's movement and the new anti-austerity movements. In Spain the Citizen Audit campaign set up a gender committee, while in Greece a women's meeting was held coinciding with the International Conference on Debt and Austerity in Athens in May 2011. All these initiatives have sought to highlight the specific impact austerity measures have on women and mark the rebirth, albeit limited, of the women's movement in the framework of resistance to austerity. They have also tried to bring an overall gender perspective to the analysis of the functioning of capitalism, work, and welfare state policies. One of the working documents of the Gender Committee of the Platform for the Citizen Audit of Spain's Debt points out:

> One of these invisible debts is the gender debt, the debt society has with regard to women. Women are creditors, in particular, in regard to the state and companies, as it is they who perform the care work that enables the reproduction of workers. Although many women have a double workload, only one part is recognized, whereas the other is neither socially acknowledged nor remunerated. As long as we live in a capitalist patriarchy, the debt owed to women will not be recognized or, of course, paid back. (Comisión de género de la PACD 2013b)

This feminist anti-austerity movement is faced simultaneously with two challenges: achieving specific visibility in this new context and impregnating all the rising social struggles with the gender perspective and its demands.

The initiatives to provide the debt audit movement with a feminist perspective are thus part of a more general attempt by feminist activists to endow the struggles against austerity with a gender perspective. In Spain, for instance, the origin of such efforts can be traced back to the activity of feminist groups during the occupation of the squares in May–June 2011 when what came to be called the 15M or *indignados* movement erupted. At the beginning, this movement did not have a specific gender dimension to its slogans, language, or demands, nor did it refer specifically to the particular problems faced by women in the crisis. In many of the main occupied squares and camps specific feminist working groups were set up, such as the Feministas Indignadas in Barcelona and the Gender Commission in Madrid. They were the result of a linking-up between the preexisting feminist movement and a new generation of women activists who developed a feminist consciousness. The work of these feminist committees played a decisive role in gradually introducing a gender perspective into the 15M movement in regard to both the impact of the austerity policies and sexual and reproductive rights. This was no easy task and was not without its problems. The gender perspective, in terms of language and practice, penetrated deeper into the movement as the movement grew in strength and maturity. Nevertheless, the gender perspective entered the 15M movement in a limited and contradictory way. Some of the most visible flaws in gender terms (e.g. the use of sexist language in meetings) were corrected, but a feminist perspective didn't truly permeate the movement in terms of its conceptualization of social inequalities and definition of priorities and demands. And what advances it made were always the result of the ongoing political pedagogy carried out by the feminist working groups within the movement (Ezquerra 2012b).

Conclusion

The combination of including nonpayment of debt among the claims of the movements opposed to austerity policies, on the one hand, and specific campaigns by the public, on the other, has led to the debt issue being situated at the center of the resistance to structural adjustment in southern Europe, where it is possible to say that democracy has been replaced by debtocracy. In other words, what we are seeing in the region is the dictatorial government of creditors and their allies, which, in the name of debt payment, is rapidly doing away with people's social, economic, and democratic rights—rights established under social democratic regimes for the past four decades.

Behind these dynamics, there is a project, not yet coherent or finished, aimed at changing the social model and reorganizing social relationships for the benefit of financial capital. For powerful banking interests, the social regulations that still exist in the old continent act as an impediment to the international competitiveness of the European economy and an annoying burden they would like to get rid of. Somehow we are witnessing a logic of "Latin Americanization" of the societies of southern Europe in terms of inequality, polarization, the deterioration of working conditions, and the degrading of public services and political participation.

The current cycle of resistance to austerity is essentially defensive; it is a collective reaction to an across-the-board attack against a particular social model. But this underlying defensive dynamic contains within it certain elements of an offensive nature in that they are disruptive and have the capacity to upset the routine functioning of the institutions. Although the resistance has so far not been able to achieve a significant number of victories that would enable it to accumulate enough forces to launch a counterattack, there have been victories. But these victories have been partial, very defensive (for example, putting a halt to household evictions in Spain thanks to the action of movements like the Mortgage Affected People Platform, or PAH in its Spanish acronym), and still lodged within an overall context of the advance of adjustment policies (Antentas and Vivas 2012).

The all-out offensive against social rights and liberties, the intensity of structural adjustment, and continued repression may unleash two alternative scenarios that are in fact going to be intermingled until one or the other definitively wins out. The first would see the austerity policies bulldoze their way unstoppably ahead, crushing all resistance as they go and consolidating an increasingly oligarchical and plutocratic political system and a society in which capital reigns unrestrained, trade unions and social movements are marginalized, and social inequalities of all kinds continue to increase. The second would be for the austerity screw to be turned so tightly that the magnitude of the ensuing tragedy produces a boomerang effect in society, exacerbating the legitimacy crisis of the political and economic institutions and opening up the way for a paradigm shift and a change of model in a democratic and egalitarian direction.

In the Mediterranean periphery of Europe, in Greece, Portugal, and Spain, what started out as an economic and financial crisis has gradually turned into an extremely serious social crisis and also a growing political crisis affecting the legitimacy of the political regimes established in the 1970s. All major crises have historically been resolved by a reorganization of social relations. As Daniel Bensaïd (2010) reminds us, "A way out of the crisis leading to the emergence of a new productive order and a new regime of accumulation does not depend on the economy alone. It requires new balances of forces, new geopolitical relations, new institutional and juridical devices." The question is therefore not so much whether we will come out of the crisis or not, but how we will come out of it and in which direction. A crisis is always a turning point in a society's historical trajectory. It is a watershed. But the course society takes from there is not marked out in advance; it depends on the balance of forces between social classes and social groups. And although at the moment the balance is heavily tilted in favor of the financial powers, the endgame still has to be played out.

Josep Maria Antentas is member of the Department of Sociology of the Universitat Autònoma de Barcelona (UAB) and member of Centre d'Estudis Sociològics sobre la Vida Quotidiana i el Treball (QUIT)—Institut d'Estudis del Treball (IET).

Esther Vivas is member of the Centre d'Estudis sobre Moviments Socials in the Universitat Pompeu Fabra in Barcelona.

Both are authors of *Planeta indignado* (Barcelona: Sequitur, 2012), about the *indignado* movement in the Spanish state and Occupy, and *Resistencias globales* (Madrid: Editorial Popular, 2009), about the movement against corporate globalization.

Note

1. *Editors' note:* See in this issue "Woman Is an Object Without History," a review of David Graeber's *Debt*, by Annie Spencer.

Works Cited

Adelantado, José, ed. 2000. *Cambios en el Estado del Bienestar: Políticas sociales y desigualdades en España*. Barcelona: Icaria.

Antentas, Josep Maria, and Esther Vivas. 2012. *Planeta indignado*. Madrid: Sequitur.

Balanyá, Belén, et al. 2002. *Europa SA*. Barcelona: Icaria.

Bensaïd, Daniel. 2010. "Crises d'hier et d'aujourd'hui." In *Karl Marx: Les crises du capitalisme*. París: Demopolis.

CADTM (Committee for the Abolition of Third World Debt). 2008. *¿Quién debe a quién?* http://www.quiendebeaquien.org/spip.php?article940.

———. 2010. *La deuda, maná del cielo para los acreedores y una tragedia para los pueblos.* http://www.cadtm.org/Juntos-para-imponer-otra-logica.

Camargo, Joao. 2013. *Que se lixe a Troika!* Lisbon: Deriva.

CCOO. 2013. "Se feminiza la destrucción de empleo público." FITEQA-CCOO http://www.fiteqa.ccoo.es/fiteqa/Conoce_FITEQA:Prensa:Notas_de_prensa:513780—Se_feminiza_la_destruccion_de_empleo_publico.

Comisión de género de la PACD. 2013a. "La deuda de género: La expropiación del trabajo y del cuerpo de las mujeres." http://www.quiendebeaquien.org/spip.php?article2542.

———. 2013b. "La deuda de los gobiernos es con las mujeres no con los bancos." *Setmanari Directa* 308:5–6.

Ezquerra, Sandra. 2011. "Miradas feministas a los efectos de la crisis." *Viento Sur* 114:91–98.

———. 2012a. "Acumulación por desposesión, género y crisis en el Estado español." *Revista de Economía Crítica* 14:124–47.

———. 2012b. "Feminist Practice in the 15-M Movement: Progress and Outstanding Issues." http://www.opendemocracy.net/sandra-ezquerra/feminist-practice-in-15-m.

Husson, Michael. 2010. "Refundación o caos." *Viento Sur*, March 31. http://www.vientosur.info/articulosweb/noticia/index.php?x=2821.

INE. 2011. *Encuesta de empleo del tiempo 2009–2010.* Madrid: Ministerio de Economía y Competitividad.

Jiménez Fernández, A., and R. Martínez-Pardo del Valle. 2013. *La economía sumergida en España.* Madrid: Fundación de Estudios Financieros

Juventud Sin Futuro. 2011. *Juventud sin Futuro.* Barcelona: Icaria.

Kouvelakis, Stathis. 2011. "Golpe de Estado europeo frente al levantamiento popular." *Viento Sur*, November 18. http://www.vientosur.info/articulosweb/noticia/index.php?x=4570.

Lapavitsas, Kostas. 2010. "Comisión internacional de auditoria de la deuda griega." *Viento Sur*, December 26. http://www.vientosur.info/articulosweb/noticia/? x=3433.

Larrañaga, Mertxe. 2009. "Mujeres, tiempos, crisis: Combinaciones variadas." *Revista de Economía Crítica* 8:113–20.

Medialdea, Bibiana. 2010. "La UE al desnudo." *Viento Sur* 110:47–57.

Mitralias, Yorgos. 2011. "Frente a la deuda: El apetito viene auditando . . ." *CADTM*, August 20. http://www.cadtm.org/Frente-a-la-deuda-El-apetito-viene.

Pedrol, Xavier, and Gerardo Pisarello. 2005. *La Constitución furtiva.* Barcelona: Icaria.

Piñero, Griselda, Olivier Chantry, and Iolanda Fresnillo. 2011. "La deuda llega a Europa, tras devastar el Sur." In ¿Quién debe a quién? Vivir en deudocracia. Barcelona: Icaria.

Pisarello, Gerardo. 2011a. Un largo Termidor. Madrid: Trotta.

———. 2011b. "Una (contra)reforma constitucional servil." Sin Permiso, September 6. http://www.sinpermiso.info/textos/index.php?id=4398.

Rancière, Jacques. 2006. El odio a la democracia. Buenos Aires: Amorrortu.

Rodríguez Cabrero, Gregorio. 2004. El Estado de Bienestar en España. Madrid: Fundamentos.

Toussaint, Éric. 2012. "Indignadas e indignados del mundo entero: Unámonos." CADTM, January 1. http://www.cadtm.org/ Indignadas-e-indignados-del-mundo.

Toussaint, Éric, and Damien Millet. 2010. Debt, the IMF, and the World Bank: Sixty Questions, Sixty Answers. New York: Monthly Review Press.

Vivas, Esther. 2007. En pie contra la deuda. Barcelona: El Viejo Topo.

Honey Flies

H. Lynnette Barr

it has me.

it has me   in pictures
          in histories
          in searches
it has me   frozen into statuses
          and blog posts
          and chat logs
                some small sticky substance
                (like you'd find on flypaper)
                i got on my hands
                     and never washed off.
it has me   in belongings
                though that's my own fault
                and i could chew through them
                     if needed.
it has me   in the fly
          that buzzes
          with incessant need
                (i die a little every time)
          if i silence the buzz
          it rings if i cut the ring
          it cries
                with silent guilt
                from angry voices within

WSQ: Women's Studies Quarterly **42: 1 & 2 (Spring/Summer 2014)** © 2014 by H. Lynnette Barr. All rights reserved.

      demanding why i didn't answer
             didn't respond
             didn't bother

it has me   in papers
     in signatures
     in documents
       i didn't have much choice
       but to fill out
       with a name
         a location
         a ten-digit number
           supposed to stand
           in place of me
             staples of society
             stuck cleanly
             through my clothes
             and then my wrists

it has me   in loans
     in payments
     in debt
     worse in jobs
       in money
       in need
it has me   every time
     i hand over a bill
     to pay for food
       for shelter
       for friends
     worse when i have to use a card.

i wonder if it had Walden
  of course it did that's a place

it has me   in physics
     in spaces
     in every cell of my body
       like a fly stuck in honey
       (did you know they all

              die and get replaced
              at some point)
it has me   in curves
      in skin
      in veins like cord
              to keep me tied in here
              little knots hidden
              under a cloth faint blue
              and barely seen.
it has me   in synapses
      in dendrites
      in frontal lobes
      worse   in serotonin
           in dopamine
           in norepinephrine
                    or more specifically
                    an imbalance of them
                    that has me   off kilter
                              off walls
                              off ledges
                              on meds.
it has me most of all in clocks
              in arms wrapped around my waist
              in hands around my neck
              in faces staring into mine

digitally it's even worse.

it has me   in soft glows to put me to sleep
        in morning shrieks to wake me
        in sliced lines that switch
              to siphon away
              seconds minutes
              hours years
      i wonder if i could break it
      off my wrists and reach
      my hands into its face
      i wonder if the numbers

would cut me slice me
as i strangled it
and they switched
switched
switched

it wouldn't do any good.
without clocks still

it has me   in a planet hurtling
in a frenzied spinning
in a fly that breeds and dies and lives
it has me   in cosmos
in black holes
in evolution
it has me   in coffins
in placenta
in lipstick
it has me   in traps
it has me   by the mouth
it has me   by the hand

and it will have me
when i am dead.

H. Lynnette Barr is a communication and writing student in Denver, who writes poetry, sketch comedy, angry essays on pop culture, and weekly blog posts. She also performs in an improv theatre troupe and teaches at a community-based youth theater. Her hobbies include mimicking human speech and coughing at the symphony.

Global Health: The Debts of Gratitude

Nora J. Kenworthy

It permits us always to say: "Careful, you think there is gift, dissymmetry, generosity, expenditure, or loss, but the circle of debt, of exchange, or of symbolic equilibrium reconstitutes itself according to the laws of the unconscious; the 'generous' or 'grateful' consciousness is only the phenomenon of a calculation and the ruse of an economy. Calculation and ruse, economy in truth would be the truth of these phenomena."

Jacques Derrida, Given Time: I. Counterfeit Money

In early April 2013, Madonna's ongoing troubles with Malawi boiled over in a spat with President Joyce Banda that aired across the Internet (Gumede 2013; Ross 2013). Without delving into the disputed details of Madonna's pitfalls trying to "do good" (Fisher 1997) in the country, it is worth repeating a small part of the lengthy statement released by President Banda's office as Madonna departed Malawi in a flurry of complaints, her public relations team still sparring with critics (Ross 2013). The statement, which President Banda later said she had neither seen nor approved, nevertheless resonated so powerfully with many in the country that few expected a retraction (Harding 2013; "Joyce Banda Disowns" 2013). An early section reads: "Granted, Madonna has adopted two children from Malawi. According to the record, this gesture was humanitarian and of her accord. It, therefore, comes across as strange and depressing that for a humanitarian act, prompted only by her, Madonna wants Malawi to be forever chained to the obligation of gratitude. Kindness, as far as its ordinary meaning is concerned, is free and anonymous. If it can't be free and silent, it is not kindness; it is something else. Blackmail is the closest it becomes" (Ross 2013).

To focus solely on Madonna's sense of entitlement or her misbehavior here is to miss the larger source of Malawians' anger and take all-too-easy aim at the pitfalls of celebrity philanthropy. African leaders and their citizens are no strangers to the "obligation of gratitude" incurred while at the receiving end of philanthrocapitalism, development schemes, or humanitarian aid. Even the most elementary student of theories of exchange will remind us that no gift is merely a symbol of generosity but is embedded in complex relations of hierarchy and expectations of reciprocity (see Derrida 1992; Graeber 2001; Mauss 1990). The language of "obligation" and "blackmail" reflects the ways in which "gifts" become debts, and charity creates subtle forms of peonage. What is notable in this incident—and indeed, vaguely titillating for critical Western observers—is that Banda steps so boldly outside her role in the contrived theater of aid recipiency.

Even on the eve of African independence, however, Frantz Fanon (1963) unmasked the dangers of colonial charity:

> And when we hear the head of a European nation declare with hand on heart that he must come to the aid of the unfortunate peoples of the underdeveloped world, we do not tremble with gratitude. On the contrary, we say among ourselves, "it's a just reparation we are getting." So we will not accept aid for the underdeveloped countries as "charity." Such aid must be considered the final stage of a dual consciousness—the consciousness of the colonized that *it is their due* and the consciousness of the capitalist powers that effectively *they must pay up* (59; emphasis in the original).

Fanon reframes the seeming generosity of the developed nations as material and psychological reparations. Here, the final step toward liberation requires a psychological shift, in which the mystifications of charity fall away, and what is given becomes what is owed.

The perceptual shift Fanon once anticipated seems long forgotten, buried under layer upon layer of initiatives for the betterment of the Global South. More recently, the vast expansion of global health programs has provided a new platform for the mystifications of donation, aid, and generosity. Although many recent critiques of global health endeavors have emphasized their unintended costs, and the exacerbations of inequalities and hierarchies they can elicit (see, for example, Benatar 2005; Crane 2011, 2013; Lewis 2007; Swidler 2009), a more explicit focus on debt may help us to fully grapple with the obligations and disenfranchisements that continue to arise despite the good intentions, "best practices," and humanitarian ideals of global health enterprises (Bornstein and Redfield 2011; Elyachar 2006).[1]

In this brief critique, I attempt to elaborate some of the ways in which pernicious forms of debt accompany global health efforts, drawing on my own work in Lesotho. Obligations and unfair exchanges enter the calculus of global health programs in myriad and unexpected ways, particularly at the level of aid agreements and donor expectations (Adams, Novotny, and Leslie 2008; Baylies and Power 2001; Esser and Keating Bench 2011; MacKellar 2005; Nguyen 2010). Here, however, I focus on three dynamics that are centrally important for recipient-citizens but often overlooked in global health research: first, the voids created by what is *not* given, or recognized as deserved, in priorities and projects; second, the unforeseen costs of partnership; and third, the democratic deficits of global health governance. First, however, I briefly describe how global health projects emerge from earlier debts and inequalities between countries of the Global North and South.

Forms of Debt

Contemporary global health crusades have not emerged in a vacuum: they remain bound up in postcolonial histories of debt and deficit policy in poor countries. In response to the "third world debt crisis," neoliberal policies were embedded in structural adjustment programs (SAPs) as conditionalities on loans for already indebted countries. As many scholars have noted, SAPs dismantled social services, with devastating effects on health systems and population health (Fort, Mercer, and Gish 2004; Pfeiffer and Chapman 2010). Not only were such impacts foreseen, they were upheld as necessary: free market ideologies insisted that if only cash-strapped governments would adopt austerity policies, development would follow. Market reform and development, therefore, were seen as precursors to wealth-driven population health improvements (Sparke 2013).

Even as austerity policies proved disastrous in most countries, and as the World Bank carefully recalibrated its messaging in recent decades, free market ideologies were hardly left by the wayside. Instead, as Matthew Sparke (2013) argues, a "New Washington Consensus" is emerging that promotes global health programs as integral to future development. Make people more healthy, so the new ideology goes, and they will be more productive. What is insidious about this new global health ideology is that it inverts the discursive linkage between wealth and health (and between poverty and illness). Rather than conclude that poverty is a structural cause of illness, it promotes the idea that a better biological functioning of citizens will be sufficient to stimulate economic growth. In the slogans of global health institutions such as the Gates Foundation ("We believe every person deserves the chance to live a healthy, productive life"), Sparke asserts, we can discern a causal chain built on techno-biological interventions that become free market "fixes": pills, productivity, prosperity (364–80).

Interestingly, it is the histories of third world debt that allowed the flourishing of many public emergencies and rampant health disorders to which global health now so urgently responds (see Fort, Mercer, and Gish 2004; Pfeiffer and Chapman 2010). Nor are the effects of austerity limited to poor countries: a recent example of the effects of fiscal policy on public health comes from Greece, where extreme austerity measures were implemented in the wake of the global financial crisis; infant mortality rose by 40 percent after 2008, and rates of new HIV infections more than doubled during a six-month period in 2011 (Stuckler and Basu 2013, 77–90). Debt creates the founding conditions for global health efforts (and the exceptional measures they often employ) but also contributes to its ideologies and means of response. Johanna Crane (2013) demonstrates how the persistent global inequalities between donors and recipients, patients and providers, and researchers and those researched retain an inherent value for knowledge production and the enterprises of global health science, which so often relies on diseased but underserved populations for research. At least certain aspects of the global health industry, then, profit from global inequalities exacerbated by debt even as they purport to ease disease burdens. This helps explain, in part, why wealth redistribution is so rarely included in programmatic interventions, even as more and more attention is paid to inequities (Commission on Social Determinants of Health 2008).

It is against this backdrop of more widely recognized linkages between debt and global health that I hope to highlight some more subtle patterns of obligation and debt. My own research on the political ramifications of HIV scale-up and broader global health programs in Lesotho (Kenworthy 2013) has repeatedly brought me face-to-face with the strange kinds of debts incurred when good works do less good, and cost much more, than recipients initially hope. Much of my fieldwork, conducted between 2008 and 2011, focused on communities, patients, clinicians, and support groups as they interacted and came into contact with HIV policy, donors, nongovernmental organizations (NGOs), and campaigns. At the time, the so-called scale-up of HIV programs was vast, a dizzying deployment of HIV money, resources, programs, and ideologies. But I found myself most often in social landscapes of hopes deferred, labors unrecognized, and promises unfulfilled—as organizations and initiatives circulated rapidly through clinical and communal sites, conferring programs and technologies and pharmaceuticals, but rarely the means of robust or secure survival. These are patterns of symbolic and political—as well as economic—deficit. They created the kinds of resentment and distrust that accumulate when gestures of charity are not wanted, not at all what was hoped for. It is to these debts of "gratitude" that I now turn.

The Void Between Need and Desert

Global health initiatives have earned criticism for emphasizing program priorities that do not always align with recipients' most urgent or important needs (Esser and Keating Bench 2011; MacKellar 2005; Shiffman 2006). At a systemic level, this priority mismatch is fueled by the politicization of health initiatives, competition among donors and organizations, and thriving ideologies about what is best for recipient nations. As global health funding continues to expand, these priorities seem to go through wavelike shifts, as donors move en masse from one issue area to another. This, combined with "vertical," or "silo," programming to address specific issues (rather than broad-based determinants of health and health system weaknesses) (Ooms et al. 2008; Pfeiffer and Nichter 2008), ensures that the lived experience of "global health" for recipients is one of shifting terrains, fragmented responsibility, and persistent inequalities.

There is much we could highlight here, but allow me to focus on two dimensions of global health priorities. First, much of the effort in global health is directed toward shuttling technologies, drugs, educational programs, or behavioral interventions into the minds and bodies of the sick or potentially sick in developing countries (Parker 2000). What it does not typically provide (though of course there is great variability in programs) is redistribution of goods, resources, or revenue to the poor. As a result, much of what filters down to patients or communities is of little recognizable value, no matter how much patients appreciate once-scarce antiretro-viral therapies, or NGOs use social marketing to distribute public health goods (Pfeiffer 2004).

By contrast, the proliferation of jobs, vehicles, and resources for NGO and government programs reeks, from the perspective of citizens, of a sinister misdirection of funds. As one of my informants put it, "Funding comes for TB, for HIV, but it only goes for their fancy hairstyles in Maseru," referring to the intricate, frequently changing hairstyles of civil servants and NGO employees in the capital (Maseru) who seem to profit so visibly from the funding of HIV and AIDS. And community care workers, referring to the HIV test kits they transported back to clinics during Lesotho's national testing campaign, angrily reminded me, "We are the ones who are bringing [the government] the blood!" These workers speak literally of the spots of blood on the HIV tests they collect during community testing drives and bring into the government clinics, and of the sick patients they send to clinics for testing. But "bringing [the government] the blood" draws on more sinister perceptions of how the government attains power and HIV money, the uses to which the bodies of the sick are put, and care workers' own complicity in these processes. Such dialogues reference pervasive beliefs in southern Africa that the rich gain power and wealth through occult practices of consuming and using the bodies or blood of the poor (Ashforth 2005, 41; Ranger 2006; Bayart 2009).

The government here is portrayed as a consuming power, using the diseased blood of patients in order to obtain funds for HIV. Common rumors in Lesotho echo such sentiments: many claim that the government ensures HIV test results are positive so it can count more and more people as HIV positive—and thus continue securing HIV funding. These perceptions hold a telling mix of fact and fiction: in many ways it is the testing, counting, and regulation of bodies by which the government is able to retain its grasp on HIV funding flows. In the "HIV Corner" at a local clinic supported in part by donor funds, an elderly gentleman with HIV and TB invoked the oft-used language of eating as he explained that funds never seem to reach those in need:

> We are living under oppression [khatello], because you know that when [NGOs] come and tell us, "We'll do this and that," . . . They come to us—and we realize that this is the way that they eat from us. Because the money that they receive will be coming from other countries and they will be saying that they are doing something for us, but these are

just empty promises. . . . These other countries think they are giving aid [*phallela*] to these people [living with HIV], but the aid never reaches them. *They eat from us.*

This ghastly sentiment, coming from a man whose own body bore the distinctive curves and hollows of advanced HIV and TB, is expressed in a dual language. Here, the "consumption of the poor" (Farmer 2000) denotes metaphorical, as well as pathogenic, ways that the bodies of the sick are being "eaten" (see similar discourses in Ferguson 2006, 73; Kalofonos 2010). From the debt of things owed but not given emerges a new illness variant, where the wasted figures of the sick embody suspicions about who eats, who does not, and what (or whom) is being consumed.[2]

Second, dialogues of sustainability, medical rationality, and accountability often translate, at local levels, into unmet desires and obligatory sacrifices. This is reflected in antiretroviral therapy (ART) trainings that encourage patients to eat protein and nutrient-rich diets that they cannot afford but that physical hunger and clinical expertise obligate them to attain (Kalofonos 2010; Marsland 2012). Or there is the policy put forth recently by a UNICEF representative in response to Lesotho's acute food crisis, in which UNICEF would *fail* to provide enough nutritional support to households in crisis. "It doesn't even cover 40% of household needs," the representative reported confidently, "and it's on purpose, by the way. Because we don't want to create a welfare state" (Magubane 2012). Fears of dependency among aid agencies continue to rewrite the historical conditions of Lesotho's entrenched food insecurity (Ferguson 1994). There is no room here for the kinds of debts carried over from colonialism— in this case, Lesotho's loss of fertile lands and ensuing reliance on food imports—and sustainability-minded policies create new, terrifying debts for those families facing the gaping void of their remaining 60 percent of household needs. Taken together, these policy legacies represent, in the words of Ferguson (1994), the continuing "anti-politics" of development enterprises; but they also evoke forms of what we might call, drawing on Freire (1970), an "anti-conscientization" as citizens internalize and repeat the ideological justifications for the debts by which they are bound. This is reflected as poor neighbors in Lesotho accuse each other of being "lazy" and dependent, citing what is popularly called a "culture of handouts." It is when recipients fail to see such ideologies as problematic—fail to see those missing nutrients or unfair distributions as resources they are owed, services they deserve—that the real debts of gratitude begin to take root.

The Costs of Partnership

Other authors in this special issue point to the ways in which debt has become a grounds for establishing legitimacy and, moreover, membership in social and political worlds.[3] Debt is only one of the conditions under which the institutions of late liberalism partition aspects of citizenship, replacing them with shifting, temporary bonds of partnership (Povinelli 2011; Schild 2000). Certainly, partnership acts as currency among those who rely on aid projects for survival (Swidler 2009). But strivings for partnership seem like residual echoes of what James Ferguson (2006) calls "haunting claim[s] for equal rights of membership in a spectacularly unequal global society" (174–75). Increasingly, many global health partnerships have not produced the kinds of membership that would entail rights, entitlements, or even varieties of citizenship but rather the kinds of membership rooted in inequality, supplication, and debt. Ann Swidler (2009), for example, argues that funding reconfigures and reinforces patronage politics among AIDS organizations in sub-Saharan Africa. Vinh-Kim Nguyen's (2010) research from West Africa demonstrates how antiretroviral therapies provided in a context of scarcity enact a damaging politics of triage, eliciting new subjectivities through "therapeutic sovereignty." As a Westerner, I found myself unwittingly drawn into recipients' perceptions of what partnership meant: "Maybe you are just like these people," one interviewee said upon meeting me, "who are just using us— saying you are doing things for the sake of people with HIV, talking to us, and maybe you are going to get some funds [because of it] and they will be no use to us!"

Many global health initiatives draw on post–Cold War celebrations of civil society (Comaroff and Comaroff 1999; Igoe and Kelsall 2005) and thus pay great attention to the power of community and the productive value of participation. Particularly in Africa, many interventions rely on the efforts of relatively unskilled, community-based workers as a means of providing low-cost labor for projects, disseminating particular kinds of knowledge, ensuring patient compliance, and encouraging mutual support (Beeker, Guenther-Grey, and Raj 1998; Low-Beer 2010). Much of this work is carried out by women, and while these are unmistakable new labors, many efforts go underrecognized and unpaid (Callaghan, Ford, and Schneider 2010; Govender 2013; Tlali 2009). Although forms of care work and community health outreach vary widely, in places like Lesotho, labors are inadequately reimbursed, with "stipends" often promised but rarely and inconsistently granted.

By institutionalizing care work as global health efforts undertaken in the spirit of volunteerism and goodwill, community-based global health strategies simultaneously transform labors into charitable efforts, economically undermine the value of such work, reinforce gender stereotypes, and obscure the conditions of poverty, gender inequality, and desperation that produce such labors.[4] In the absence of more formal, institutionalized social safety nets, community-based workers whom I accompanied were often forced to fill gaps in social provision from their own slim resources, doling out money for medicines, transport, and orphan care. 'M'e 'Makabelo, an unpaid treatment supporter in a peri-urban village in which I worked, was one of many who faced the problem of how to support patients on HIV and TB treatment without supplemental resources. Some of her patients would arrive at her door, medicines in hand, and refuse to take their pills until she shared her own household's food with them. "I know that this patient shouldn't take the treatment without eating, or on an empty stomach," she explains, "[so] I enter inside my house, and share the bread I have made for my children, which is not even enough [for them]. . . . And I am left there with the drama of replacing that portion [of the bread] for my child." 'M'e 'Makabelo's neighbor engages in a bizarre practice of claims-making, eking out nutritional survival by impinging on the generosity of his neighbors, making claims about what he deserves, not to the state but to his resource-strapped caregivers, arguing that without food, the toxicity of the medicines he takes will kill him. An irony of much aid at these microcosmic levels is that, even as it purports to help those in need, it can cast local workers into further nets of obligation and create hungers for patients that cannot be filled. In the absence of broad political entitlements, the needs of neighbors and patients become obligations to be fulfilled by care workers themselves.

Thus, one of the most remarkable social phenomena of community health interventions in Lesotho is the tension between mutual care and mutual vulnerability. Support groups—first imagined by Western agencies as psychosocial associations for eliciting better biomedical outcomes— often come to resemble mutual aid societies, whose members organize hoping to gain access to new global health resources but frequently find themselves burdened by the financial weight of members' illnesses and deaths (Marsland 2012). Since many organizations and granting agencies view support groups as productive associational venues for the dissemination of knowledge or the rollout of specific projects, their goals are unlikely to closely align with those of support groups, whose most proximate concerns are survival, food security, and assistance for dying members (Marsland 2012; see also Kalofonos 2010).

In one support group whose meetings I attended for nearly a year, members constantly fought about how to divide scant resources to support multiple sick and dying members. Organized as a group by the clinic, most members initially had only their HIV status in common. They quickly found that new forms of social organization also created more people for whom they were potentially responsible. In one heated meeting, a frustrated group member suggested that they bring the corpse of one of their deceased members—for whom they could not afford funeral expenses—to the steps of the Department of Social Welfare to protest the department's lack of support for those affected by HIV. While NGO-community partnerships in global health expand the responsibilities of citizens to each other as well as to transnational entities, they rarely extend the obligations of global health agencies to meet needs that are crucially important to citizens, as what citizens typically want are social services and basic goods that fall outside organizational mandates and conflict with ideologies of sustainability. Evidence above and elsewhere points to the pervasive absence of social safety nets, such that even as global health programs treat the body, they fail to safeguard the person.

The forces causing such a dismantling of responsibility for social goods and basic needs are complex. What is worth noting here are the ways in which such partnership arrangements institutionalize collective vulnerability and decentralize obligations to care, even when they also show positive program outcomes and promote social solidarity. Partnership itself can take on the appearance of well-orchestrated theater, as organizations or donors sporadically appear, carry out dialogues or give out goods, and then, in the words of my informants in Lesotho, "disappear." Citizens tend to be aware of the roles they are expected to play in such dramas—to be the supplicant, thankful community, endorsing any plan that brings in resources. These rituals discourage more open dialogues about complex needs and desires, limiting opportunities for equitable dialogue and priority-setting, even as they purport to endorse participatory approaches. As Sarah White (1996) argues, participatory efforts "may be the means through which existing power relations are entrenched and reproduced"

(6); other development critics have called participation a "new tyranny" (Cooke and Kothari 2001).

Democratic Deficits

Not surprisingly, the final horizon of these debts is a political one. As partnerships frequently exacerbate and reinforce power inequalities between citizens and donors, weakening their voices in priority-setting, global health apparatuses participate in an unwitting dismantling of the state. This is not simply an emptying out of the state, nor can it be attributed only to surging support for NGOs and civil society organizations. Rather, in Lesotho, the funding cycles, short-term time horizons, and vertical implementations of a project culture disrupt and partition off the social contract, relieving the national government of direct obligations to citizens and sending citizens themselves scrambling to procure participation in one project or another for survival. Many do not succeed at all in meeting shifting program criteria. What results is a vast disruption of political landscapes already marred by earlier incursions of colonialism, development, and structural adjustment. Recipiency replaces entitlement; biopolitics and the administration of promises replace the social contract. I want to suggest that the debts of gratitude are more often enacted here through the relations between donors, organizations, and recipients, a dynamic that enforces the crucial misrecognitions of gift exchange (Derrida 1992).

In some cases, these dynamics add fuel to old patterns of hierarchy (Smith 2003; Swidler 2009). In other cases, citizens observe the seeming complicity of governments in these new arrangements and conclude that the close working partnerships between donors and ruling parties look a great deal like nepotism and corruption. When the U.S. Millennium Challenge Corporation (MCC) offered an enormous grant to Lesotho in 2008, opposition parties and citizens took to the streets in protest, arguing that their government did not deserve the money and was too corrupt to qualify for MCC selection criteria, and claiming that the grant would only further corrupt politics. Global health money provides support to ruling parties in myriad ways, even when donors are painstaking in their efforts to reduce corruption.

Because policies have largely come from donors, and donors require new efforts of accountability from recipient states, the normal patterns of accountability between states and citizens are disrupted. It is little wonder that citizens, bound up in the politics of charity, find themselves saddled with a deficit of power. Nor is it surprising that these debts seem ephemeral, secondary compared to the urgent material debts of life lived at the margins. Much as moments of resistance from my informants are important to note, they are incomplete and ineffective in the new power arrangements encouraged by global health initiatives. Few citizens can afford, as President Banda can, to step outside the theater of recipiency and name it false. Perhaps the best and only recourse to the disenfranchisements of charity is the one offered by Aminata Sow Fall (1981) in her novella *The Beggar's Strike*, in which the indigent poor of a West African city contest the government's efforts to evict them by refusing to accept alms. It is only in their refusal that their necessity—as vessels for the charity required in order to be a good Muslim and also to be considered a fully fledged citizen—is demonstrated. Sometimes, the book seems to argue, the poor guard the gates to power as well as those to salvation.

Conclusion

My intent here is to initiate a reconsideration of global health politics through the lens of debt and, in doing so, to extrapolate how charity and the debts of gratitude affect recipients of global health aid. These are, of course, very broad strokes. Global health takes many forms, and the efforts of organizations and programs demonstrate great variability; there are many praiseworthy exceptions to these generalizations. While I speak here of my observations in a single country, they echo the findings of many scholars from across numerous disciplines. I offer this piece as a reflection, a rethinking of the dynamics of gift, obligation, entitlement, and membership among recipient citizens.

Fanon (1963) reminds us that debt more often lies in the Global North, rather than the South. As long as global health is understood and practiced as a gift and an intervention, it may be difficult to convince Fanon's (1963) "unfortunate peoples" that they need not "tremble with gratitude." Although the long-lasting effects of colonialism, global inequalities, and structural adjustment programs have confined large portions of the world's poor to lives damaged and foreshortened by illness, we still rarely conceive of global health efforts as anything more than works of generosity and goodwill. But as Derrida (1992) argues, "The 'generous' or 'grateful' consciousness is only the phenomenon of a calculation and the ruse of an economy"—parts well played by both parties, but nonetheless a cunning fiction. Renewed attention to justice and rights in global health makes some headway in recognizing health as a debt owed; such efforts should continue to be supported. Yet evidence from Lesotho and elsewhere indicates that even well-intentioned global health efforts have far-reaching and unexpected consequences, leaving in their wake new debts, obligations, and forms of peonage for recipients. We urgently need to attend to these broader injustices as well: it is not just reparations, but a balancing of power and voice, that is owed to those at the receiving end of global health endeavors.

Acknowledgments

This material is based upon work supported by the National Science Foundation under grant number 1024097, the US Fulbright IIE Program, and the American Association of University Women American Fellowship. I am indebted to the Ministry of Health and Social Welfare for research clearance, the National University of Lesotho for research support, and, most importantly, to colleagues and informants in Lesotho for their insight and assisitance. Finally, I am especially grateful to Rosalind Petchesky, as well as an anonymous reviewer, for feedback on earlier drafts of this paper.

Nora J. Kenworthy is an assistant professor of nursing and health studies at the University of Washington, Bothell. Her research focuses on global health politics and the effects of HIV programs on relations between citizens and the state in southern Africa.

Notes

1. As one example of unintended costs, scholars at Yale University recently published compelling evidence that UN intervention in Haiti after the earthquake was directly related to, and indeed, a cause of, the deadly outbreak of cholera that began in 2010 (See: Transnational Development, Global Health, and Association Haitiënne 2013). The more recent harms in post-earthquake Haiti are expertly contextualized by Petchesky (2012).
2. Of course, the notion of "being eaten" is not a new illness idea in Lesotho, where certain expressions of illness translate literally as, "I am eaten," or, "where are you eaten?" But the physical manifestations of AIDS and TB, and the suspicions of corruption arising from the influx of HIV/AIDS and global

health funding, reinforce the linkages between "eating" as unfair consumption of resources, "being eaten" as illness, and the emaciated bodies of the sick appearing to have been "eaten away."

3. *Editors' note:* See, in the present issue, Larisa Jasarevic, "Speculative Technologies: Debt, Love, and Divination in a Transnationalizing Market"; Monica Johnson, "The Adventures of Dorrit Little"; and Jodi Kim, "Debt, the Precarious Grammar of Life, and Manjula Padmanabhan's *Harvest.*"

4. I do not intend to downplay the equally important role of generosity and solidarity that motivates many volunteers but instead wish to emphasize that such selflessness coexists with acute wants.

Works Cited

Adams, Vincanne, Thomas E. Novotny, and Hannah Leslie. 2008. "Global Health Diplomacy." *Medical Anthropology* 27(4):315–23.

Ashforth, Adam. 2005. *Witchcraft, Violence, and Democracy in South Africa.* Chicago: University of Chicago Press.

Bayart, Jean-Francois. 2009. *The State in Africa: The Politics of the Belly.* 2nd ed. New York: Polity.

Baylies, Carolyn, and Marcus Power. 2001. "Civil Society, Kleptocracy, and Donor Agendas: What Future for Africa?" *Review of African Political Economy* 28(87):5–8.

Beeker, Carolyn, Carolyn Guenther-Grey, and Anita Raj. 1998. "Community Empowerment Paradigm Drift and the Primary Prevention of HIV/AIDS." *Social Science and Medicine* 46(7):831–42.

Benatar, Solomon R. 2005. "Moral Imagination: The Missing Component in Global Health." *PLoS Med* 2(12):1207–10.

Bornstein, Erica, and Peter Redfield, eds. 2011. *Forces of Compassion: Humanitarianism Between Ethics and Politics.* Santa Fe, NM: School for Advanced Research Press.

Callaghan, Mike, Nathan Ford, and Helen Schneider. 2010. "A Systematic Review of Task- Shifting for HIV Treatment and Care in Africa." *Human Resources for Health* 8(1):8.

Comaroff, John L., and Jean Comaroff, eds. 1999. *Civil Society and the Political Imagination in Africa: Critical Perspectives.* Chicago: University of Chicago Press.

Cooke, Bill, and Uma Kothari. 2001. *Participation: The New Tyranny?* New York: Zed Books.

Commission on Social Determinants of Health. 2008. *Closing the Gap in a Generation: Health Equity Through Action on the Social Determinants* of Health; Final Report of the Commission on the Social Determinants of Health. Geneva: World Health Organization. http://www.who.int/social_ determinants/thecommission/finalreport/en/index.html.

Crane, Johanna. 2011. "Scrambling for Africa? Universities and Global Health." *Lancet* 377(9775):1388–90.

———. 2013. *Scrambling for Africa: AIDS, Expertise, and the Rise of American Global Health Science*. Ithaca: Cornell University Press.

Derrida, Jacques. 1992. *Given Time: I. Counterfeit Money*. Chicago: University of Chicago Press.

Elyachar, Julia. 2006. "Best Practices: Research, Finance, and NGOs in Cairo." *American Ethnologist* 33(3):413–26.

Esser, Daniel E., and Kara Keating Bench. 2011. "Does Global Health Funding Respond to Recipients' Needs? Comparing Public and Private Donors' Allocations in 2005–2007." *World Development* 39(8):1271–80.

Fanon, Frantz. (1961) 1963. *The Wretched of the Earth*. Trans. R. Philcox. New York: Grove Press.

Farmer, Paul E. 2000. "The Consumption of the Poor: Tuberculosis in the 21st Century." *Ethnography* 1(2):183–216.

Ferguson, James. 1994. *The Anti-politics Machine: "Development," Depoliticization, and Bureaucratic Power in Lesotho*. Minneapolis: University of Minnesota Press.

———. 2006. *Global Shadows: Africa in the Neoliberal World Order*. Durham, NC: Duke University Press.

Fisher, William F. 1997. "Doing Good? The Politics and Antipolitics of NGO Practices." *Annual Review of Anthropology* 26:439–64.

Fort, Meredith P., Mary Ann Mercer, and Oscar Gish, eds. 2004. *Sickness and Wealth: The Corporate Assault on Global Health*. Cambridge, MA: South End Press.

Freire, Paulo. 1970. *Pedagogy of the Oppressed*. Thirtieth Anniversary ed. New York: Continuum Press.

Govender, Indira. 2013. "Funding Crisis Looms Large." *Mail and Guardian*, March 28. http://mg.co.za/article/2013-03-28-00-funding-crisis-looms-large.

Graeber, David. 2001. *Toward An Anthropological Theory of Value: The False Coin of Our Own Dreams*. New York: Palgrave Macmillan.

Gumede, William. 2013. "Malawi President Joyce Banda: When Madonna Met Her Match." *Independent*, April 12. http://www.independent.co.uk/news/ people/profiles/malawi-president-joyce-banda-when-madonna-met-her-match-8570613.html.

Harding, Andrew. 2013. "Malawi's President 'Furious' After Madonna Criticised." *BBC*, April 12. http://www.bbc.co.uk/news/ world-africa-22123841.

Igoe, Jim, and Tim Kelsall. 2005. *Between a Rock and a Hard Place: African NGOs, Donors, and the State.* Durham, NC: Carolina Academic Press.

"Joyce Banda Disowns State House Harshly-Critical Statement on Madonna." 2013. *Malawi Voice,* April 13. http://www.malawivoice.com/2013/04/13/joyce-banda-disowns-state-house-harshly-critical-statement-on-madonna-54671/.

Kalofonos, Ippolytos. 2010. "'All I Eat Is ARVs': The Paradox of AIDS Treatment Interventions in Central Mozambique." *Medical Anthropology Quarterly* 24 (3):363–80.

Kenworthy, Nora J. 2013. "What Only Heaven Hears: Citizens and the State in the Wake of HIV Scale-Up in Lesotho." PhD diss., Columbia University.

Lewis, Bradley. 2007. "New Global Health Movement: Rx for the World?" *New Literary History* 38(3):459–77.

Low-Beer, Daniel. 2010. "Social Capital and Effective HIV Prevention: Community Responses." *Global Health Governance* 4(1): 1–18.

MacKellar, Landis. 2005. "Priorities in Global Assistance for Health, AIDS, and Population." *Population and Development Review* 31(2): 293–312.

Magubane, Khulekani. 2012. "SA to Prevent Lesotho Famine?" *iAfrica,* November 6. http://business.iafrica.com/businessday/825733.html.

Marsland, Rebecca. 2012. "(Bio)Sociality and HIV in Tanzania: Finding a Living to Support a Life." *Medical Anthropology Quarterly* 26(4):470–85.

Mauss, Marcel. 1990. *The Gift: Forms and Functions of Exchange in Archaic Societies.* 9th ed. New York: Norton.

Nguyen, Vinh-Kim. 2010. *The Republic of Therapy: Triage and Sovereignty in West Africa's Time of AIDS.* Durham, NC: Duke University Press.

Ooms, Gorik, Wim Van Damme, Brook Baker, Paul Zeitz, and Ted Schrecker. 2008. "The 'Diagonal' Approach to Global Fund Financing: A Cure for the Broader Malaise of Health Systems?" *Globalization and Health* 4(1):6.

Parker, Richard G. 2000. "Administering the Epidemic: HIV/AIDS Policy, Models of Development, and International Health." In *Global Health Policy, Local Realities: The Fallacy of the Level Playing Field,* ed. Linda Whiteford and Lenore Manderson, 39–56. Boulder, CO: Lynne Rienner.

Petchesky, Rosalind. 2012. "Biopolitics at the Crossroads of Sexuality and Disaster: The Case of Haiti." In *The Ashgate Research Companion to the Globalization of Health,* ed. T. Schrecker, 169–90. Burlington, VT: Ashgate.

Pfeiffer, James. 2004. "Condom Social Marketing, Pentecostalism, and Structural Adjustment in Mozambique: A Clash of AIDS Prevention Messages." *Medical Anthropology Quarterly* 18(1):77–103.

Pfeiffer, James, and Rachel Chapman. 2010. "Anthropological Perspectives on Structural Adjustment and Public Health." *Annual Review of Anthropology* 39(1):149–65.

Pfeiffer, James, and Mark Nichter. 2008. "What Can Critical Medical Anthropology Contribute to Global Health?" *Medical Anthropology Quarterly* 22(4):410–15.

Povinelli, Elizabeth A. 2011. *Economies of Abandonment: Social Belonging and Endurance in Late Liberalism*. Durham, NC: Duke University Press.

Murray, Colin, and Peter Sanders. 2005. *Medicine Murder in Colonial Lesotho: The Anatomy of a Moral Crisis*. Edinburgh: Edinburgh University Press.

Ranger, Terence. 2006. "Medicine Murder in Colonial Lesotho: The Anatomy of a Moral Crisis by Colin Murray; Peter Sanders." *Journal of the International African Institute* 76(2)267–68.

Ross, Elliot. 2013. "Madonna vs Joyce Banda: Celebrity Deathmatch (Philanthropy Edition)." *Africa Is a Country*, April 11. http://africasacountry.com/2013/04/11/madonna-vs-joyce-banda-celebrity-deathmatch-philanthropy-edition/.

Schild, Verónica. 2000. "Neo-liberalism's New Gendered Market Citizens: The 'Civilizing' Dimension of Social Programmes in Chile." *Citizenship Studies* 4(3):275–305.

Shiffman, Jeremy. 2006. "Donor Funding Priorities for Communicable Disease Control in the Developing World." *Health Policy and Planning* 21(6):411–20.

Smith, Daniel Jordan. 2003. "Patronage, Per Diems, and the 'Workshop Mentality': The Practice of Family Planning Programs in Southeastern Nigeria." *World Development* 31(4):703–15.

Sow Fall, Aminata. 1981. *The Beggars' Strike; or, The Dregs of Society*. London: Longman.

Sparke, Matthew. 2013. *Introducing Globalization: Ties, Tensions, and Uneven Integration*. Malden, MA: Wiley-Blackwell.

Stuckler, David, and Sanjay Basu. 2013. *The Body Economic: Why Austerity Kills*. Philadelphia: Basic Books.

Swidler, Ann. 2009. "Dialectics of Patronage: Logics of Accountability at the African AIDS-NGO Interface." In *Globalization, Philanthropy, and Civil Society*, ed. David C. Hammack and Steven Heydenmann, 192–220. Bloomington: Indiana University Press.

Tlali, Sophia. 2009. *Lesotho Report: Making Care Work Count; A Policy Analysis*. Johannesburg, South Africa: Gender and Media Southern Africa.

Transnational Development Clinic, Global Health Justice Partnership, and Association Haitienne de Droit de l'Environment. 2013. *Peacekeeping Without Accountability: The United Nations' Responsibility for the Haitian Cholera Epidemic*. New Haven, CT: Jerome N. Frank Legal Services Organization, Yale Law School, Yale School of Public Health.

White, Sarah C. 1996. "Depoliticising Development: The Uses and Abuses of Participation." *Development in Practice* 6(1):6–15.

Feminist Indebtedness

C. H. Browner and Carolyn Fishel Sargent's *Reproduction, Globalization, and the State: New Theoretical and Ethnographic Perspectives.* Durham, NC: Duke University Press, 2011.

Michelle Murphy's *Seizing the Means of Reproduction: Entanglements of Feminism, Health, and Technoscience.* Durham, NC: Duke University Press, 2012.

Heather Munro Prescott's *The Morning After: A History of Emergency Contraception in the United States.* New Brunswick: Rutgers University Press, 2011.

Chikako Takeshita's *The Global Biopolitics of the IUD: How Science Constructs Contraceptive Users and Women's Bodies.* Cambridge, MA: MIT Press, 2011.

Claire McKinney

Both the historical ties between development aid and population control technologies and the material ties between feminist political health claims and expert-controlled and capitalist-distributed reproductive technologies reveal the centrality of debt to the formation of particular responsibilities and potential freedoms. How does such indebtedness inform feminist pursuits of freedom when the practical terrain is the body? We take on debt acknowledging our responsibility to adhere to the terms of the debt, while seeking new freedoms through the material advantages indebtedness confers. How can a feminist technoscience contend with these paradoxical formations of control and liberation?

The four books under review trace the historical, geopolitical, and economic aspects of reproductive technology and highlight where feminist agendas fit within these complex formations. To varying degrees of success, each grapples with how the shifting ideologies of women as a population to control, as a population to exercise control, and as a population of citizen-consumers has tied the experience of reproduction to technoscience in both productive and dangerous ways. It is undoubtedly the case that feminist reproductive health politics is indebted to profoundly antifeminist technological developments. Margaret Sanger, the early and influential advocate of birth control, shifted her focus from the diaphragm, which she thought would fail to limit the fertility of the poor

 WSQ: Women's Studies Quarterly 42: 1 & 2 (Spring/Summer 2014)

in the United States and in the global South, to a hormonal contraceptive pill (Takeshita, *Global Biopolitics*, 38–39; Prescott, *The Morning After*, 11). Eugenic and neo-Malthusian, the global development agenda was crucial for the initial funding and development of reproductive technologies that were also key components of the political demands for women's reproductive freedom. Today, as analyzed in various essays in Browner and Sargent's *Reproduction, Globalization, and the State*, the debt-creating development aid radically influences the provision of reproductive health care in family planning programs, AIDS clinics, and refugee camps across the globe, often in contradictory and nonfeminist ways (Gutmann 2011; Richey 2011; Whiteford and Eden 2011).

Chikako Takeshita's *The Global Politics of the IUD* provides a fascinating look into the development of IUDs, a technology that "embodies the paradox of the simultaneous possibility of giving women control over their bodies and taking it away from them" (5). The belief of development experts that women in the global South constituted a population in need of scientific control allowed for the development of IUDs in ways that glossed over dangerous and painful side effects. These ignored side effects ironically undermined the widespread adoption of IUDs that international aid agencies desired. Takeshita demonstrates that the IUD as a method of coercive reproductive control relied on the need to justify the IUD as a technology suitable for the global North as well. After the removal from the U.S. market of the Dalkon shield after it resulted in over ninety thousand injured women in the United States, "IUD advocates were concerned that Western donors and the U.S. government might be accused of wrongdoing if they continued to distribute a contraceptive method that was no longer being sold to American women" (101). Thus, the search for the correct U.S. consumer for IUDs and marketing of IUDs such that women in the United States would use them was part and parcel of the justification of fertility control abroad. Takeshita's careful tracing of the shifts in how the subjects appropriate for IUD use were understood provides illuminating insight into the contradictory life of the IUD as a simultaneously feminist, neo-Malthusian, and neoliberalist instrument of reproductive choice and control. The complex stance toward the IUD slightly fades in the later chapters of the book, as Takeshita sees the main problem with current IUDs as lying in racially inequitable marketing, while she espouses a normative belief that "the disappearance of the IUDs from the market [is] equivalent to losing reproductive choice" (78). Despite her call for feminists to remain always conflicted (168), Takeshita's complex history of IUDs falters in its implicit faith in the provision of choice in the market as necessary for a feminist health agenda.

The same faith in neoliberal provision of reproductive technologies underlies the history of emergency contraception in Heather Prescott's *The Morning After.* Prescott charts a similar shift in understanding emergency contraception from the disease model of pregnancy seen in "the worldwide population crisis and the 'epidemic of unwed pregnancy in the United States'" (126) to a reproductive rights model "aimed at increasing women's birth control choices" (3), though she does not link the two models as mutually reinforcing. Instead, she argues that the continued expanded access to and health care workers' awareness of emergency contraceptives "represent a major rapprochement between major population groups, representatives from the pharmaceutical industry, and members of feminist women's health advocacy groups" (6). What remains unexplored are the terms through which this rapprochement was won and what had to be given up in its pursuit. For Prescott, the questions now facing emergency contraception center on whether dedicated emergency contraception marketing by pharmaceutical companies will be covered by health insurance schemes and be made available without health care worker intervention. What gets lost in Prescott's sanguine appraisal of the rapprochement is that another model of feminist self-help has disappeared from the terrain of emergency contraceptive provision. The Yuzpe method involved a higher dosage of commonly used oral contraceptives for postcoital contraception. Thus, as Reproductive Health Technologies Project board member Felicia Hance Stuart did, one could "cut up packets of oral contraceptives and place the Yuzpe regimen dosage in an envelope along with typed instructions on how and when to use the pills for postcoital contraception" (83). It was only the belief among some advocates that "the best way to spread knowledge about [emergency contraception] was to persuade pharmaceutical companies in the United States to manufacture and market a dedicated product" that tied women's health advocates to a less do-it-yourself and resistant strategy of emergency contraception provision. While Prescott's history details the evolution of the struggle for emergency contraception, the framing of the project provides no sense of what a political, instead of market-driven approach, to women's reproductive health might look like.

In contrast, *Seizing the Means of Reproduction* provides exactly such an historical look at resistant projects. Michelle Murphy's history of the 1970s feminist health movement, focused on its instantiation in Los Angeles, is a fascinating look at how a conscious feminist politicization of particular protocols and technologies simultaneously relied on and resisted capitalist formations, medical expertism, and family planning regimes. It is only with the depoliticization of feminist health concerns and the "NGO-ization" of feminism that the understanding of women's reproductive health as a kind of counter-conduct wanes. Because of her focus on the 1970s, Murphy also documents a shift in the development strategies away from the coercive population strategies of the 1960s and toward a neoliberal "supply side" strategy, whereby picking "the right market practices" would result in "even the peasant woman" choosing to consume birth control, thereby accomplishing "the enlargement of human freedom by extension of family-planning programs" (165). While this faith in the provision of the right technologies to accomplish neoliberal goals may describe the current efforts of numerous NGOs focused on women's health, some feminist NGOs resist this reduction of women's health to a technological problem. Notably in Murphy's text, the Women and Development Unit and the International Women's Health Coalition reject Pap smears as a tool because they fail to address the power imbalances, both between men and women and between the global North and South, that are the real cause of "reproductive tract infections." Thus, while the NGO-ization of feminism can result in abandoning political contestation of the terms of reproductive control, it need not require such stances as long as feminist concerns remain at the fore. Murphy's balanced and detailed examination of the shifts in the tactics and investments of the women's self-help health movement is a crucial resource in understanding how the presence and absence of different types of feminist politics shape reproductive health landscapes.

Of course, questions of when and how such concerns are formulated are enmeshed in the technoscientific and localized terrain of reproductive health. Murphy, Prescott, and Takeshita's work can tell us little about how particular reproductive technologies are taken up, resisted, and navigated in contexts across the globe defined by different state, religious, economic, and kinship formations. *Reproduction, Globalization, and the State* takes as its task to provide a global ethnographic investigation of women and men's agency in the context of reproductive technologies. As its editors define it, agency is "the socioculturally mediated capacity to act" though "in reality exercising agency does not necessarily produce an unequivocally positive outcome." They ask, "In what sense is the term agency even meaningful when the very acts in question, although 'agentive,' may be destructive or rooted in the exigencies of survival (e.g., 'survival sex,' pressure to produce only sons, aborting female fetuses)?" (13). Thus, though there may be subversive and resistant strategies for dealing with stem cell research, assistive reproductive technology, fetal diagnosis, female genital cutting, and AIDS care regimes (just a few of the many topics examined in this volume), agency can also manifest in participating in potentially harmful or harm-producing reproductive activities. But this volume does highlight that reproductive technologies provide the basis for particular forms of social cultivations, while particular actors also transform the meaning and use of those technologies. As Susan Erikson notes in her innovative ethnography of the multiple global inputs to the availability and use of ultrasound in Germany, "The uneven distribution of ultrasound use in pregnancy throughout the world . . . attests to ultrasound as a praxis requiring both social cultivation and technological capacity" (30). Similarly, Claudia Fonseca presents a fascinating piece on the ramifications of state-funded paternity tests in Brazil that have resulted in a de-emphasis on women's sexual history in paternity suits and a reinforcement of a purely biological sense of paternal responsibility. Fonseca reveals that when individuals understand themselves as only consumers of genetic technology, the question of why one ought to be invested in a genetic understanding of kinship exclusive to other meanings of kinship fades from view.

What all these texts illuminate is how the indebtedness to reproductive technologies has produced multiple forms of responsibility and freedom. Inseparable from the construction of certain women as capable of exercising responsible choice and others as requiring coercive control, feminist political responses to these technological formations require an active reflexivity such that the terms of our indebtedness do not leave us as uncritical consumers. While the professionalization of feminism both in the United States and in international NGOs risks creating a view from above that accepts the terms of the provision of reproductive health, a purposeful dedication to view technology as only a means to feminist opposition to the colonization of the body can maintain a reproductive health agenda as a powerful force for global social justice.

Claire McKinney is a PhD candidate in political science at the University of Chicago. Her dissertation charts the ethical turn in reproductive politics in the United States in relation to current bioethical and legislative debates.

Works Cited

Erikson, Susan L. 2011. "Global Ethnography: Problems of Theory and Method." In *Reproduction, Globalization, and the State: New Theoretical and Ethnographic Perspectives,* ed. C. H. Browner and Carolyn Fishel Sargent, 23–37. Durham, NC: Duke University Press.

Fonseca, Claudia. 2011. "Law, Technology, and Gender Relations: Following the Path of DNA Paternity Tests in Brazil." In *Reproduction, Globalization, and the State: New Theoretical and Ethnographic Perspectives,* ed. C. H. Browner and Carolyn Fishel Sargent, 138–54. Durham, NC: Duke University Press.

Gutmann, Matthew. 2011. "Planning Men Out of Family Planning: A Case Study from Mexico." In *Reproduction, Globalization, and the State: New Theoretical and Ethnographic Perspectives,* ed. C. H. Browner and Carolyn Fishel Sargent, 53–67. Durham, NC: Duke University Press.

Murphy, Michelle. 2012. *Seizing the Means of Reproduction: Entanglements of Feminism, Health, and Technoscience.* Durham, NC: Duke University Press.

Prescott, Heather Munro. 2011. *The Morning After: A History of Emergency Contraception in the United States.* New Brunswick, NJ: Rutgers University Press.

Richey, Lisa Ann. 2011. "Antiviral but Pronatal? ARVs and Reproductive Health: The View from a South African Torwnship." In *Reproduction, Globalization, and the State: New Theoretical and Ethnographic Perspectives,* ed. C. H. Browner and Carolyn Fishel Sargent, 68–82. Durham, NC: Duke University Press.

Takeshita, Chikako. 2011. *The Global Biopolitics of the IUD: How Science Constructs Contraceptive Users and Women's Bodies.* Cambridge, Mass: MIT Press.

Whiteford, Linda M., and Aimee R. Eden. 2011. "Reproductive Rights in No-Woman's Land: Politics and Humanitarian Assistance." In *Reproduction, Globalization, and the State: New Theoretical and Ethnographic Perspectives,* ed. C. H. Browner and Carolyn Fishel Sargent, 224–38. Durham, NC: Duke University Press.

PART II. **DEBT IN EVERDAY LIFE**

The Adventures of Dorrit Little

Monica Johnson

The Adventures of Dorrit Little was created by Monica Johnson to capture the story of an average student debtor in the United States today. The title is a reworking of Charles Dickens's serial novel *Little Dorrit,* which told the tale of the first child born into an English debtor's prison in the mid-nineteenth century. Additional chapters of Dorrit's story can be found at dorritlittle.com.

Monica Johnson is a comic artist living in New York City. She completed *Dorrit Little* as part of her degree in the Integrated Media Arts MFA Program at Hunter College. In 2010 she created EDU Debtors Union, an organization for student debtors that argues the need for union representation for student debtors.

WSQ: *Women's Studies Quarterly* 42: 1 & 2 (Spring/Summer 2014) © 2014 by Monica Johnson. All rights reserved.

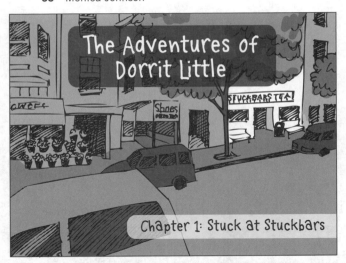

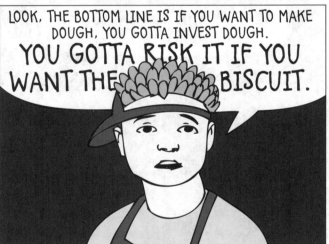

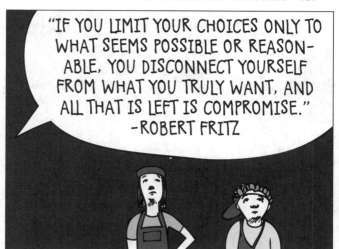

Will Dorrit sign her student loan offer and take a gamble on grad school?

See what happens at dorritlittle.com.

Douloti the Bountiful

Mahasweta Devi
Translated by Gayatri Chakravorty Spivak

—Where have you come from, Somni?

—They brought me from Barha village.

—Did they say they would marry you?

—Why should they? I was already married.

—Already married?

—Yes yes. And I have my man at home.

—How did you come?

—Was there another way? My man took two hundred rupees from him, to get land. Hoo, in a year it became four thousand rupees. Then the god said to my man, You won't be able to repay, you are a kamiya. Send your wife. Your debt will be repaid in five years, your wife will return home with money in hand. I kept my son with my husband and came here.

—And the boy?

—He is in Barha. The god has lots of land in Barha.

—How many children do you have here?

—Three.

Somni put her hand to her cheek and said, "See what a strange thing. I was married in childhood, and I stayed with my man for so long. I had only one son. And Latia made me the mother of three sons in a row.

—Those sons?

—They lie around in the marketplace. They beg. They don't let you live with your child, and clients come up to one month before birth. Then I can't for three months.

—Then?

—The god lends money.

WSQ: Women's Studies Quarterly 42: 1 & 2 (Spring/Summer 2014) © 2014 by Gayatri Chakravorty Spivak. All rights reserved.

—Doesn't he let you keep them?

—No no, would he? When I am burnt up, I go see them. Rooti's son too is Latia's son. And it was Latia's *truck* that hit him and crippled him. As a cripple he gets more begging. He got a shirt too.

—How long will you stay?

—Who knows. As long as it pleases the god.

—Then?

—Then I'll beg. There's nothing in my body anymore. Will I be able to work hard anymore? For four-five years thirty clients a day. I'll beg.

Acknowledgments

This excerpt from Mahasweta Devi's short story "Douloti the Bountiful," translated by Gayatri Chakravorty Spivak, is from *Imaginary Maps: Three Stories by Mahasweta Devi* (New York: Routledge, 1995), 63. Published by permission of the translator. All rights reserved.

Gayatri Chakravorty Spivak is university professor at Columbia University. Her most recent books are *Other Asias* and *An Aesthetic Education in an Era of Globalization*. She was the 2012 Kyoto Prize laureate in Art and Philosophy and a Padma Bhushan awardee for 2013. She trains teachers and guides ecological agriculture in western Birbhum District, West Bengal, India. The daughter of a feminist mother, she is involved in feminism across the spectrum.

The Kind of Life You Always Wanted

Justin Boening

You have finished what you set out to,
                                    given up
        on desire, preferring
                            the silent commerce
of unwinding wire
                    from a spool,

and you have invited sadness,
                            like a child hiding
underneath a boathouse,

                            called catastrophe a horse
that waited for you to ride him,
                            too tired
        to pull at his mane.

Who's brought you
                        to this far off country? What strangers
have gathered in your house
                        to see you off?
Who's forgotten to wear
                    one's best, wingtip shoes?

(You have). This kind of life
                        has its rewards: little

WSQ: Women's Studies Quarterly **42: 1 & 2 (Spring/Summer 2014)** © 2014 by Justin Boening . All rights reserved.

is recorded, little
        is remembered long.

It finds you on foot,
        looking familiar, wearing a new suit,
apologetic with a pocketful
        of sweaty money.

It pops open your trunk,
        when you're drunk and shirtless
    in the moonlight,

claps twice, then scoops flocks
        of red-and-gray fan-tailed warblers
into the smoke, into night,
        until you swear to him
    you've done as you were told.

Born in the Adirondacks, **Justin Boening** is the author of *Self-Portrait as Missing Person*, which was selected by Dara Wier for the Poetry Society of America's National Chapbook Fellowship. His poems and reviews have appeared or are forthcoming in a number of journals, such as the *Atlas Review*, *Boston Review*, *Colorado Review*, and *Lana Turner*. A graduate of Columbia University's School of the Arts, Boening currently lives in Lewisburg, Pennsylvania, where he is Bucknell's 2013–14 Stadler Fellow.

Habitual Exit

Jayanti Tamm

Amy placed the brown package along with the rest of the mail on the circular coffee table. She expected her five-year-old to grab and pull the parcel, but Janie remained in place, her cotton pajamas with pink and green frogs sagging off her tiny frame. Perhaps the basic brown mailer envelope—no color, glitter, or stickers—triggered Janie's suspicions about the lack of fun it contained. As Amy examined the handwriting, she knew instantly who it was from. Although she'd received few written mementos from Renaldo, the compact script with letters squeezed together as though not wanting to risk being alone, was unmistakably his. His fake return address offering further confirmation: *666 Anyplace, Your town, U Suck of A.*

"Mommy, is it for me?" Janie asked.

"Yes, jellybean. It's for you," Amy said, holding out the package for Janie to see. "It says right here. 'To J-A-N-I-E.'"

Janie repeated the letters, confirming her name.

"Maybe it's a birthday gift," Amy said.

"But my party is over before yesterday."

"You mean your birthday party already happened," Amy said. "Two weeks ago." No matter how times Amy went over the concept of time with Janie, her daughter failed to comprehend. On particularly challenging days, Amy wondered if Janie purposefully persisted in intersecting the past, present, and future, determined to smear them all together just as she did her finger paints.

"Is it my birthday again?"

"No," Amy said. The last thing she needed was Janie expecting another load of cheap plastic dolls with garish makeup and oversized breasts. She

WSQ: Women's Studies Quarterly 42: 1 & 2 (Spring/Summer 2014) © 2014 by Jayanti Tamm. All rights reserved.

handed the package to Janie, who, after a pause, took it in her tiny hands. Janie shook it, and when nothing clanked or rattled, she handed it back, asking her mom to open it.

No card, no wrapping. Typical. Amy scanned the envelope once more, checking the stamps and closure seal if there were any additional scribbles, any clues intending to be found. It had been over two years since she'd last seen him sprint away from the restaurant where they'd met for lunch. There'd been no further contact.

Inside, folded into the bottom of the envelope was a pink shirt.

"I see something pink," Amy said, knowing anything pink would rev up Janie's interest. Janie stepped closer.

"Ta-dah!" Amy said, smiling at the unexpectedness of his gesture. She imagined him clutching the gift at a crowded post office somewhere, shuffling forward in his black Doc Martens and purple laces.

Amy unveiled the grand surprise as Janie craned for a full view. There it was. Silk-screened across the front of the mini pink T-shirt was a glittery rainbow sprouting from heart-shaped clouds. Beneath the rainbow's arc, two magical white unicorns were gleefully humping.

Amy had first met Renaldo fifteen years ago in a nightclub on the frayed outskirts of Washington, DC. It was the period in her life she privately referred to as her "lean years,"—she was four sizes thinner and her sense of displacement had made her feel nearly transparent with insignificance. She'd never wanted to be in DC, but when Bill, her fellow clubgoer and boyfriend, graduated college and landed his first job in the nation's capital, he wooed her to accompany him. With this job, an entry-level position in financial planning with low pay, Bill had brimmed with pride at the prospect of what he envisioned as their future. He'd prepared Amy's favorite dinner—potato pancakes with lemon meringue pie for dessert—and after he cleared the plates, he got down on one knee and had asked her to move with him. When she'd started giving him reasons why it was a bad idea— the heat, the distance from New York City, the heat, the distance from New York City—he brought up sacrifices made by famous couples throughout history: Cleopatra for Anthony, Juliet for Romeo, Nancy for Sid.

"Didn't all of those end badly?" Amy had asked.

"But think of all the good years they had first."

Bill had refilled their pair of unmatched wineglasses, and Amy drank until the very word itself—"sacrifice"—morphed into hilarity. The more she said it—*sacrifice, sacrifice, sacrifice*—the more it just sounded like "sack," and all she could imagine was herself stepping inside an enormous itchy burlap sack. Soon, she was laughing so hard that her entire body shook, offering her confirmation.

"Let's go dancing tonight," Amy said to Bill when he unlocked the door to their third-floor apartment. It had been four months since their move to Washington. Amy had waited for Bill's return all afternoon, combing through the *City Paper*, DC's free weekly alternative newspaper, circling and highlighting what she declared was their ideal itinerary for the evening. The pages spread across what functioned as their coffee table, an old piano bench that she'd rescued from garbage night and spray painted black. In DC, she was perpetually bored.

"No cover charge before eleven," she said, attempting to placate his ever-present concern about their humble budget.

"How 'bout we stay home? Rent a movie? Snuggle in for the night?" Bill asked, twirling his tie over his head like a corporate cowboy.

Amy frowned, circling again and again the listing from the club the Catacombs that promised a night of Goth-Industrial spun by DJ Nosferatu with a live performance by GrindGirls until the pen tore the paper. He owed her. She'd agreed to move. She'd packed up, waved farewell, and unpacked as a stranger in a city with no job, no friends. She'd tried looking for jobs. Sometimes. She'd print her résumé—with her recent degree in anthropology—and mailed it to some nonprofits that had something to do with intentions toward clean water in Africa or vaccinations against multisyllabic diseases in South America, but she'd had no luck. When Bill had gingerly suggested that she might remove her nose ring and dye her hair, she had twisted her silver rings in disapproval, vowing not to perpetuate encourage those who discriminate by changing. Bill himself had surprised her when he had arrived home earlier that month with a new squared crew cut, leaving his dyed black locks, the ones she used to braid, remaining only in photographs held up by tiny magnets on the refrigerator.

"Fine. I'll go myself," Amy had said, expecting that Bill would follow her or, at the very least, turn up at the club during "Love Will Tear Us Apart," their favorite song, and dance in circles around her.

He didn't.

But Renaldo did.

"That one's bat shit crazy!" Renaldo had said to Amy, stepping forward to intervene just before an oversized man holding a drink and sloppily spinning, nearly collapsed onto her.

"No problem," Renaldo said.

"I hadn't said thank you." Amy said.

She noticed his black eyeliner puddled below his dark eyes.

"What?" he asked.

As he leaned closer so he could hear her over the music, she thought she smelled Elmer's glue.

"I hadn't said thank you," Amy tried again.

"You won't owe me anything."

From that night, they were a duo. In Renaldo, Amy had found the perfect playmate. Like her, he swam through time without having to return for work, appointments, or deadlines. Like hers, his days accommodated any whim from the prior night without repercussions. No matter Amy's suggestion, Renaldo always answered the phone before it finished its first full ring as though he'd been sitting in his room with his palm cradling resting on the receiver, waiting. He then appeared, at the apartment door, ringing the bell incessantly, dressed in an over patched black leather coat and emptied backpack.

Often on weeknights, Renaldo would appear unexpectedly for dinner, and they'd all eat together, a makeshift family. Always ravenous, Renaldo gobbled up his food without pause, as though anything that had been placed before him would vanish, if he braked, even for a second. After dinner, Bill would bid them good-bye, joking that curfew was at ten, as Amy and Renaldo headed out to a club. The arrangement suited Bill as well—Amy happily could haunt the nights with a companion, leaving Bill to focus on work and join them on the weekends. Amy sensed Bill felt grateful knowing she wasn't alone. Since meeting Renaldo, she'd felt less lost. She'd started going to the farmer's market to buy brightly colored vegetables and had even gone on a second interview at an international adoption agency.

At times when Amy and Renaldo ventured out to the cramped clubs where the blue-Mohawked DJ spun ethereal music encased in beats, Amy stood along the wall and watched Renaldo dance. Through the smoke machine's haze, Renaldo didn't appear human. Instead, he was a windup doll, cranked to the maximum, where the notch, if forced to turn even the slightest, would snap. He jerked and flailed, far too fast for the amplified rhythm. Kicking and hopping, he wore the same combat boots, Amy presumed, from his days of military service, now fastened with fat purple laces. His eyes stared at no one, sweating until his black T-shirt clung to the form of his muscled back and stomach, and the tight black jeans melted onto his legs. If he came close enough and the spotlight hit just right, she'd see the raised grid of thick scars near his brown wrists. She had never asked him about that because she sensed he'd tell her it was from some tragic fall while training for the Olympic equestrian team or else in an accident wrestling a swordfish in the Florida Panhandle. He'd dance for hours, oblivious of the thinning and swelling of the crowds, until Amy found she wasn't having fun anymore, that it all felt suddenly brittle and sad, and she'd have to stop him by bracing him with both hands to report that she wanted to leave. She'd had enough.

Fifteen years after their first encounter, the truths Amy knew about Renaldo were few and far between. In fact, she still doubted that Renaldo was his real name. At the time they met, Renaldo lived at the Walter Reed military hospital. He'd given her conflicting stories about why he'd been discharged and returned from his base patrolling the border that divided North and South Korea like a tight waistband. Always suspicious of the military, Amy viewed the armed forces as an overpriced charade, a maddening spectacle professionally packaged in stars and stripes. Whether Renaldo had indeed been honorably discharged after a Humvee accident or he hadn't, what did it matter?

"Honorable discharge? The military's the only place that has the balls to call vaginal spew 'honorable.'" Renaldo said, slurping spoonfuls of Amy's attempt at curry.

Amy had laughed so hard that she'd spilled the watery concoction onto her new black and purple corset.

During that time with Renaldo, he'd always have her laughing. His stories were funny, unapologetic, and raw. While shopping for thrift store finds to be transformed into Goth fashions, Renaldo reenacted stories about growing up in a rented room in the ghetto of Paterson, New Jersey. According to Renaldo, his earliest memories were of his mother bribing him to wait on the building's front stoop until the sessions with her male clients ended.

"She'd set me up with her suitcase of wigs and hair rollers, and I'd be all good. I had the beehive down. The up-do. They were mad stylin'" he'd said, explaining how he'd wear them and dance, jutting out his hips for a convincing wiggle.

But when Amy would ask more questions, he'd skip years and stories and start in again. This time, starting years later, as an enlisted soldier, living on base in Korea. Sometimes Amy would try to rewind, to reposition him to fill in the missing years, but he'd break his own hesitation with a recharged urgency of something else entirely, and his dark eyes would widen in anticipation at the next opportunity to present Amy a slice of absurdity for them to share. He'd then launch into stories of the members of his battalion, the freckled homophobic Southern Baptists and sunburned born-again Texans.

"These guys hated the gays. Like really hated the gays. They'd all be in the rec room bloodying up their fists punching the penis-looking punching bags, yelling, 'Fag! Fag!' And then later, they'd hook up with each other in the showers. Isn't that funny?"

According to Renaldo, he'd kept his gayness well hidden. He told Amy that he'd trudge out with the rest of the drunk soldiers to the sad tittybars along "Hooker Hill," filled with young Korean girls who didn't have enough titties to squeeze.

It felt good to laugh, to laugh at someone or something remote from her own circle of frowning concerns—overdue student loans, overwrought parents—at her formless life. As if needing it himself, Renaldo was always ready to provide comic relief for her. And at that point she needed it. With Renaldo, she felt justified in day trips to Baltimore to scour cloudy plastic cases of used CDs, searching for rare European import singles. Later, at the prominent Baltimore Harbor Hotel, they'd convince the chambermaid they'd left their key to the pool area in their room, and they'd swim and lounge, taking extra piles of prim laundered towels as pillows, until it was finally late enough to dress up in layers of velvet, lace, and leather and dance at a club until dawn. In his company, there was no such thing as squandered time; he invested feverishly in the day and night at hand; to the present he was wholly committed.

In addition, he found Amy's sacrifice for love outstanding.

"It's the shit I want," Renaldo said one day as he accompanied Amy to pick up Bill's shirts from the dry cleaner.

"Clean shirts?" Amy asked.

"Mad love. You. Him. The move. The whole thing. You gave it all up for him, for love."

Amy didn't have the heart to correct the errors, to clarify that the only reason she agreed to pick up Bill's shirts from the dry cleaner was that she couldn't deal with the thought of having to wash, dry, and, God forbid, iron Bill's endless cycle of button-downs in subtle hues of grays and blues, that she'd never been on board for the move, that she still resented Bill for her acceptance of it, and finally, and probably worse, that she had given up nothing. She had had nothing in the first place to give up. Her relationship with Bill was what provided her a costume, a veneer of honor, of, yes, sacrifice. But she didn't tell Renaldo any of it, and his blissful ignorance and his gift of bestowing purpose upon her put her even more in his debt.

One night Renaldo showed up at Amy and Bill's apartment with a bloody nose. Seeing the burst of red, Amy tried hard not to overreact, to remember this was just boys being boys.

"He fought like a little girl!" Renaldo said. "Check out these scratches. It was fuckin' hysterical."

The story that followed was yet another elaborate tale involving some defective guy. These stories inevitably turned out badly. And while Amy concentrated on cleaning Renaldo's scrapes with a cotton swab and antiseptic, Renaldo chuckled as he spun the yarn of this latest dud, who turned compulsive, pushing for more until Renaldo showed up at the guy's job at Juicy Juice in the Pentagon Shopping Mall to end it once and for all.

"Smells good in here." Renaldo suddenly said, sniffing the air hungrily. "You cooking soup?"

Over the course of their friendship, Renaldo was prone to coyly disappear. No notice. No warning. No thanks. No good-bye. Maybe this was cyclical, the drama games of extended youth. *Look at me. Look at me. Now you see me. Now you don't.*

The first time it happened was shortly after Amy announced that Bill had been transferred to Philadelphia and that they would be moving at the end of the month. As though to avoid being the one left behind, the next week, Renaldo gushed about his move in three weeks to Austin. The circumstances always remained vague and the contact information never properly worked. A disconnected phone number. Return-to-sender letters. In the aftermath of his absence, a possibility that, this time, he might never resurface, that, this time, he'd have decided he'd had enough. But then, just when she'd assumed she'd lost him for good, he'd reappear—Tigger-like, boinging on his zany tail with hilarious stories about how pathetic the Goth music scene was in Austin, and how pitifully the Texan Goths dressed.

Each time he reappeared, he acted the same, as though he'd emerged unscathed from the past, unaware that time had moved forward in his absence. With his black hair still shaved on the sides and clumped above his forehead into gigantic spikes like a triceratops's, he'd boast about obtaining new track releases from Siouxsie and the Banshees and, flashing his unsteady row of yellowed teeth, announce the big, big news that he'd *finally* found a DJ who played full sets devoted to Current 93.

Two years ago when Amy discovered in her inbox an email from Renaldo, she frantically clicked it open. He wrote of having found, at last, his true calling, in Jesus, and of finally renouncing the evils of his past ways. He declared himself a changed man, proved by his recent marriage to Mindy, a God-fearing woman he'd met at church. They were embarking on a new life together, in God's love, and he was reaching out to Amy to see if there was even the remote possibility that, she too, might have been saved.

"Bullshit," Amy said, not believing it for a second. "Bill! Renaldo's back!" she shouted.

Bill rushed in from the next room, where he was painting the nursery for their soon-to-be second daughter the color of a Creamsicle.

"What's it this time?" Bill asked, peering at the computer monitor for the punch line.

"A born-again straight church guy!"

Together, laughing more than they had for what felt like years, Amy and Bill collaborated on a lengthy reply. With her belly too large for her to be close enough for comfortable typing and her feet and ankles too swollen for them to remain on the ground, Amy dictated while Bill alternately typed and rubbed her bloated legs, which rested across his lap. The unexpected excitement of Renaldo's message, interrupting both of them, felt like a rare chance to be jointly nostalgic. They had come a long way, Amy thought, looking around at the cathedral ceiling in their recently renovated five-bedroom Victorian. Bill's promotion to senior financial analyst, followed by the move to Long Island, and then the birth of Janie, their now three-year-old who was already in bed, at times made their days in Washington feel so remote that she'd question if they happened at all. Who were those people? What had they wanted? Bill placed his paint-flecked hand gently against her belly, against the still-contained internal bundle, due to be delivered by cesarean section at the end of summer, and together, they laughed.

"Should we ask Renaldo to be the new baby's godfather?" Bill asked, feeding another unopened credit card offer into the paper shredder.

"You're joking, right?" Amy asked, folding washcloths and receiving blankets into picnic squares.

"It might be good for him," Bill said.

"That's not how it's supposed to work," Amy said.

She stopped to watch Bill shred an advertisement for an elaborate home security system where a blonde mother, a blonde father, and two even blonder daughters smiled inside a house while a brown-skinned man dressed in black with the mandatory robber's mask peered longingly through the window.

They had been looping endlessly on this issue. As devout atheists, it had been hard enough to figure out godparents for Janie, and now, having to discover, once again, that there were no decent candidates made Amy wince. All possible options were desperately flawed, and she knew that she had only herself to blame. After years of consciously rejecting the trappings of responsible circles, she felt exposed. The lack of an appropriate choice of godparent for her daughter appeared to her as clear evidence of her wasted past, of her extended sloppy and reckless years of fitful roving.

"It might be great for him. Just what he might need to get him to turn that corner. It could be just the perfect thing. Besides, it's really not such a big deal," Bill said. "Without the religious part, it wouldn't entail any of the formal hoopla of a ceremony. So there wouldn't be anything to mess up," he said, continuing to maul documents and junk mail alike.

"You're supposed to select someone who will be good for the baby," Amy said. "Someone to look out for and take care for the baby. Not the other way around."

Since Renaldo's latest reappearance, when he announced he was moving to New York, this time, it felt different. His antics and his delights in his near misses lacked humor. This time, Renaldo's misadventures—two bucks short of subway fare, his boasts of near capture by the MTA cop when he'd jumped the turnstile—only added to Amy's overwhelming sense of late pregnancy fatigue.

When Renaldo was overwhelmed at Bank of America while trying to open his first checking account, Amy returned with him, filling out the paperwork on his behalf. Later, after lending him three hundred dollars, Amy had sat Renaldo down for a talk about his future. She then found herself hunched over the computer, fabricating Renaldo's résumé, concocting job titles, duties, and dates in an earnest, scrupulous font.

After Renaldo found a sublet of a sublet in Washington Heights on craigslist, Amy and Bill provided themselves as references, knowing contacting his former landlords and getting the room was an impossibility. He never invited them to his apartment, and when Amy offered to help him settle in, he joked that his mattress was on the floor, and since he owned nothing, there was officially nothing needed to settle.

For Renaldo's thirty-fifth birthday, she bought him a set of sheets and comforter for which he never thanked her. She found herself packing him lunches, bundling items inside a recycled Target plastic bag, a few oranges and bananas, some cashews, and an unopened package of cheese.

"I think I might have had enough of Renaldo," Amy said to Bill one night after Renaldo had left their house, leaving his wet towel on the guest room floor and not having stripped the bed. With Janie finally asleep upstairs, Amy hoped she and Bill could just sit, park themselves on the beige suede couch and suspend the nagging additional duties of the polite grown-up world to which she finally happily and exhaustedly belonged— of thank you notes and play dates and babysitting. She knew that she couldn't, of course. The mothering, she realized, could never be turned off. She was now immersed in the life of protective worries about her family. Somewhere after her wedding to Bill, she'd done it, committing without regret to her firm adherence to the role of wife, of mother. She'd lodged herself into the realm of formal, scripted baby-proofed expectations. She reshifted, listening to Bill's approaching footsteps to her, his wife, the one wearing a scar like a necklace across her pubic bone that would soon be reopened.

"I thought this was part of the deal." Bill said.

"What deal?" Amy asked.

"That all of this is paying off that debt. For DC and all," Bill said.

Amy chose to ask Renaldo to be godfather at the Pirogue Palace. Once the only destination for postclub nourishment in the hour still too early for a proper breakfast, the Pirogue Palace never closed, and despite the dizzying corporate gentrification of the neighborhood, its existence seemed petrified—its cracked vinyl booths, grease-stained Formica tables, and graffiti-covered bathroom stalls—an archeological wonder. Back when she and Renaldo drove to Manhattan for special club nights, morning always ended at a booth in the Pirogue Palace.

That afternoon, Amy inched through traffic all the way from Long Island, and by the time she was looping around blocks searching for a metered spot to park her SUV, Janie was whining that she wanted to go home.

"Janie, keep your shoes on," Amy said, herding her into a brown vinyl booth toward the back of the restaurant. "It's filthy in here."

Janie flicked them onto the sticky ground, bouncing on the cushion's uneven springs. Amy regretted not schlepping the ballerina bag stuffed with quiet management tools—Aqua-Doodle, the mini LaLaLoopsy figurines, and Janie's Pixie Hollow Fairies sticker book. With no kids menu or crayons to draw on a placemat, the waitress squinted when Amy asked for a kid's cup of apple juice.

When Renaldo entered, Amy detected his slight pause as though he needed to verify that the middle-aged mother, bloated and pregnant again, was indeed the same woman who had once squished into vinyl pants and thigh-high patent leather boots. Her purple hair long gone, now the color of summer mulch was tied into a loose bun. She waved as though to confirm. He nodded.

"Did you hear the new Batlashes song? It's a killer," Renaldo said, pulling out tiny black earphones from his ears.

"The who?" Amy said, trying to work her way out of the booth to give him a hug.

He wore a black jacket, way too heavy for May, and sweat leaked down his face. His black hair was still swooped into an elaborate pompadour split into sharp spikes, but at the temples it threaded, revealing patches of scalp. His face was slightly puffy as though he'd endured exposure to harsh climates.

He unzipped his jacket, dragging his sleeve to wipe his nose.

"Look, Mommy, a cartoon!" Janie said, pointing excitedly at Renaldo.

Amy ignored her, trying to ease herself into mild comfort by asking if he wanted to share an order of spinach pirogues like the old days.

"Mommy, a cartoon!"

Amy rolled her eyes, signaling to Renaldo that this, the constant interruptions, the attention-mongering, the energy thieving, was the perpetual state of her current life.

"There!" Janie leaned across the booth, balancing her bony knee on the table, directing her finger at Renaldo's chest.

"Stop that behavior now!" Amy said, prying Janie off the table and pushing her into the seat.

"Some days, I swear," Amy said and then stopped.

The cartoon was on Renaldo's T-shirt—an enormous image of the Prophet Mohammad stared directly at her, his turban an elaborate bomb with a lit fuse at the top.

"Like it?" he said, unable to contain his playful delight.

Amy scanned the neighboring booths and tables, hoping they were vacant.

"Yikes. Are you trying to start a jihad at this restaurant? Do me a favor, zip that back up."

"No can do." He drank his entire glass of water. "Look at you," he said, laughing and pointing to her chest, "bustin' out all over the place."

"I'm a one-woman dairy farm," Amy said, reminding herself to have fun. It was, after all, a long drive here, and it would be one back. Besides, this would be her last outing to the city for a long time, until after the baby was born. "Moo."

"Mommy said *moo*!" Janie laughed.

"Your mommy's a cow!" Renaldo said playfully.

"Yeah! Moo! Moo! Mommy, moo!" Janie said. When Renaldo laughed with her, Janie wanted more.

"OK," Amy said, holding the menu. "That's enough."

"Look at you all blonde and cute," Renaldo said, pretending to snap a picture of Janie.

"I wear big-girl underpants!" Janie said.

"I do too!" Renaldo said.

After the waitress took their order, Janie stood up in the booth to start jumping.

"Can you do this?" Renaldo asked. Taking the sugar packets, he constructed a house.

Janie watched, mesmerized, as the chimney, roof, and front door took shape.

"Who lives in it?" Janie asked.

"I do," Renaldo said.

Janie extended her tiny hand toward him, and he silently traced it as she watched in wonder.

At that point, it all made sense. Bill was right. She'd ask him about being the godfather later, maybe during a stroll around the old neighborhood. Amy saw how it could work, how, entrusted with a role in the safekeeping of Janie, of supplying wonderment and diversion from the trappings of the predictable, that Renaldo could fortify himself in the process.

By the time they'd finished dessert—strawberry ice cream for Janie and Renaldo and a decaf iced coffee for Amy—she remembered the meter had expired. She dug through her pocketbook searching for her coin purse.

"Get your coat on now, Janie. I've got to go feed the meter," Amy said, heaving her pregnant body out of the booth.

"Stay, stay." Renaldo stood up. "I got it." He was up before she could protest.

"I want to feed the meter!" Janie said.

"She probably thinks it's an animal," Amy said.

"You want to feed the hungry meter with me?" Renaldo asked.

"Yeah!" Janie squealed.

"No, Janie, you stay here," Amy said.

"But I want to feed the meter!" Janie said.

"I got this," Renaldo said with a wink. "Come on." He motioned to Janie. "Let's feed the beast."

"You sure?" Amy asked.

Janie reached up for Renaldo's hand.

"Let's go, Pinky."

"Gray SUV. Pink car seat. Two blocks down," Amy said.

After waddling to the bathroom, she returned, paid the bill, and left her traditional overtip to compensate for the mess left above and below the table. She felt the baby inside nudging with what felt to be either an elbow or knee. Deciding to enjoy the wait, the momentary silence, Amy eased herself onto a counter stool. From there, the front windows allowed her a view of the street where a gray delivery truck double-parked, knotting traffic. On the crowded sidewalk shuttled people intent on being somewhere else. The baby ruffled against her left side. Amy pressed her hand upon her taut belly, an offered response—you OK in there?—for their ongoing silent dialogue. She smiled, feeling happily full. Her belly, her life. The expression of not being able to have more, of feeling that anything additional should cause her to burst, never felt as accurate.

The sun slanted through the glass. There was plenty of time, Amy decided, to extend the afternoon. No need to rush onto the highways toward home. An hour or two longer and Janie would be worn enough to catapult into deep car slumber, mouth open, head drooping from her pink safety seat. From Amy's vantage point, securely harbored, the commotion outside the restaurant windows appeared both distant and pressing. With this second pregnancy, she noticed she could never turn off the maternal watch guard. Somehow she was now permanently wired to be on constant patrol, taking notice of every infant and child in the area. This neighborhood that she used to tumble upon, roaming with Renaldo still drunk when the clubs closed at dawn now appeared solely as an encapsulated baby zone, the makeup-smudged postrevelers replaced by purposeful parents. Outside, she saw a father with a backward baseball cap pushing a stroller with one hand while sipping an oversized coffee with the other. From the opposite direction, a blonde man with a long ponytail and with a baby strapped on his chest, stopped to the right of the restaurant to talk on the phone. Another dad navigated past, holding hands with wobbly toddler twins in matching striped shirts. Amy hadn't remembered there ever being so many dads when she and Renaldo used to wait out time along these blocks, but of course there must have been. She just hadn't cared and hadn't noticed. Now, every man, it seemed, was a dad, yelling to pigtailed, skipping children instructions to slow down before the approaching curb. She smiled, hoping that Renaldo had noticed the wealth of hip dads and that in the noticing, he'd want to a part of it, too. With Janie, she decided, he'd have an instant invitation to the sanitized city of playground access and ice cream trucks. It was community, connection, belonging. A purpose and grounding, and she could gift that to him.

"You're all good," Renaldo said, returning with his hands lost in his jacket pockets. Sweat sparkled across his wide forehead. He hopped onto the stool beside Amy and swiveled a full circle.

He spun round again. The simple joy of turning, a momentary wonder, and he, as always, was receptive to it without the slightest tinge of self-consciousness. If Janie were there, she'd do the exact same thing. Amy suddenly looked at the empty space around him.

"Where's Janie?" she asked.

She peered at the straight row of empty stools.

Renaldo shrugged on third spin cycle.

Amy clutched his crusted leather jacket, arresting his motion. He laughed at the hint of a game—I go, you stop. She squeezed his arms, alerting him that this never was a game. Too dizzy from motion, his distracted eyes avoided focus.

"Now. Where is she?"

She rose too fast. Her belly hit the counter.

"Oh, God! Where the hell's Janie?" Amy gasped.

She reached wildly at nothing.

Renaldo turned to look at the restaurant's front door as though the explanation was as simple as locating the entrance. Amy stepped back, away from him. A rush of all she'd need to do. A police report. Janie Ivy Bradenton. Thirty-five inches. Thirty-two pounds. Blonde hair. Wearing? Wearing? She couldn't remember. How could she not remember? She'd picked out the clothes; she'd dressed her. Pink? It had to have been pink. A dress. Maybe pants. Sneakers? Definitely shoes. Oh, God. She had no idea. The police would need specifics, and she had none. Who was she with, they'd ask. They'd need to know. It was critical. Who was she with at the time? What exactly was the nature of the relationship?

"She didn't make it back?" he asked, still seated.

"Make it back?" The casualness of his words caused a cramp in her left side. Amy winced, searching the booths just in case Janie had slipped in and was playing table cave. She moved to the half of the restaurant with booths. The diners stared at the enormous woman attempting to squat beneath their booths. Legs and legs and more legs. No Janie.

"Can I help you with something?" someone asked.

Amy knew that she wouldn't find Janie ducking behind the cash register or twirling around the umbrella stand and instantly her body shook. With dread she realized she and Bill hadn't prepared Janie for this, for any of it. They'd never had the stranger danger talk, because it was irrelevant to their lifestyle. Janie had never been entrusted to anyone who'd release her. Janie didn't know where she was, her home address, or last name. What was she wearing? What did she have on? Amy had done this. This was all her doing.

She imagined calling Bill's work, shouting at the receptionist until Bill picked up, and then telling him she'd lost Janie. How could you do that? He'd want to know. They'd all want to know. Amy lunged toward the exit, not hearing, not seeing anything other than all the horrors, the predators she imagined who'd scooped up her firstborn and, at this very second, were leading her down rusty metal stairs below the sidewalk.

"She wanted to run back. Show how fast she was," Renaldo said inches behind her.

Renaldo. For a second, she couldn't remember who he was and why he was there. Then it came back to her. Renaldo.

"And you LET HER?" Amy screamed.

A couple entering stepped away, allowing Amy clear passage. Pedestrians crossed with eyes locked on their phones. A woman walked a bony dog with an enormous cone around its neck. The delivery truck pulled away, coughing black pollution upon the sidewalk.

Amy turned to look at Renaldo because everything had come to this. A three-minute venture of safekeeping, an impossible charge. He faced south, as though still unsure it was the direction he'd come from only moments before. Inside, she felt every memory of him evaporate, a total deletion of his record of appearances and disappearances upon her life, instantly erased. Imbecilic and reckless, he didn't deserve the sculpted burdens and pleasures of grown-ups. Shaking violently, Amy screamed for Janie above the noise. From the corner of her eye, she saw Renaldo sprint off to the left in pursuit. But this time, Amy knew, this time she'd never let him return. This time, even after Janie emerged, cheeks flushed, and triumphant at her running skills, the distance had become too vast, the span irreparable, and to imagine that it could be done was a phantasm. Amy knew it was finally over. In that one instant, her debt was wholly and irrevocably forgiven.

Jayanti Tamm is the author of *Cartwheels in a Sari: A Memoir of Growing Up Cult* (Crown, 2009). She is currently working on a novel.

PART III. WOMEN'S WORK AND THE "SOCIAL NECESSITY DEBT"

Poverty, Middle-Class Poverty, and the Tyranny of Debt: Excerpt of "Poverty" by Ira Steward, 1873

Stuart Ewen

Below is a selection from an essay titled "Poverty," written by Ira Steward, a machinist turned labor organizer who was a key founder of Grand Eight Hour League of Massachusetts. Steward was an influential activist and a leading American figure in the struggle to improve the general living conditions of working men and women and to bring an end to the poverty that he saw as a pervasive product of industrial capitalism as it expanded exponentially in the years following the Civil War.

This essay first appeared in 1873, in the Fourth Annual Report of the Massachusetts Bureau of Labor Statistics, published under the stewardship of Carroll D. Wright, who would later become the first U.S. commissioner of labor. Wright was one of the United States' most influential early sociologists and believed that a combination of statistics and critical analysis could help bring about "the amelioration of unfavorable conditions" affecting a growing swathe of the country's population. During his leadership in Massachusetts, the bureau's reports promoted the idea that an informed populace was the best route to bringing about social and economic justice. "Any means which the Legislature can adopt which will add to the information of the people on subjects which concern their daily lives are of untold value," he wrote. "To popularize statistics, to put them before the masses in a way which shall attract, and yet not deceive, is a work every government which cares for its future stability should encourage and enlarge."

Under Wright's direction, the Massachusetts Bureau of Labor Statistics sought to enlighten laboring people that they might be in a position to comprehend the scope of injustice and bring about the reforms that indus-

WSQ: Women's Studies Quarterly 42: 1 & 2 (Spring/Summer 2014) Introduction © 2014 by Stuart Ewen. All rights reserved.

trial society required. The bureau worked to publicize a wide range of ideas and was at the forefront of highlighting the conditions of women as they entered the factory system and the business office workforce. "As woman has the power given her to support herself, she will be less inclined to seek marriage relations simply for the purpose of securing what may seem to be a home and protection," he wrote.

In tune with Wright's goals for the Bureau of Labor Statistics, Ira Steward's "Poverty" presented a wide-ranging and sophisticated perspective on poverty as it afflicted various sectors of society, attempting to draw connections between people who didn't necessarily see themselves connected to one another. And in this essay he addressed issues of gender inequality as a pivotal component of economic hardship, noting, "Poverty . . . falls most crushingly on woman. In all countries and in all ages among the middle and lower classes, she has worked harder, and for less pay, than men."

The selection from Steward's "Poverty" that is excerpted below is less direct in terms of what Charlotte Perkins Gilman would call "sexuo-economic" relations. Yet it is no less pertinent to intertwined matters of class and gender. And, written in 1873, it is remarkably prescient regarding the ambiguous position of the middle class life even into the present.

In this passage, Steward moves beyond the idea of poverty as conventionally understood and opens up an illuminating examination of what he termed "middle class poverty." Here he vividly describes the life of an American middle class that has been uprooted from its traditional identity as made up of small entrepreneurs and property holders and has become a population of salaried employees, better dressed than paupers or the laboring poor, but living lives fearfully positioned at the brink of poverty. The marginally better pay that they earn, Steward argues, is little more than what it takes for them to maintain the appearance that they are not poor, that they are among the prosperous sectors of society. As Steward dissects the contours of middle-class poverty, he notes that going into debt in order to maintain the illusion of affluence is an essential component of its anatomy. And this debt is a stranglehold that haunts them while being, at the same time, a prerequisite for the illusions that stand at the heart of their public identity.

As more and more women were becoming employed as clerical office workers in the later decades of the nineteenth century, this investment in appearances became an increasingly important element of their job description. For women, the imperative to maintain appearances was forged by a combination of both sexual and economic constraints. This remains true today. A 2012 British study of how working women spend their salary indicated that they spend one-fifth of their income on clothing, feeling a greater pressure to maintain and compete over appearances than their male counterparts (London 2012).

Another of Steward's arguments, seen below, offers a fascinating speculation on the political and economic consequences of middle-class poverty. While middle-class salaries were certainly greater than the wages of laborers, and both of these exceeded the economic welfare of pauperized classes, Steward argues that the cost of managing and maintaining poverty was more expensive to society than the cost of including middle-class amenities as a component of salaries. As he puts it, "The cheaper style of living of the pauperized class does not cost them as much as it costs to satisfy the pride, ambition, and changing fashions of the middle classes. But the difference will be more than paid for by the taxable public, in police, courts, and asylums. The dress and habits of living of the lower classes are not cheap, in the broad and comprehensive meaning of that word."

In this brief extract, Steward opens up an analysis of class that moves far beyond a purely materialist interpretation of the term, and suggests that the ideological divide separating the middle class from the poor is one that is more political than economic, serving to maintain a sector of the population that, in spite of its proximity to poverty, is encouraged to nervously emulate the interests and lifestyles of wealth while denying any connection to those who are more easily deemed poor. In so doing, middle-class appearances, sustained by deeper and deeper debt, serve to maintain and buttress the inequities of the social order.

—Stuart Ewen

From the Massachusetts Bureau of Labor Statistics
Report, 1873 • House No. 173
Ira Steward

Poverty is the great fact with which the Labor movement deals. The problems that now most disturb and perplex mankind will be solved when the masses are no longer poor.

Poverty makes the poor poorer, and independence impossible. It corrupts judges, ministers, legislators, and statesmen. It decides marriages, shortens human life, hinders education, and embarrasses progress in every direction. It gives rise, directly and indirectly, to more anxiety, suffering, and crime, than all other causes combined. Poverty crams cities, and their tenement-houses, with people whose conduct and votes endanger the republic. The "dangerous classes" are always poor.

There is a closer relation between poverty and slavery than the average abolitionist ever recognized. Whether a man should own himself, or whether he should own enough else to supply his natural wants, are both questions concerning his natural and inalienable rights. The great motive for making a man a slave was to get his labor, or its results, for nothing; and the abolition of slavery did not abolish this disposition. The motive for employing wage-labor is to secure some of its results for nothing; and, in point of fact, larger fortunes are made out of the profits of wage-labor, than out of the products of slavery.

Poverty originated slavery; for in the older times, as the only and last refuge from utter destination, men sold themselves into bondage. But poor people now accept the position of public paupers. The pauper's body cannot be sold, but how much is a human being worth to himself, or to society, who can call nothing his own but his body? Under certain circumstances, extreme poverty has resulted in death; and under the vilest system of bondage ever known, the slaveholder could do nothing worse than to kill his slave.

All the distinction it is possible to make between poverty and chattel slavery, is the difference between a natural right, and a natural necessity. We call liberty a natural right; and food and shelter, that we may not starve or perish, natural necessities; but whether a natural right is more or less sacred than natural necessity, is a question that decides, when answered, how close the relation is between slavery and poverty.

The anti-slavery *idea* was that every man had the right to go and come at will. The Labor movement asks how much this abstract right is actually worth, without the power to exercise it.

An abstract right, admitted, is correct in theory, but the masses are not theorists; and so many theories fail, finally, that most people dispute or distrust them until they are reduced to practice. Those who write books may be able to tell precisely how much was done for the average laborer, when, for example, his right to go across the continent was finally conceded by emancipation; but the laborer himself will never give a satisfactory account of this "right," until he actually goes across the continent, obtains larger views, sees home with its many local and narrow considerations, from abroad, and, as it were, takes a new parallax of life.

The laborer instinctively feels that something of slavery still remains, or that something of freedom is yet to come, and he is not much interested in the anti-slavery theory of liberty. He wants a fact, which the Labor movement undertakes to supply.

But has not the middle class its poverty— a poverty that should excite the most anxiety, and the most searching inquiry? They are a large majority of the people, and their poverty is generally carefully concealed.

All who have barely enough to keep up appearances are just the ones to cover up the fact that they have nothing more. They are ranked among the middle classes; and their power to cover up their poverty, is made to argue that they are not poor.

The middle classes have the strongest motives for never making any parade or public complaint of their poverty. To advertise one's self destitute is to be without credit that tides so many in safety—to their standing in society—over the shallow places where ready resources fail. To be without credit and without resources, is to be dependent upon charity whenever employment fails, or sickness prevents employment, and to depend upon charity is an advertisement of one's destitution and poverty that the public is very slow to forget.

> *"Dimes and dollars, dollars and dimes,*
> *An empty pocket's the worst of crimes."*

To betray or confess the secrets of one's destitution is also regarded, in some measure, as a sign of incapacity, for, as the world goes, the poor man is an unsuccessful man; unless like Professor Agassiz, or William Lloyd Garrison, whose reputations are otherwise assured, he cannot afford to "stop to make money."

The poverty that publishes or argues one's incapacity closes many a door to more profitable or advantageous situations or promotions. The more expensive and superior style of living adopted by the middle classes, must therefore be considered in the light of an investment, made from the soundest considerations of expediency—considering their risks and their chances—and from motives even of self-preservation, rather than from the mere desire for self-indulgence, or because the middle classes are not poor. Very few among them are saving money. Many of them are in debt; and all they can earn for years is, in many cases, mortgaged to pay such debt—"debt that increases the load of the future, with the burden which the present cannot bear."

In the faces of thousands of well-dressed, intelligent, and well-appearing people, may be seen the unmistakable signs of their incessant anxiety and struggles to get on in life, and to obtain in addition to a mere subsistence, a standing in society. If men have nothing but a bare living, they are in condition to believe, at any critical moment, that they have something to gain from public disorder.

The cheaper style of living of the pauperized class does not cost them as much as it costs to satisfy the pride, ambition, and changing fashions of the middle classes. But the difference will be more than paid for by the taxable public, in police, prisons, courts, and asylums. The dress and habits of living of the lower classes are not cheap, in the broad and comprehensive meaning of that word.

Stuart Ewen is distinguished professor in the Department of Film & Media Studies at Hunter College, and in the PhD programs in history, sociology and American studies at The CUNY Graduate Center (City University of New York). He is generally considered one of the originators of the field of media studies, and his writings have continued to shape debates in the field.

Works Cited

London, Bianca. 2012. "Suited and Loubouted: Women Spend a Fifth of Their Salary on Work Clothes Every Year." *Mail Online*, October 1. Updated January 15, 2013. http://www.dailymail.co.uk/femail/article-2211278/Women-spend-staggering-4k-work-clothes-year—FIFTH-salary.html.

Gendered Transactions:
Identity and Payment at Midcentury

Lana Swartz

According to company lore, the idea for Diners' Club[1], the first "universal charge card," emerged in 1949 when Frank X. McNamara, a New York City businessman, was dining out with a client and realized that he had forgotten his wallet at home. He was able to sneak to off to call his wife, who drove in from Long Island "with cash in her pocket and a hot look in her eye" (and, in some accounts, "curlers in her hair") so that he could pay for the meal and avoid embarrassment and potential loss of business (Sutton 1958). While he waited, the story goes, McNamara decided that this sort of thing should never happen again, that any "responsible businessman" should be able to sign a tab for a restaurant everywhere (Linehan 1956).

The Diners' Club origin story is powerful, often repeated, and probably apocryphal (Simmons 1995). But like most good marketing myths, it demonstrates the imaginary from which Diners' Club emerged: who the founders thought their consumers were and what their needs and aspirations might be. Even if McNamara never left his wallet at home, the tale reveals the context that animated the Diners' Club card. The commuting businessman, the expense account dinner, and the suburb and the housewife in it were all interrelated midcentury American inventions, and the charge card, like the highway that the unnamed Mrs. McNamara drove in on, became an infrastructure that helped make them possible.

To understand this infrastructure, it is crucial to know that the Diners' Club card was not, as it is sometimes described, the first credit card. Although the terms were sometimes used interchangeably, the Diners' Club card was not a credit card but a charge card. In fact, it preceded the credit card by at least fifteen years. Unlike later, true credit cards, the Diners' Club card was not tied to an account of revolving credit. It did not allow members to carry a balance, and it charged yearly membership fees instead of interest. For the first few decades, most of its revenue came from merchant fees.

It has been quite convincingly argued that consumer debt has been, and continues to be, a powerful social force in American life (see, for example, Mandell 1990; Cohen 2003; Nocera 1995; Martin 2002; Hyman 2011). Very little attention, however, has been given to payment infrastructures themselves, that, in fact, are not always tied to debt. This essay foregrounds *payment* as distinct from, but in relation to, *debt*. Payment systems, as Bill Maurer (2012b) puts it, are the "plumbing" of modern economies.[2] Attending to debt alone misses the pipes for the water that flows through them. Furthermore, studying the history of payment systems such as the Diners' Club card is essential for encountering new and emergent payment systems, which increasing rely less on debt and more on other revenue models, notably those that trade on the value of identity in the form of personal transactional data.

Payment is always already a vector of identity. It is a tool used to perform and determine identity. It is one of what Michel Foucault (1998) called "technologies of the self," those techniques through which "selves" are performed and policed according to available discourses. The way people pay marks them and marks the nature of their economic agency in everyday life. Particular payment instruments construct particular social relations. Georg Simmel (1900), for example, argued that modern money—which can be understood, in this sense, as a payment instrument—made people strangers, but it also made it possible to interact, trust, and pay as strangers. Like national currencies, payment forms define territories and foster within them a "common economic language with which to communicate" (Helleiner 1998, 1414).

Crucially, payment tools produce difference. Paying with a jar of pennies or a debit card that benefits the Sierra Club or a large wad of cash or a black American Express Centurion each produces distinction and meaning. This process is reciprocal: payment forms are marked by those who use them and also by the context in which they are used. Payment can be used to create or dissolve social ties, as in courtship expenses and alimony, respectively; to manage and limit intimacy, as in payments to therapists and sex workers; or to establish or maintain inequality, as in "women's wages" (Zelizer 1994).

Payment is an interface between dichotomous spaces that define identities: the economy and the individual, the market and the home. Modern payment systems also depend on underlying structures that knit the financial to the personal, producing interoperabilities with other information systems that manage the self: there is a reason that payment card fraud is more commonly referred to as "identity theft." Payment produces transactional identities. Transactional identities are networks of relations between people, institutions, and discourses. They are performed at the moment of transaction and authorize who can pay and be paid by whom and where. These identities are also constituted by transactional records and influence how those records are marshaled, how they are able to count.

This essay is not intended to be a comprehensive history of payment systems in the United States but rather a pathway through the history of gendered transactional identities. Unlike consumer debt, the third-party private payment system was a symbol of modernity and masculinity. For women, it dramatized tensions between compartmentalization with, dependence upon, and navigation through institutions, including both marriage and the corporation. As debt became more compulsory, credit cards were normalized through gendered depictions of the family as an economic unit. Credit cards, in their payment function, then became the venue for feminist activism over financial identity. By way of conclusion, this essay examines new payment systems, demonstrating how gendered identity has become an even more explicit part of their value proposition.[3]

A "Symbol of Inexhaustible Potency"

Most histories of credit cards in the United States are situated almost completely within the financial sector (see, for example, Mandell 1990; Wolters 2000). Louis Hyman, in *Debtor Nation* (2011), likely the most comprehensive history of debt in American life, traces the origin of credit cards to early retail accounts. He argues that Americans learned to shop on credit much earlier, at department stores using in-house lines of revolving credit that were accessible through metal Charga-Plates (Hyman 2011). These department stores frequently opened accounts for women who could demonstrate sufficient income. Hyman dismisses Diners' Club's impact, arguing that it was less relevant to the popular use of credit payment. He writes, "Businessmen did not matter nearly as much as suburban housewives in the creation of the credit card" because "America's shift to the credit card began with shopping at the local department store, not on a business trip" (Hyman 2011, 145).

Indeed, this is not surprising, as debt, Hyman demonstrates, has long been feminized. Anecdotes about young female office workers buying luxuries on department store credit—"a fur coat with a mortgage"—were common anticredit narratives of the 1920s (Hyman 2011, 38). They were also seen as feminizing: the unsuccessful use of credit was thought to sap male vitality; in one cautionary tale from 1922, it transformed a "success" into a "deadbeat" who has "lost nerve and his wit" and developed "gray hairs and lines in [his] face from worry" (qtd in Hyman 2011, 41). Excessive debt was seen as the fault of "weak husbands" who failed to control their wives (Hyman 2011, 41).

Perhaps because Diners' Club was in fact not tied to debt, and Hyman's project concerns the role of debt in American life, his account does not sufficiently deal with the Diners' Club card, at times conflating it with the bank credit cards that would emerge later. I would like to augment Hyman's account with one that shifts the focus away from *debt* and places it instead on *payment*. If Hyman's housewives had learned to pay at department stores with Charga-Plates linked to revolving credit, their husbands (or sons) learned to pay at restaurants, hotels, gift shops, rental car lots, and other businesses all over the country with cards linked to charge accounts. If department stores taught people to pay on credit, Diners' Club taught people to pay through an independent third party whose business was payment itself.

Paying with the Diners' Club card was an overt performance of identity as much as an economic transaction. In contrast to earlier department store lines of credit, the Diners' Club charge card overtly sought to serve as a form of a payment for the modern man. A 1957 study on payment cards (which seems to have been widely circulated, if not fabricated, by the Diners' Club public relations team) reported that the charge card had become "a symbol of inexhaustible potency" (Jones 1958, for example). It enabled the holder to demonstrate his trustworthiness and membership—to be *known*—anywhere the card was accepted. The "inexhaustible potency" stemmed not from credit-worthiness but the ability to use a privileged payment infrastructure.

Diners' Club was indeed like a club. It marked the cardholder as a member of an elite group that could be trusted to employ the modern convenience of paying later. Businessmen were able "to avoid the unpleasantness of asking for a receipt in front of guests by flashing a credit card" ("Services" 1963). The elimination of "vulgar cash" added a "pleasant, club-like feeling that comes from walking into a beanery and paying with a card instead of cash" (Sutton 1958). Those without the card, it was assumed, "were enormously impressed by the kind of man whose signature on a three-figure night club check was as valid as the Secretary of the Treasury's on a three-figure bank note" (Sloane and Sloane 1958). The club was no longer limited in space and time to a particular building in a particular city, but spread out through the merchant network. Of course, some memberships in the "club" were more equal than others: although Diners' Club did not discriminate on the basis of race, the card was of limited use to African Americans, who faced de facto discrimination when their cards—technically not "legal tender"—would be turned down by merchants ("Negro Still Has Hotel Problem" 1958). Even elite African Americans could unexpectedly be relegated to cash-only status.

Diners' Club also offered an infrastructure that made spending more easily documented—so-called country club style billing—and therefore recognizable to institutions. For example, entertaining clients for business purposes had long been tax deductible, but starting in the late 1950s, it had to be thoroughly documented. At the end of every business cycle, Diners' Club sent members a consolidated statement that was "in orderly contrast to the promiscuous scattering of bills" (Grutzner 1958). This was the "perfect way to squelch the doubting Thomases at the Bureau of Internal Revenue" (Tucker 1951). The source of the payment card's totemic "inexhaustible potency" was not wealth alone; it came from a vision of perfectly bureaucratized identity as luxury living.

"Of Course the Diners' Club Is for You"

Although it may have been intended primarily for the "responsible businessman," rather than his wife, Diners' Club was quickly adapted for use by middle- and upper-class married women. In 1959, Diners' Club opened a special "Women's Division" (*Diners' Club Magazine* 1959). A contemporary commentator speculated on the future of charge cards, imagining that "perhaps with some misgivings, but with some sense of 'inexhaustible potency,' the subscriber may watch his wife head for the supermarket, drug store, or dress shop clutching a universal credit card that is truly universal" (Brown 1958). This "inexhaustible potency," if only by proxy, characterizes the use of Diners' Club by affluent, married, presumably white women in this period. Women did not typically hold Diners' Clubs accounts of their own. Their cards were usually supplementary to their husbands' account. Women were an economic appendage of their husbands, but their spending using the Diners' Club card was positioned as an extension of their husband's success, not a weakening force like department store credit.

Although they were hailed as married and not employed outside the home, women were not encouraged to use their Diners' Club card for expenses related to home labor or the family. Instead, Diners' Club marketing imagined a world of adult-only luxuries and convenience (Coates 1962). "Of course the Diners' Club Card is for you," a 1959 ad in *Vogue* assured. It continued, "From your early hairdresser appointment, through lunch and on to an afternoon of shopping for clothes, hats, shoes, accessories, gifts—your personal Diners' Club card is a welcome companion" ("Of Course" 1959). The Diners' Club card was as fitting an emblem of the stylish, mature lifestyle of the woman pictured in the ad as her pearls and gloves. Women were hailed as individualistic consumers, but always in reference to an implied, compulsory husband and to a distinct classed and raced transactional identity.

In her study of Cold War–era domesticity, Elaine Tyler May (1988) argues that strategies of "domestic containment" placed the nuclear family structure and traditional gender roles as central to democratic society and American prosperity (91). The metaphor of "containment" can also be applied to Diners' Club, which, even as it tied women's economic identity to that of their husbands, emphasized the distinction between the respective financial domains of men and women, the city and the suburb. On the Diners' Club application, a prospective member could choose how to compartmentalize his accounts by indicating whether he wanted his personal account to be sent to his home or business address.

Even as Diners' Club compartmentalized male spending, it allowed husbands to maintain more precise surveillance if not control over that of their wives. It was also enlisted as a filter to mediate conflict over this spending. A 1956 *New York Times* article describes a man calling the Diners' Club office and asking a representative to cancel his wife's card (Grutzner 1956). "She's been taking all her friends to lunch," he said. The representative tells the man that his wife will be notified that he's requested the cancelation of her card. "'Me?' whispered the suddenly alarmed spouse. 'Look, lady, don't get me in the middle!'" The joke trades on the ironic promises of the card: control, convenience, containment, compliance.

"White Collar Girls" and "Lady Executives"

Although the Diners' Club Women's Division was introduced with uses that were more aligned with leisure than with work, it was granted not just to wives of existing cardholders but to "women business executives" as well (*Diners' Club Magazine* 1959). Just as married women's cards were usually supplemental to their husbands', these working women rarely held Diners' Club cards issued to them in their own right. Instead, these were often corporate cards held in conjunction with employment. In the 1950s and 1960s, there is evidence that working women were frequent users of the card, but they are not present in its marketing. Professional women were not envisioned by Diners' Club as members, but in everyday use, their membership came with privileges that both expanded and circumscribed their economic agency.

As an infrastructure, Diners' Club also offered a practical tactic for women attempting to navigate new professional roles. "White Collar Girl," a 1950 advice column, advocated the card for "women executives who find it embarrassing to reach for the check when taking a male client to dinner" (MacKay 1950). Although it was customary for vendors to pay for their client's meal, many male clients would have felt uncomfortable allowing a female executive to pay for his dinner. By using her Diners' Club card, a woman would be able to tactfully imply that it was the company and not she herself who would be picking up the tab. The Diners' Club card served as a technology of the self that marked the working woman as an authorized agent of her employer and facilitated her ability to carry out her role as such.

Working women also found other tactical uses for the card. Some working women who did hold company cards were able to use the Diners' Club infrastructure to augment their low wages and extract additional resources from their employers. In 1964, future *Cosmopolitan* magazine editor Helen Gurley Brown (1964) in frank terms advised working women to make extensive use of their company Diners' Club card: "Bosses," she wrote, were "miserable paranoids about raises and indulgent sugar daddies about expenses." Women who were granted company Diners' Club cards were determined to be a kind of worker better paid in quasi-secreted gifts than in increased salaries. They were economic appendages of a patriarchal and sometimes paternal organization.

In a 1959 *Life* feature on Diners' Club, among the typical members profiled was the "lady executive" (Breen 1959). Although she holds an "important executive position," she often "finds no more than a dollar in her purse on the night before payday." On such occasions, this "chic black-haired divorcée" goes "alone to a leading restaurant, drinks a couple of cocktails, orders a good dinner á la carte, enjoys a bottle of wine, and finally signs a check, which, with a generous tip, usually comes to about $25. She arrives home well fed and content—with her dollar bill intact." The Diners' Club card served as a "comforting ace-in-the-hole" when she—no doubt paid less than her male peers—needed it. The card was described, once again, as a "symbol of inexhaustible potency" that came with her professional success. It marked her as a particular kind of woman: one whose classed and raced relationship to both marriage and her employer glamorized her and permitted her to be alone and in public in a way that otherwise might not have been possible.

"Sunny Blonde with a Credit Card"

Diners' Club was the only successful universal payment card for nearly two decades, but by the late 1960s, it had begun to lose its market dominance. It was challenged on the high end of the market by American Express. It was also challenged on the low end of the market by the first true credit card. By 1965, Bank of America began to license its BankAmericard to small banks nationwide (Stearns 2011). Unlike Diners' Club and American Express, BankAmericard was tied to a line of revolving credit. Also unlike these predecessors, BankAmericard did not at first require an application (Nocera 1995). Instead, Bank of America mailed out mass "drops" of credit cards, a practice that was ultimately outlawed in 1970, but not before the American market had been saturated by over one hundred million largely unsolicited credit cards (Nocera 1995).

Unlike Diners' Club, BankAmericard overtly courted the unmarried, employed female consumer. In 1965, purportedly to test the limits of their merchant network, Bank of America advertised: "Girl wanted for experimental research project by leading financial concern" ("It's Back to Budget" 1965). They hired "sunny blonde" Ann Foley, a "pretty secretary," to live for one month "without touching any money" ("Credit Card" 1965; "It Was Fabulous" 1965). During her month of living on a BankAmericard, Foley traveled throughout California, visiting Disney World and buying "a $150 wig, a dress, a yellow polka dot bikini, sport clothes, a stuffed alligator, and a toy mechanical dog" ("Merry Ball" 1965).

This first major publicity stunt for BankAmericard reads like a near homage—or perhaps parody—of the creative, tactical ways working women had already been using charge cards for the past decade. Foley's efforts to avoid using any cash at all were described by press as "resourceful" and "adventurous" ("Give Her Credit" 1965). Like the "lady executive" at a nice restaurant on her last dollar before payday, Foley chose to "live the fabulous life" that month because it was the only option ("It Was Fabulous" 1965). She stayed in motels to avoid paying rent and ate only at "marvelous" restaurants" ("Credit Card" 1965). In fact, she reported missing all the inexpensive things that could not be put on the card: "I'm getting awfully tired of good food. I can hardly wait to go back to eating hot dogs" ("Merry Ball" 1965). Foley's use of the card for pleasurable expenses that she ultimately could not afford normalized and romanticized—infused with a new "potency"—the previously sub rosa uses of payment cards by working women.

If Helen Gurley Brown's employer had been a "sugar daddy" for padded expense reports or at times of need, Bank of America was Foley's fairy godmother. She had a "merry ball" for a month, driving a "Cinderella coach" in the form of a rented convertible ("Merry Ball" 1965). As in a fairy tale, Foley's enchanted period came to an abrupt end when, after thirty days, her "magic purse snapped shut promptly at midnight" ("Secretary" 1965). In ordinary circumstances, Foley and those like her would have no such benefactor. Foley, who spent $1,728.88 in one month on her BankAmericard, said that she had been living on $275 a month before (Porter 1965). She explained, "I'll be going back now to that kind of budget, or it might be even a little lower, but I'll survive" ("Merry Ball" 1965). Publicity stunts aside, the only fairy godmother or sugar daddy most working women could hope for was their own future paycheck. Working women who had held company Diners' Club cards were dependent on the generosity of the corporation, even as it undervalued their contributions. Those who held these BankAmericards were promised a kind of pseudoliberation that came with high interest rates.

"Think of It as Money"

By the early 1970s, as Hyman argues, debt in all its forms had come to be seen as more of a right than a privilege. It was, as one congressman put it, "the cornerstone upon which our enviable U.S. standard of living rests" (qtd. in Hyman 2011). The newly common credit-based payment cards integrated debt more fully into everyday life. The payment card, now tied to an account of rotating credit and seen as a necessity, became a point of access to a store of "money" in the form of debt rather than a system of deferred billing. The early 1970s BankAmericard "Think of It as Money" advertising campaign is indicative. A series of billboards and print ads encouraged consumers to dissolve the mental barrier between money stored in a savings or checking account and money "stored" as debt as part of a line of credit. Consumers had to be retrained to think of credit cards not as a "symbol of inexhaustible potency" but as a stored resource that could be used to pay for things. It traded on the idea of money as both a store of value and a medium of exchange.

But unlike the first-round BankAmericard, credit cards became more difficult for women and minorities to get. Because the male head of household was normalized as the primary holder of the credit card, advertisements addressed the family and its individual members differently from how Diners' Club had. In its credit-backed form, the payment card was marketed as household money. One credit card advertisement simply displayed the phrase "Dresses/Drugs/Dishes" with an arrow pointing to a credit card ("Dresses/Drugs/Dishes" 1960). Another billboard describes the credit card as "always equal to school needs," unlike, it is implied, the amount of money in a checking or savings account ("Always Equal" 1960). Through consumers being encouraged to "think of it as money," the credit card became not a "symbol of inexhaustible potency" but a stopgap "equal" to exactly the amount of unmet need.

As money for the household, the new credit cards were marketed not just to women, who were likely to be making domestic purchases, but also to married men, who would most likely procure the card. One billboard showed a man holding newborn triplets—"Think of it as money. For the unexpected" (1972). Another showed a man painting a wall—"Think of it as money. For the home" (1972). The credit card united the masculine act of "breadwinning"—bringing new money into the household—and the feminine act of home economics, using that money to buy things for the family. Whereas Diners' Club had summoned separate but interconnected male and female spheres, credit cards addressed husbands and wives together.

This discursive reunion of marital finances mirrored married women's actual lack of independent economic identity. In earlier eras, women of all marital statuses had been able to open credit accounts at department stores. Although women had usually been treated as an appendage of their husband or employer by Diners' Club, charge accounts were not regarded as compulsory for adulthood, as credit—including credit cards—had become. But by the early 1970s, even as women were entering the workforce in larger numbers, women of all marital and employment statuses faced barriers to having their own credit accounts. Single working women often had the easiest time but found that upon marriage, their accounts were subsumed into that of their husbands and their credit history and income no longer counted, even if they continued to work. As one woman put it, "In the eyes of the credit department, it seems, women cease to exist, and become non-persons, when they get married" (Hyman 2011, 194). Upon divorce, credit "follow[ed] the husband," even if, during the marriage, the wife had paid the bills or even been the primary earner (Hyman 2011, 193).

"Credit-Worthy People"

This situation was seen as untenable by many women, and many feminist organizations sought regulatory solutions. These efforts—alongside similar work by civil rights activists—culminated in legislation such as the 1968 Consumer Protection Act and then the 1974 Equal Credit Opportunity Act. Hyman describes how many feminists understood that new laws would not necessarily bring about change in actual credit departments, where lending decisions were made by low- and midlevel employees. For this reason, they pressed for greater use of quantitative actuarial science and more universal credit surveillance in making lending decisions because these nascent forms of credit scoring were seen as more transparent and less discriminatory. In short, "good credit" should be gender blind.

But, as Hyman as points out, although white feminists often drew parallels between their own economic subject position and that of poor and Black Americans, they were often affluent and highly educated. As he puts it, "Credit for these professional, married women was not a strategy of survival but an expression of class privilege, economic independence, and pride" (Hyman 2011, 203). Further, "blind" actuarial credit decisions would not be a useful solution for poor women and black Americans, for whom structural social problems would have resulted in a low score. Feminist activists' umbrage at being denied independent credit was related to "being treated like a poor person" (Hyman 2011, 203). He describes one advertisement from the National Bank of North America that proclaimed, "Whether you're a Miss., Mrs., or Ms., we make loans to all credit-worthy people," and showed a blonde woman with shopping boxes holding up her left fist in a gesture of resistance and unity (qtd. in Hyman 2011, 202). The advertisement won a "positive image award" from the National Organization for Women, which may have been less concerned with the social factors that contributed to whether a person would be deemed credit-worthy or not.

This is certainly a valid critique, resonant with a larger critique of the American feminist movement's general failure to account for race and class. However, the mid- to late twentieth-century feminist complaint may be understandable as more than a mere expression of "class privilege" or "pride" when seen through the lens of payment as a technology of the self. Economic independence is not just an issue of survival; it is an issue of agency in everyday life. In fact, many of the stories Hyman uses to describe the indignities faced by women seeking credit from this period hinge on its payment function and its relationship to identity, even though these are not his primary concerns. The shopping experience in general was frequently described as a source of frustration. Upon marriage, women usually had to reapply for any credit cards they held, allegedly in order to determine if they would continue to work. If not, the card would be reissued in, as one bank executive put it, "papa's name" (qtd. in Hyman 2011, 197). At department stores where women had held accounts and shopped for years, it was a "gross insult to their personhood" to be asked to reapply (Hyman 2011, 194). A payment card tied to credit in one's own name and an appeal to computerized credit scoring represented an attempt to align identities—public and private, lived and bureaucratic.

Imperfect Dopplegängers

Today, charge cards and credit cards remain common forms of everyda payment, but the financial arrangements undergirding these systems have grown more diverse and complex since the 1970s. In contrast to the simple heuristics found on the early Diners' Club application, newly interoperable financial networks render individual payment histories as streams of transactions to be compared, clustered, and classified at much finer levels of granularity than were previously imaginable. Feminists of the 1960s and 1970s sought inclusion in systems of bureaucratized finance because they recognized the central role of payment in the production and maintenance of an independent identity, but they could not have anticipated the mechanical scrutiny to which their everyday economic activity would one day be subjected. As the "plumbing" of payment grows more complex, the infrastructure of these private systems—and transactional identities they produce—is perhaps more important to understand than ever.

The close relation of payment and identity—recognized and taken advantage of by the early female adopters of Diners' Club—is currently being positioned as a newly exploitable source of value by the payments industry. Organizations that control payment infrastructures frequently assert ownership over the transactional data they carry. The record of payments—rather than simply the fees associated with their delivery—has become an important source of revenue for new payment system business models (Maurer 2012a). Payment is increasingly being assembled as part of social media, rather than financial, services. Transactional data sets are put into conversation with other data sets: web browsing history, locative information collected by cell phones, the relationships suggested by social network services.

Through these processes, a transactional identity gains new materiality and is transformed into a market segment. Personal data can be used—if we accept heady promises of "big data" advocates—to figure out what kind of paper towels we buy, what kind of coupons we want, when, according to our purchases, we enter our second trimester of pregnancy (Duhigg 2012). The new "potency" of payment lies in its power to create market-based identity categories, filter people into them, and hail them accordingly. But data often conjures imperfect doppelgangers. For example, in 2011, there was a small controversy when many women working in tech-

covered that Google, on the basis of the predictive
...ssociated with their accounts, believed them to be
...1). Gender is reified, and sloppily, by the systems that
...er of their value proposition.

...scholars have taken note of the proliferation of "algorithmic
...ystems on the social web (Cheney-Lippold 2011), little atten-
...yet been paid to the use of transactional data to track highly tar-
...ed advertising messages through to an actual point of purchase, in real
location and time, the so-called holy grail of marketing (Swartz 2013).
One newspaper columnist writing in 1959 imagined private payment systems as a "subtly insidious refinement of modern living" that may produce
a new kind of two-class society, divided between those able to "use a single
glistening comprehensive card to charge everything from soap to automo-
biles, and those other unfortunates who must degrade themselves by actually fingering grimy, old-fashion dollar bills" (Walker 1959). He could not
have predicted how complex an ecosystem of both payments and identities associated with them would emerge. As payment twists away from the
now-familiar debt relation, it remains to be seen what new transactional
identities will follow.

Acknowledgments

Initial research for this project was conducted in a seminar led by Vanessa
Schwartz and Daniela Bleichmar at the University of Southern California.
It was presented at the Feminist Scholarship division of the 2013 Inter-
national Communication Society conference. Additional feedback and
assistance came from Amelia Acker, Kevin Driscoll, Mary Dickson, Sarah
Banet-Weiser, Manuel Castells, Morgan Currie, Larry Gross, Josh Laurer,
Bill Maurer, Taylor Nelms, and MacKenzie Stevens.

Lana Swartz is a doctoral candidate and the Wallis Annenberg Fellow in Communication, Technology and Society at the Annenberg School for Communication and Journalism at the University of Southern California. She received a master's degree in
comparative media studies from the Massachusetts Institute of Technology in 2009.

Notes

1. "Although the use of the possessive, plural apostrophe has changed and been inconsistently applied over the years, in its early decades, the company was known as 'Diners' Club.'"
2. Maurer is the leading scholar on the forms and functions of payment. For more on payment, see Maurer 2012a, 2012b.
3. This essay primarily focuses on gender and, to a lesser extent, its intersections with race. The very important, much larger, and quite complicated issue of race and payment is treated in detail in an in-progress work by the author.

Works Cited

"Always Equal to School Needs." 1960s. Valley National Bank. http://library. duke.edu/digitalcollections/oaaaarchives_AAA0878/.

Breen, Herbert. 1959. "The Great Credit Card Spree: Charge Plans Make Cash Unstylish." *Life*, June 1.

Brown, Helen Gurley. 1964. *Sex and the Office*. New York: Barricade Books.

Cheney-Lippold, John. 2011. "A New Algorithmic Identity: Soft Biopolitics and the Modulation of Control." *Theory, Culture and Society* 28:164.

Coates, Paul. 1962. "New Credit Card Game Shows Youngsters How to Live It Up." *Los Angeles Times*, April 12.

Cohen, Lizabeth. 2003. *A Consumers' Republic: The Politics of Mass Consumption in Postwar America*. New York: Vintage Books.

"Credit Card + Foley = $1500." 1965. UPI Wire. Published in the *Pittsburgh Press*, May 14.

Diners' Club Magazine World-Wide Listings. 1959. July.

"Dresses/Drugs/Dishes." N.d. [early 1970s]. Valley National Bank Credit Card. http://library.duke.edu/digitalcollections/oaaaarchives_AAA1824/.

Duhigg, Charles. 2012. "How Companies Learn Your Secrets." *New York Times*, February 16.

Foucault, Michel. 1998. *Technologies of the Self: A Seminar with Michel Foucault*. Amherst: University of Massachusetts Press.

"Give Her Credit." 1965. *Nevada Daily Mail*, May 2.

Grutzner, Charles. 1956. "Living High Without Money: All the Traveler Needs Is a Thing Called the Credit Card." *New York Times*, December 2.

———. 1958. "All Over the Globe—on Credit: American Express and Diners' Club Carve Up Delayed-Payment Tourist Market While Travel Agents Ponder Their Futures." *New York Times*, November 2.

Halzack, Sarah. 2011. "Who Does Google Think You Are?" *Faster Forward* (blog), *Washington Post*, June 17. http://www.washingtonpost.com/

blogs/faster-forward/post/who-does-google-think-you-are/2011/06/17/
AGQVXxYH_blog.html.

Helleiner, Eric. 1998. "National Currencies and National Identities." *American Behavioral Scientist* 41:1409–36.

Hyman, Louis. 2011. *Debtor Nation: The History of America in Red Ink.* Princeton: Princeton University Press.

"It Was Fabulous: Secretary Ends Free Vacation on Credit Card." 1965. UPI Wire, May 14.

"It's back to budget living now for Ann." 1965. Associated Press, May 15.

Jones, Dave. 1958. "Credit Card Climb." *Wall Street Journal*, February 21.

Linehan, John. 1956. "Diners' Club: Picking Up Tabs Can Be a Lucrative Business." *Barron's National Business and Financial Weekly*, January 9.

MacKay, Ruth. 1950. "White Collar Girl, Use Your Lunch Hour Wisely Is Advice from the Author of Make Mine Success." *Chicago Daily Tribune*, October 13.

Mandell, Lewis. 1990. *The Credit Card Industry: A History.* Boston: Twayne.

Martin, Randy. 2002. *Financialization of Daily Life.* Philadelphia: Temple University Press.

Maurer, Bill. 2012a. "Late to the Party: Debt and Data." *Social Anthropology* 20(4):474–81.

———. 2012b. "Payment: Forms and Functions of Value Transfer in Contemporary Society." *Cambridge Anthropology* 30(2):15–35.

May, Elaine Tyler. 1988. *Homeward Bound: American Families in the Cold War Era.* New York: Basic Books.

"Merry Ball of Living on Credit Card Ends." 1965. Associated Press. Published in the *Palm Beach Post*, May 14.

"Negro Still Has Hotel Problem." 1959. *Memphis Tri-State Defender*, March 14.

Nocera, Joseph. 1995. *A Piece of the Action: How The Middle Class Joined the Money Class.* New York: Simon and Schuster.

"Of Course the Diners' Club Card Is for You." 1959. Diners' Club advertisement, *Vogue*, September 1.

Porter, Sylvia. 1965. "Living on Credit Only." *Sarasota Journal*, May 28.

"Secretary Spends Vacation on Credit Card." 1965. UPI Wire. Published in *Middlesboro Daily News*, May 18.

"Services: Embarrassment Is Wonderful." 1963. *Time*, February 22.

Simmons, Matty. 1995. *The Credit Card Catastrophe: The 20th Century Phenomena That Changed the World.* New York: Barricade Books.

Sloane, Bob, and Shirley Sloane. 1958. "Travel Industry Eyes the Pay-Later Plan." *Hartford Courant*, November 9.

Stearns, David. 2011. *Electronic Value Exchange: Origins of the VISA Electronic Payment System.* London: Springer.

Sutton, Horace. 1958. "Just Write It on the Tab, Joe." *Washington Post and Times Herald*, September 21.

Swartz, Lana. 2013. "Goodbye, Wallet: The Phone Will Take It from Here." *Media Fields Journal*, September 6.

"Think of It as Money. For the Home." 1972. BankAmericard advertisement. http://library.duke.edu/digitalcollections/oaaaarchives_BBB3429/.

"Think of It as Money. For the Unexpected." 1972. BankAmericard advertisement. http://library.duke.edu/digitalcollections/oaaaarchives_BBB3413/.

Tucker, Carl. 1951. "Credit System Lures 40,000 Eaters-Out in 1st Year of Operation; Diners' Club Has Big Attraction: Ready Made Expense List to Show Tax Collector." *Wall Street Journal*, March 28.

Walker, Gerald. 1959. "Life a la Carte: Credit cards make it easy to live it up— and pay later." *New York Times*, November 8.

Wolters, Timothy. 2000. "'Carry Your Credit in Your Pocket': The Early History of the Credit Card at Bank of America and Chase Manhattan." *Enterprise and Society* 1: 315–54.

Zelizer, Viviana. 1994. *The Social Meaning of Money*. New York: Basic Books.

Lean Back: Lessons from Woolf

Sheryl Sandberg's *Lean In: Women, Work, and the Will to Lead*. New York: Alfred A. Knopf, 2013.

Rebecca Colesworthy

A while back, a colleague and I were rehashing the anticipatory buzz and backlash inspired by Facebook COO Sheryl Sandberg's then forthcoming *Lean In: Women, Work, and the Will to Lead*. My colleague, knowing that I work on Virginia Woolf's writing, speculated, "It's kind of like *A Room of One's Own*, right?" In part to be polite but mostly to conceal my embarrassment at having no clue what she meant, I more or less agreed: "Yeah, that's really interesting."

What exactly she had in mind, I am still not sure. But the notion that Woolf's manifesto for women's creative freedom could have anything in common with what I imagined to be Sandberg's postfeminist information age success manual stuck with me, so much so that I preordered *Lean In* despite my anxiety about supporting a cause with which I was pretty certain I would not be on board. Having now read it, I cannot help but think that my co-worker was onto something. Sandberg's feminism *is* kind of like Woolf's feminism—at least to a point.

As I probably should have realized off the bat, both Woolf's and Sandberg's feminisms are constrained by class in complex and sometimes problematic ways, and for this and related reasons each writer has been charged with elitism. Queenie Leavis's scathing review of Woolf's other feminist classic, *Three Guineas*, is exemplary in this regard. Woolf, Leavis observed, "is quite insulated by class" and, by her own account, "has personally received considerably more in the way of economic ease than she is humanly entitled to" (1938, 203–4). Sandberg similarly acknowledges her own economic ease, admitting that it somewhat limits her scope: "Parts of this book will be most relevant to women fortunate enough to have choices about how much and when and where to work" (10). Ultimately, however, Sandberg downplays and even disavows the role of class in dividing her interests from those of other women. In the context of the book, this disavowal is supposed to be justified by her faith that having more women in positions of power will bring about the institutional changes necessary to gender equality: "If we can succeed in adding more female voices at the highest levels, we will expand opportunities and extend fairer treatment to all" (10). How such institutional change would work is not Sandberg's focus and she is straightforward about this. She focuses instead on the "internal obstacles" that hold women back (9). By encouraging women to "lean in"—*sit at the table; make your partner a real partner; don't leave before you leave*—Sandberg aims to close what she sees as an ambition gap between men and women: "I continue to be alarmed not just at how we as women fail to put ourselves forward, but also at how we fail to notice and correct for this gap" (36). It is because Sandberg's foremost concern is with the ways in which women have internalized gender biases and thus undercut their own potential that she is taken by some to be blaming the victim.

For the record, I actually do not think Sandberg is guilty of blaming the victim—though it bears underscoring that the biggest "victims" with whom she deals are working moms who fail to climb all the way to the tops of their professions. Truth be told, most working women and mothers are simply not on the scene here. As Sandberg herself notes, hopeful and heartfelt invocations of a general female "we" notwithstanding, "the vast majority of women" are neither in nor on their way up to her position, but "are struggling to make ends meet and take care of their families" (10).

What intrigues me is how Sandberg, in outlining various internal obstacles that hinder women's advancement, in effect joins Woolf in giving priority to the individual over the collective. The Marxist cultural critic Raymond Williams argued that Woolf, along with her fellow members of the Bloomsbury Group, most of all privileged "the unobstructed free expression of the civilized individual"—the great irony being that they were a *group* devoted to individualism (1980, 165). It seems fair to say that the unobstructed free expression of individuals, particularly women— what Woolf, in an epistemological vein, calls the "freedom to think of things in themselves"—is precisely the end at which *A Room of One's Own* aims (1957, 39). Woolf's basic claim in *A Room of One's Own* is materialist: the production of poetry and fiction depend on intellectual freedom, and intellectual freedom in turn "depends on material things," namely, five hundred pounds a year and a room of one's own (108). If literature by women is harder to come by than literature by men it is because "women have always been poor, not for two hundred years merely, but from the beginning of time" (108).

Woolf's materialism, which translates into both a practical sense of economic necessity and a philosophical attunement to the role of class and material factors in shaping personal experience, can be extraordinarily troubling. In a letter to Margaret Llewelyn Davies introducing an anthology of biographical writings by members of the Women's Co-operative Guild, Woolf describes herself as a "benevolent spectator," "irretrievably cut off" from members of the guild: "They want baths and money. To expect us, whose minds, such as they are, fly free at the end of a short length of capital to tie ourselves down to that narrow plot of acquisitiveness and desire is impossible. We have baths and we have money" (1931, xxi, xxvii). Woolf's tone is far from transparent here. She is too shrewd a thinker not to be self-ironizing in her snobbish superiority, and yet there is a certain sincerity to these reflections, a real sense of an unbridgeable class divide. This divide does not foreclose political kinship, but it does change its character. After all, the guildswomen are not beyond sympathy for Woolf; rather, her sympathy is "fictitious" (xxviii), rooted in imagination instead of reality and experience. This notion of fictitious sympathy is itself troubling for the way it turns the other into an abstraction, a mere object of reflection. And yet Woolf is always asking whether such violent instrumentalization of other people might be a feature of human relations in general, one that a heightened sensitivity to the material fact of alienation and class differences might actually help to defuse.

If I sound sympathetic to elements of Woolf's materialism and, by the same token, her feminism, it is not because I think her politics are beyond reproach but because I think there is an invaluable distinction to be drawn between *Lean In* and texts such as *A Room of One's Own* and *Three Guineas*. Whereas for Sandberg leaning in is the condition of economic equality, economic equality for Woolf is the condition of leaning *back*, of taking the critical distance necessary to see the complex interrelation of capitalism, sexism, and imperialism. Leaning back, then, need not correspond to a lack of ambition, as Sandberg and some of her supporters have implied. If anything, I am suggesting, with Woolf, that we, as feminists, should be *more* ambitious—that our ambition should not be limited to getting ahead in a capitalist system that makes it difficult if not impossible for so many women and men just to get by.

Here I have to say, I find many elements of *Lean In* to be important and convincing. Having taught young women at the undergraduate and graduate levels who spoke of feminism strictly, and sometimes contemptuously, in the past tense, I am beyond thrilled that a woman in a position of power is publicly embracing the term. And I thoroughly agree that women should be more confident and need to better advocate for themselves.

Equally admirable is Sandberg's criticism of the onerous myth of "having at all," which she swiftly debunks on the all too evident and yet routinely ignored ground that, alas, "no one has it all." Rebecca Traister (2012), writing in response to Anne-Marie Slaughter's controversial 2012 article in *The Atlantic*, has shrewdly argued that the notion of "having it all" confuses liberation with satisfaction. It confuses, in other words, "a righteous struggle for greater political, economic, social, sexual and political parity" with "a piggy and acquisitive project." While Traister could not be more right, we should not be especially surprised by this widespread confusion. After all, our conception of freedom in the United States in part owes a debt to John Locke's identification of property as the metaphor par excellence for freedom. Following Locke, freedom is paradoxically presumed to be inalienable to the individual and in need of protection by the state. It is something we have and yet its possession is precarious, which may be why, from a psychoanalytic perspective, we ceaselessly fret about its being taken away and preemptively foist it on others.

Sandberg, for her part, replaces the notion of having it all with the notion of doing it all, shifting from an ideal of ownership to an ideal of action. Doing it all, like having it all, turns out to be impossible, but that is ultimately beside the point. Although Sandberg appears to sidestep the confusion of liberation and satisfaction, her conception of equality is still rooted in economics. Indeed, the shift from "having" to "doing" in effect enables Sandberg to bring a more exacting managerial eye to bear on her own expenditure and use of that most precious resource, time. Denouncing perfectionism because it is not only ill-fated (remember Icarus!) but also counterproductive, Sandberg notes becoming "much more efficient" when she stopped working twelve-hour days in the office, more able to "maximize my output" at work *and* at home: "when I remember that no one can do it all . . . I am more productive at the office and probably a better mother as well" (129, 138).

Fair enough—and perhaps true. But what we are left with is a feminism that cannot—and in its will to lead, will not—think and act beyond the ideology of the market. Nothing is beyond measure here. Life, like work, is gauged in terms of losses and gains, trade-offs and payoffs, with an eye toward maximum productivity and profit. Again, we should not be especially surprised by this fact. Sandberg is a businesswoman (and mentee to Larry Summers and she worked at the World Bank and she has degrees in economics and business and so on and so on). The problem is that if feminism fails to reflect on or take seriously the absolute colonization of everyday thought and praxis by capital, monetary or otherwise, it is bound to reproduce the very inequalities it aims to overcome. Thus, when Sandberg gives women the seemingly salutary advice to "be more open in taking risks in their careers," we not only should recall that having the choice to take risks is itself a rare privilege but also should hear an echo of the risk-driven financial industry that has helped widen the class divide between creditors and debtors, rich and poor—that is, between Sandberg and "the vast majority of women" (61, 10).

Other writers have used terms like "corporate feminism" and "trickle-down feminism" to describe Sandberg's politics, underscoring her failure to account for the practical issues facing most working women. I mean to stress a related point about the ideological limits of her feminism.

There is a fascinating moment in Sandberg's 2010 TED Talk when she shares an anecdote about taking a class in European intellectual history with her roommate (a woman) and her brother during her senior year at Harvard. The story is supposed to exemplify women's tendency to downplay and underestimate their abilities and achievements: Sandberg and her roommate, despite working hard all semester, presumed they had underperformed on the final exam; her brother, despite not working hard all semester, presumed he aced it; in the end, they all got As. The story is repeated in the book, although here Sandberg mentions different course material. References to the Hegelian dialectic and Locke's theory of property in the talk are mysteriously replaced by references to Schopenhauer's conception of the will, the Freudian id, and Kant's distinction between the sublime and the beautiful (32–33). They are replaced, in other words, by less obviously *political* references. There is another key difference between the talk and the book. In the talk, Sandberg (2010) frames the story thus: "When I was in college, my senior year, I took a course called 'European Intellectual History.' *Don't you love that kind of thing from college; I wish I could do that now"*—the implication, of course, being that Sandberg has no time for such leisurely activities as studying European intellectual history. The banal opposition of academia and the "real world" in the talk serves the same function as the shift to psychoanalysis and aesthetics in the book: it assures us that intellectual history is just that—history, a thing of the past. Locke, Freud, Hegel—how telling that Marx never makes the cut!—these thinkers cannot speak to or of the present. Their thought is superfluous, irrelevant, especially to the everyday concerns of working moms.

Yet these moves also do something else: by treating intellectual history and "that kind of thing" as mere objects of study, Sandberg obscures the extent to which her own thinking—her cost-benefit analysis and the "hard data" on which she consistently relies—is itself part of a larger intellectual history. The economics in which she was trained and the innumerable studies she cites, despite their seeming unassailability as scientific fact, are part of a historical struggle of ideas in which some objects, methods, and findings are given value over and against others. The bottom line, then, is that *Lean In*, despite its nominal opposition to the status quo, is on the winning side of a battle that imaginative and critical thinking—or, simply put, the humanities—has long been losing.

For Woolf, women are particularly well positioned to fight this battle, to critique dominant social structures and effect social change, not because of some inveterate quality of their sex, but because their traditional exclusion from the rights of citizenship and public life (politics, education, religious institutions, the professions) gives them a distinctive vantage point. The prevailing metaphor for Woolf's gender politics, as for Sandberg's, is spatial: women, as Woolf claims in *Three Guineas*, are Outsiders. It is their position outside society, combined with their then newly earned suffrage and economic independence, that enables them to see "the same world . . . through different eyes" (2006, 22).

Reading *Lean In* alongside Woolf's writing thus makes painfully clear the intellectual costs of Sandberg's feminism. Crucial though overcoming internal barriers may be, we should not presume that those barriers stop at issues like confidence. If there is a struggle in which feminism must engage in the quest for equality, it is not just the personal and institutional struggle to balance work and family but the routinely obscured struggle between the universal ideology of the market and its spectral outside. To this end, we might take Woolf's figuration of women's intellectual debts in familial terms as a way into rethinking the categories of "work" and "family" altogether. If, as Woolf famously suggests in *A Room of One's Own*, "we think back through our mothers if we are women" (1957, 76), then thinking back through Woolf might mean recognizing that the opposition of work and family is itself a material and ideological effect of capitalism—one we must lean back to think beyond.

Acknowledgments

I am deeply grateful to Lisa Molina for providing the inspiration behind this essay.

Rebecca Colesworthy is a visiting scholar in English at New York University. She holds a PhD in English from Cornell University and has been published in the *Journal of Modern Literature* and *Angelaki*.

Works Cited

Leavis, Q[ueenie]. D. 1938. "Caterpillars of the Commonwealth Unite!" *Scrutiny* 7(2):203–14.

Sandberg, Sheryl. 2010. "Sheryl Sandberg: Why We Have Too Few Women Leaders (speech). Recorded December 21. *Ted Talks*. http://www.ted.com/talks/sheryl_sandberg_why_we_have_too_few_women_leaders.html.

Traister, Rebecca. 2012. "Can Modern Women 'Have It All'?" *Salon*, June 21. http://www.salon.com/2012/06/21/can_modern_women_have_it_all/.

Williams, Raymond. 1980. "The Bloomsbury Fraction." In *Problems in Materialism and Culture: Selected Essays*. London: Verso. 148–69.

Woolf, Virginia. 1931. "Introductory Letter." In *Life as We Have Known It*, ed. Margaret Llewelyn Davies, xvii–xxxxi. London: Virago.

———. (1929) 1957. *A Room of One's Own*. New York: Harcourt Brace.

———. (1938) 2006. *Three Guineas*. Orlando, FL: Harcourt.

An Honest Day's Wage for a Dishonest Day's Work: (Re)Productivism and Refusal

Heather Berg

Thirty years after publishing the pivotal "Wages Against Housework," Silvia Federici revisited reproductive labor and its central role in the "unfinished feminist revolution": "The concept of 'reproductive labor' recognizes the possibility of crucial alliances and forms of cooperation between producers and the reproduced: mothers and children, teachers and students, nurses and patients" (2008, 100). The Wages for Housework movement focused on establishing reproductive work as *work* and demanding a wage for it in hopes of making the family on which capital relies so uneconomical as to bring the system to its knees (Federici 1975). An additional legacy of the movement for anticapitalist feminism remains the celebration of cross-class alliances between those served and those serving. I argue that Wages for Housework is remarkable both for the militancy of its approach to reproductive labor's organization under capital and the conservatism of its approach to the reproductive work ethic. We would be ill-equipped to resist the violence of late capitalism without a framework with which to understand unrecognized and unwaged work as *work*. However, the ethic of alliance positions workers precariously in relation to the blackmail of what I term the "social necessity debt," a configuration in which workers are evaluated based on the perceived necessity of their work to the reproduction of society. This perceived value is in turn mobilized against workers as the reason they cannot refuse work. Teaching and health care are therefore valued more highly than retail work, for example, but a teacher's or nurse's refusing work tasks or walking out midshift is assigned an ethical debt retail workers have not as yet been asked to confront. Capital extracts ethical responsibility from workers, much like labor itself. By positing a vision of community in which our interests are necessarily aligned with those of the people we serve, we enable that extraction.

In this spirit, I critique what I term "(re)productivism," an attitude toward reproductive labor that assumes that social reproduction is self-evidently good and necessary and subordinates disruptive desires and practices to its dictates. This both draws from and complicates autonomist Marxist critiques of productivism as a framework in which "the richness, spontaneity, and plurality of social practices and relations are subordinated to the instrumental and rationalist logic of productivity" (Weeks 2011, 81). That autonomists directed their critique of productivism at both capitalist and orthodox Marxist visions of social organization is key to my argument. Like socialism informed by Marxist orthodoxy, anticapitalist feminism and the Wages for Housework movement emphasize control over labor's structure and organization rather than its ethics. Extending the push from autonomist industrial workers who "didn't want control; they wanted out" (Cleaver 2000, 17), I am concerned with reproductive labor and its ethics, including but not only as they exist under capitalism.

Nearly forty years after Wages for Housework's inception, the problematics the movement identified with reproductive labor—the "blackmail whereby our need to give and receive affection is turned against us as a work duty," unclear boundaries between work and nonwork, contingency, isolation, and low pay—are paradigmatic of work that reaches far outside the home (Federici 1975, 20). Marxist feminist scholars have explored the "feminization of work," where "feminization" means both an increasing proportion of women in the labor market and the trend in which capital increasingly calls upon the affects, activities, and conditions associated with women's reproductive labor in all forms of work (Morini 2007). Working from this latter definition of feminization, I explore the corresponding feminization of symbolic debt, whereby more and more workers get saddled with the syrupy affects that have traditionally helped capital to extract the maximum reproductive labor from women.

Marxist critiques of productivism that unsettle not only the material terms of labor but also its ethics are central to efforts to disrupt the ethical economy of capitalism—an adaptive and complex system of debts and credits that pushes us to work more for less (Weeks 2011). Antiproductivism allows us to see work as a form of violence, rather than a path to self-discovery or a necessary service to the community. From there, we can begin to articulate a politics of refusal: these terms and these debts are not ours. But the assumption that productive and reproductive labors occupy distinct realms continues to plague anticapitalist thought and leaves reproductive workers ill served by the antiproductivist framework. Anticapitalist feminist interventions in the realm of reproductive labor have crucially underscored the extent to which reproductive work is necessary to capital, but most have done so while reinforcing the ethical schema that sentimentalizes reproductive labor as necessary to the social. The refusal that is radical for factory workers is antisocial in reproductive workers, and this makes unavailable to the latter many of the supports necessary to resist the material and symbolic violence of work.

The central pull of the social here makes queer antisocial thought a useful tool with which to resist the social necessity debt. Placing this body of scholarship in conversation with autonomist Marxist and anticapitalist feminist thought, I draw from these frameworks' key interventions: the refusal of the coercive pull of heteroreproductive sociality, critique of productivism and focus on workers' bottom-up resistance, and centering gendered relations in understanding how capital functions and the insistence on understanding women's reproductive work as *work* (Edelman 2004; Berardi 2009; Federici 1975). While there exists some measure of conversation between autonomist and feminist Marxisms (see, e.g., Weeks 2011) and, to a lesser extent, Marxism and feminist and queer theory (see, e.g., Hennessy 2006), my approach is unique in bringing these three bodies of scholarship together to develop a critique of (re)productivism. Thinking through social necessity debt, I draw from the work of autonomist Marxists interested in the central role of debt in contemporary capital. Working from Franco Berardi's definition of the term as a refusal of not only economic but also symbolic debt, I argue for a radical "insolvency" (2012, 16). For socially indebted workers, this insolvency could mean a refusal of the terms by which workers are assigned the ethical debts associated with the labor they perform, an insistence on an honest day's wage for a dishonest day's work.

Resources for Refusal: Theoretical Overview

Autonomists' antiproductivism, which emerged from 1970s Italian factory worker movements, moves beyond Marxist resistance to work's social organization to a critique of its very existence. Theirs is a call "*against* work, against the socialist ethics that used to exalt its dignity" (Lotringer 2004,

7). The autonomist tradition grew increasingly interested in a moment in post-Fordism in which, because of the ways in which work increasingly took on the appearance of leisure, self-expression, creativity, and the like, "the old [Fordist] distinction between 'labor' and 'non-labor' ends up in the distinction between remunerated life and non-remunerated life. The border between these two lives is arbitrary, changeable, subject to political decision making" (Virno 2004, 103). I am interested in an equally contingent border, that between labor that is subject to refusal and that which is not. Put otherwise, if we can agree that the work/life distinction can be better understood as that between paid and unpaid life, what forms of life might we opt out of? How far can we take the call against work and its ethics?

The anticapitalist feminist movement rooted in the struggle for Wages for Housework has long been concerned with the constructed boundaries between paid and unpaid life, identifying housework as "the most pervasive manipulation, and the subtlest violence that capitalism has ever perpetrated against any section of the working class" (Federici 2012, 16). By "housework," they mean not only the drudgery of domestic labor (cooking, cleaning, etc.), but also its most romanticized and naturalized elements—motherhood, love, sex. Here, I use "reproductive labor" capaciously as connoting those forms of work, paid or otherwise, that produce not things but affects, bodies, desires, social systems, and so on.[1] This includes labors as seemingly diverse as motherwork and massage, porn performance and food service, television production and volunteer community service. As with housework, which is "already money for capital" (Federici 1975, 19), I take as a given that all reproductive labor is a source of capitalist expropriation.

This critique of (re)productivism seeks to apply antiproductivism's refusal of work to reproductive labor and, in so doing, to queer antiproductivism and anticapitalist feminism. Refusal might be individual or collective: quotidian resistance to work discipline (such as absenteeism or workplace theft), more formal direct action (such as strikes), or a wholesale refusal of work (such as chosen childlessness or opting out of waged employment). I am not interested in organizing these forms of resistance hierarchically but rather in opening up a discussion about the range of struggles anticapitalist feminism might support. Wages for Housework advocates powerfully state that "to say that we want wages for housework is the first step towards refusing to do it" (Federici 2012, 19). I want to push this suggestion further by initiating a discussion of where the boundaries of that refusal can or should go. If, as the 1975 call for "Wages Against Housework" suggests, sexual "frigidity" is "absenteeism" (Federici 1975), what other reproductive labors are subject to refusal—providing meals for one's children, care for the ill, an education for one's students? What do these sorts of refusal mean for reproducer-reproduced alliances and the ostensibly compatible interests that enable them? I am not necessarily calling for these sorts of resistance, but I do contend that we lose crucial ground in the struggle if we—comrades, feminists, unionists, workers— refuse to confront them with a measure of intellectual openness. We also risk easy appropriation by capital.

Precisely because of the ways in which reproductive work serves as a model for more and more forms of labor under post-Fordist capitalism, those modes of refusal rendered impermissible to reproductive workers are also closed off to workers in other sectors. Any program designed for the prefigurative commons can be easily repackaged for the corporate community. Management trains us to regard work as a calling and the company as a family; the ethical debts assigned to mothers—love, duty, necessity—are easily assigned to workers outside the home. This is the feminization of debt.

Anticapitalist feminists have taken this issue seriously but have, I argue, responded to it with (re)productivism. For Federici, the Wages for Housework movement was able "to conceive of an anti-capitalist struggle against reproductive labor that would not destroy ourselves or our communities" (2011, 7). My point is that crucial space gets opened up when we allow at least the intellectual possibility that ourselves and our communities as we know them are not sacred. Workers may very well identify with the "social necessity debt," and I am not interested in claiming false consciousness here. Rather, I want to think about the ways we might protect ourselves from this being used by management as a lever of greater exploitation.

Queer theory gives us unique resources for exploring what we might gain from loosening our attachments to what Miranda Joseph has, in a broader context, termed "the romance of community." Joseph describes the "simultaneous support and displacement that community offers capital" (2002, xxv). I suggest that we can understand the social necessity debt as part of that which gives community its potentially coercive force. In anticapitalist feminist discourses of reproductive labor, (re)productivism emerges as the particular "discourse of community" that "seems to answer all the important questions before they have even been asked" (1). Lee Edelman seeks to critique this romantic vision by uncovering the ways in which "The image of the Child, not to be confused with the lived experiences of any historical children, serves to regulate political discourse . . . by compelling such discourse to accede in advance to the reality of a collective future whose figurative status we are never permitted to address" (2004, 11). For mainstream gay rights activists, this has meant a discourse and policy platform tailored to paying the social necessity debt (or, more to the point, winning the right to do so) via military service and participation in the nuclear family through marriage, adoption, childbearing, and child rearing. Edelman terms the future that is always dangled before us, pushing us to produce and reproduce in the *right* ways, "the Ponzi scheme of reproductive futurism" (2004, 7). We could also call this "(re)productivism" or the "romance of the commons," the prefigurative community evoked in much anticapitalist feminist and autonomist theorizing. In "Feminism and the Politics of the Commons" Federici writes that reproductive work "is the rock upon which society is built and by which every model of social organization must be tested" (2011). This, in my view, answers far too many questions before they have been asked. Reading reproductive labor queerly, that is, at a slant and with intellectual openness toward the possibility of resisting "regimes of the normal" (Warner 1999, 7), allows us to leave those questions crucially open.[2]

Autonomist Marxist rejections of productivism, Marxist feminist theories of reproductive labor, and queer critiques of "reproductive futurism" and the "romance of community" very much complement one another. Thus, autonomists Philippe Pignarre and Isabelle Stengers's description of the refusal of "infernal alternatives" and the "imperative of having to reply to the question in the terms by which it is posed" (2011, 23) could also describe radical queer critiques of homonormativity. Queer critiques of the coerciveness of "the social" can help us to see "social necessity" as an accommodationist trap. Autonomist antiproductivism, and the effort to conceive of a Marxist analysis of work under capitalism that seeks a wholesale critique of labor rather than more equal access to the means of production, is in this sense very queer.

Maurizio Lazzarato identifies debt as primary to labor's organization under capital and modes of exchange as secondary (2012, 75). His configuration of debt morality centers the ways in which debt's moral and financial economies are mutually reinforcing; debt merges waged labor and intrapersonal "work on the self" "such that 'ethics' and economics function conjointly" (1). Those labors are never complete—the debt is constantly being accrued and cannot be repaid (76). Capital compels workers to absorb the costs of the risks (financial, social, environmental, etc.) it takes. It is not so much that capital incurs debt that it then assigns to working people, but rather that capital never recognizes the debt as its own in the first place. Refusing the moral economy of debt requires rejecting the coercive promise of the future. For autonomist critics of productivism, this has meant crying foul at the idea that working much more, harder, or better will give us access to the living we've been trying to *earn*. This might mean simply availing oneself of that life by means other than those prescribed, as through forms of radical theft—what Cleaver calls "the refusal of price" (2000, 156). The force of this move is not only in its redistribution of material resources but also, and perhaps more powerfully, its refutation of the rules of the game. As queer antisocial theory reconfigures failure as resistance, autonomists have reinterpreted the alienation of humanist Marxism as "positive estrangement," "a refusal to identify with the general interest of the capitalistic economy" (see, e.g. Halberstam 2011; Berardi 2009, 24).

Against (Re)Productivism

Federici's work continues to be the vanguard of Marxist feminist thought (indeed, Marxist feminists, myself included, are indebted to her), and it exemplifies both the framework's radical potential and the areas in which anticapitalist feminist thought can be strengthened by queer critique. Federici's 1975 "Wages Against Housework" and subsequent work demystify reproductive labor, introducing economics where sentimentality otherwise reigns. The poem with which the pamphlet begins insists:

> They say it is love. We say it is unwaged work . . .
> Every miscarriage is a work accident . . .
> More smiles? More money.
> Nothing will be so powerful in destroying the healing virtues
>   of a smile. (1975, 15)

Federici's move to replace sentimentality with an analysis of classed power relations is, at its core, quite queer. We can see clear links between Federici's move to term "work" what we are told is "love" and queer critiques of the family that tie the institution to forms of capital accumulation (see, e.g. Conrad and Stanley 2010).

Lee Edelman makes explicit the links between the social, the future, reproduction, and queer failure. He calls for a response to claims of queer failure that moves beyond disproving that failure but radically embraces it: "Fuck the social order and the Child in whose name we're collectively terrorized" (2004, 29). Teachers striking for better pay who are constantly besieged by the blackmail of the social necessity debt—*what about the children*—might do well to embrace the estrangement in Edelman's entreaty. This is, again, not a question of actual children, but rather of the symbolic Child (or other care recipients) whose image is mobilized toward the terrorism of the social necessity debt. Actual children are obviously implicated in the teacher's strike, and while I do not call for harm to come to them, such a risk is not workers' burden.

But there is no place for this possibility in Federici's commons, where we are reminded that sociality is measured by its relationship to reproduction. To those who would envision a Marcusean utopia of mechanized care work in the commons of the future, Federici warns that "we cannot robotize care except at a terrible cost for the people involved. No one will accept nursebots as caregivers, especially for the children and the ill" (2011). If cost to those on the receiving end of care work is reason enough to abandon a resistive proposal, we have already surrendered, already accepted responsibility for both the labor of care and its moral terms. Such blackmail is as problematic when directed at care workers as it is when aimed at those who produce durable goods.

Federici reminds us that "at the other end of your struggle there are people not things. . . . This is why it is crucial to be able to make a separation between the creation of human beings and our reproduction of them as labor-power" (7). It is perhaps the extent to which we recognize that distinction as self-evident that we fall into the trap of (re)productivism. If late capital does not recognize a distinction between reproductive and productive labor, we also need to trouble the assumedly obvious distinction between people and things, or, more to the point, the moral systems that confer this distinction. Because of the ways in which "life [is] put to work" (Morini and Fumagalli 2010), there is no clear distinction between reproducing people *as people* and people *as workers*. Scholars have made clear that late capital extracts its greatest profits precisely from the production of people, subjectivities, and affects; this is the essence of immaterial labor (Berardi 2009, 17). If we are to take seriously reproductive work as *work* as well as the murkiness of any boundary between reproductive and productive labor, we need to approach care in a way that does not allow capital to extract more time, ethical responsibility, or emotional energy from workers. A commons in which cost to care recipients trumps costs to caregivers sets us up for just that. The customer is always right, and here, so is the Child.

I return now to the discussion of alliances with which this essay opens by way of considering how certain alliances work to put us ever more deeply in debt. What do we lose by collapsing our interests with those of the Child? Federici writes that the vision of "reproductive labor" born of the Wages for Housework movement recognizes the "crucial alliances" available to reproductive workers and "the reproduced" (2008, 100). In the spirit of "answering questions before they have been asked," the usefulness of these alliances appears to go without saying in much reproductive labor scholarship and activism. Alliances' potential benefits—caregivers and recipients alike have a stake in improved funding and conditions, workers and care recipients develop real bonds and this makes caregiving better for both, we are stronger together, etcetera—are so frequently repeated that I will not spend time rehashing them here. I neither doubt their veracity nor suggest a politics that would reject their power. I do, however, want to think about how we might imagine alliances in a way that presents more of a departure from how management wants us to see ourselves in relation to clients.

In the "What Should Our Goals Be" section of her article on revaluing care work, Evelyn Nakano Glenn posits that valuing care requires that "the work of care giving and the people involved (care receivers and caregivers)—would have to be recognized and valued. . . . Caring [would be] recognized as 'real work' and as a social contribution on par with other activities that are valued" (2000, 88). Refiguring care work as a "public social responsibility" comparable to the "obligation to earn," Glenn claims that care workers "fulfill an obligation of citizenship and are thus entitled to societal benefits" (2000, 88). This is a model that organized care workers have successfully deployed (see, e.g., Boris and Klein 2012; Pratt and Philippine Women Centre of B.C. 2012). Childcare workers, for instance, garnered public support for higher wages by "emphasizing the skill of their work as well as the *social* importance of care work" in what Dorothy Sue Cobble calls "campaigns for 'worthy wages'" (2010, 291).

The "Who We Are" section of the National Domestic Workers Alliance website centers the thoroughness with which domestic workers pay the social necessity debt: "Domestic workers care for the things we value the most: our families and our homes. They care for our children, provide essential support for seniors and people with disabilities to live with dignity at home, and perform the domestic work that makes all other work possible. They are skilled and caring professionals, but for many years, they have labored in the shadows, and their work has not been valued." The implied address here is significant—the imagined *we* of the "things we value most" is not domestic workers but rather employers. *We* have families, property, and work outside the home that relies on others' shadow labor. *They* have an introduction to the "the nation's leading voice for the millions of domestic workers in the United States" that addresses workers in third person and engages with an audience of employers ("Who We Are" 2013). There are undoubtedly areas in which the *we* of domestic workers and their employers is a unified one, but the alliance's self-description does not appear to be one. In the earlier-cited critique of the "romance of community," Joseph gets at this very problem when she asks, "What does the good society toward which 'we' are working look like? And what is the nature of the 'we' who undertakes that work?" (2002, xxiv). These questions underscore the danger of the cross-class alliance (or *community*) that worker-employer coalitions represent. I do not mean class in terms of socioeconomic status (both care workers and recipients may be working class) but rather in terms of where one is situated in a particular work relation. It seems axiomatic to point out that class in this sense affects one's view of the possibilities for work's reorganization, subversion, or refusal, but such a realization is absent in celebrations of worker-employer alliance. Certainly, the spectrum of militant activities workers have historically drawn power from—theft, laziness, work-to-rule strikes, walkouts and the like—are off the table.

Kathi Weeks describes the ways in which the reproductive-work-as-socially-valuable framework as it has emerged in liberal feminist thinking, while politically effective, uncritically appropriates capitalist work ethic discourse (2011, 67). This risk is apparent in the examples cited above: as Glenn takes for granted the idea of work as "social obligation," the organizers Cobble describes support the idea that wages need be "worthy," and the National Domestic Workers Alliance merges employer and worker perspective in a way that subsumes the latter. The risk is also pervasive in some of the most militant Marxist feminist thinking, such that here liberal and radical perspectives begin to sound alike. Following the terms of the social necessity debt, these visions of organizing evaluate workers in accordance with the social value attached to their work and limit permissible resistance to those forms palatable to workers' ostensible allies. If the bid for better wages and conditions through improving a job's social status can only ever be palliative, it is also the case that its soothing will be delivered through means both conservative and exclusionary. What of those workers who (re)produce things and people other than those *we* care about most?

Sexual Labor and the Social Necessity Debt

I use sex work as a location from which to consider the ways in which the social necessity debt renders invisible some forms of labor as it romanticizes others. Sex work occupies a margin in discourses of work and, as queer theory teaches us, margins can illuminate the perversity of the center. The fervor of anti–sex work stigma makes the affective soldiering of workers to work more obvious. For anti–sex work feminist Sheila Jeffreys, "identifying prostitution as a form of reproductive labour is a category error" because, unlike domestic labor, it is not "socially necessary. . . it is more useful to see prostitution as the outsourcing of women's subordination, rather than the outsourcing of an ordinary form of servicing work which just happens to be performed by women (2009,19)." Jeffreys's critique of the anticapitalist feminist move to define domestic and sexual labor as "reproductive" relies on a fundamentally conservative approach to both waged work and the gendered division of labor, and one out of sync with those who advanced the theory of reproductive labor. Jeffreys ignores what is perhaps the most central assumption of anticapitalist thought— work *is* subordination. Reproductive labor does not "just happen to be performed by women" but is gendered (a process not limited to female bodies) as part of the division of labor that allows capitalism to function. All the same, Jeffreys's analysis points precisely to the dangers of a (re)productivist framework that, on the one hand, elevates some forms of reproductive labor to the status of dignified and ostensibly not exploitative work and, on the other, pathologizes others that fail to meet the criteria for social necessity. Here, prostitutes have failed to pay the social necessity debt; not only does this render them abject victims, it also negates any possibility of organizing for improved working conditions, better policies, or access to vital services. As Wages for Housework advocates point out, worker organizing is difficult to imagine when one is convinced that those concerned are not working.

Much like the domestic worker organizing I critiqued, mainstream sex worker activism in the United States has largely focused on goals of legal reform and improving workers' access to rights and recognition. In so doing, it has devoted considerable attention to correcting the pervasive myths about sex workers as abject victims or amoral criminals. These efforts have had significant impacts on sex workers' lives, making space for new forms of solidarity, making legal and health resources more readily available, and, to some extent, pushing for scholarly and policy approaches that speak to workers' diverse needs and experiences (Gall 2012). The reformist approach has also, however, limited the radical potentiality of mainstream sex worker organizing, pushing workers to deliver demands in terms of redemption rather than refusal. So we see a focus on workers' altruistic (and explicitly noneconomic) motivations for entering sex work and on the contributions sex workers make to clients and the community (Berg, forthcoming). As queer critiques of marriage equality show us, redemptive bids for inclusion from historically despised groups reinforce other terrains for exclusion (Stanley 2010). In the sex work context, those renewed exclusions affect workers who, lacking the class, regional, and racial capital necessary to choose work for reasons other than economic survival, fall short of the altruistic care-worker-as-public-servant ideal. The imagined street sex worker (a poor or working-class trans- or cisgendered woman of color) for instance, is often as reviled by middle-class sex workers in the United States as she is among anti–sex work policy makers.

Activist sex workers have taken pains to show that their well-being is linked to that of care recipients and the community. As with childcare workers who focus public campaigns on children's rights to quality care, sex workers' efforts to prove that their work is "honorable" seek to pay the social necessity debt. Focus on clients' benevolence and entitlement to sexual services attempts to affix the positive affects associated with the Child (and the reproductive future it represents) to the John. Sara Ahmed's point that "emotions work as a form of capital" and become, through circulation, attached to bodies and groups, is helpful here (2004, 120). Activist porn actors focus on pornography's value as a sex education tool or relationship aid, and escorts elaborate their role in providing lonely, socially awkward, or disabled clients with care and compassion (Berg, forthcoming). Sex-positive activist Carol Queen writes, "When sexual pleasure is seen as a positive and honorable goal, much of the negative fruit of the sex industry is deprived of the soil in which to grow" (1997, 130); and Mirha-Soleil Ross claims that the "invisibility" of clients is "perhaps the political missing link to the obtainment of prostitutes' rights" (2007, 212). Certainly, stigma against the purchase of sexual services (and as Queen points out, sex in general) affects sex workers' social and legal status in very real ways, not the least of which is stigma's role in excluding sex workers from labor law.[3] But focusing on legitimizing demand, a strategy in line with the reproducer-reproduced alliance, presents problematic implications for what we do once we agree that we are talking about work.

Queers and sex workers alike (and to the extent that these groups overlap) routinely fail prescribed tests of acceptable labor and sociality. In spite of vibrant and sustained activist efforts, sex workers remain frequently scapegoated, despised, and both socially and geographically marginalized. If the goal was respectability, we have failed, and there is liberatory potential in that failure. Quoting Quentin Crisp, Judith Halberstam suggests that "if at first you don't succeed, failure may be your style" (2011, 96). If at first (and so on) sex workers have not succeeded at convincing the gatekeepers of the status quo that their existence is legitimate, "positive estrangement"—indeed, failure—may be our style. Work ethic and respectability discourses have proved anemic in the face of massive anti–sex worker drives by abolitionist feminists and their conservative allies globally; meanwhile, similar rhetorics continue to be mobilized by the neoliberal state in drives to divest teachers and other public sector workers of union protections, claims for economic citizenship, benefits, and wages. That sexual labor is particularly despised puts workers in this context in an especially vulnerable position, but the affective blackmail we find here pervades even those forms of work that enjoy widespread social acceptance. This will be increasingly the case to the extent that reproductive labor becomes more and more the model for all work. Teachers, mothers, and nannies are obviously subject to the terrorism of the Child, but even office workers, caught in the human resource trap of labor-as-sociality, are compelled to measure their demands in terms of abstract models of mutual responsibility from which capital manages to always excuse itself from.

Conclusion

Alongside the National Domestic Workers Alliance's description of "who we are" is a worker's photo with the words "domestic workers and employers are part of the same family, therefore domestic work should be valued" (Maria Morales qtd. in "Who We Are" 2013). I am concerned with the limitations of a political project premised on the deployment of this sort of romantic community. This romance is particularly vexing in the context of domestic labor, in which workers have fought for decades against the dubious honor of being claimed "like one of the family." Family can be a toxic place, both when it extracts labor via the blackmail of love and blood ties and when it emerges as an imagined community based on mutual responsibility and the work ethic. The mutuality of the wage relation is a perverse one; the social necessity debt levies its costs unevenly.

Workers' interests differ from those of the people we serve. A domestic workers' bill of rights would read differently were it not authored with the assistance of employer allies under the biopolitical objectives of the state. It might be that a teacher values time more than the most thoughtful lesson plans. A porn performer may work in adult films because they pay better than retail, not because she wants to pick up where the state left off in sex education. Claiming insolvency in the face of the social necessity debt could mean refusing to qualify our right to make demands in terms of how much we care—refusing work so that we might have "hours for what we will" (Weeks 2011, 151) rather than to avoid burnout or pave the way for our children's "refusal and the process of their liberation" (Federici 2006).

Speaking three decades after the movement's founding, Federici contended that Wages for Housework feminists "saw that our struggle was not at the expense of the people we cared for" (2006). This weakens the movement not because harm to care recipients is inevitable or desirable, but because accepting responsibility for that possibility seeks to pay a debt whose origins and terms are not ours. Perhaps our struggle *will* come at the cost of the people we care for, but we cannot be blackmailed into giving up that struggle. If harm comes to care recipients in the process of workers' resistance to the banality and violence of work, this debt belongs to capital (or whatever system has failed to make work livable), not workers.

This is a matter of reopening those questions about the labors of care that were answered before having been asked, including "Who is responsible?" Again, these debts belong to capital, and while we may count on each other to stave off the wreckage, we cannot afford to do so out of duty. Those who stay on duty off the clock to be sure the job is done do an admirable kindness for the person in need, but those who leave when pay runs out do not own the burden of work left undone. Holding capital accountable begins with refusing the fiction that we are.

Heather Berg is a doctoral student in the Department of Feminist Studies at the University of California, Santa Barbara. Her research focuses on sex work, policy, and worker organizing. Berg's dissertation looks at labor relations in the U.S. adult film industry. Her article "Working for Love, Loving for Work: Discourses of Labor in Feminist Sex Work Activism" is forthcoming in *Feminist Studies.*

Notes

1. Many in the autonomist tradition call this sort of work "intellectual" (Virno 2004, 54), "cognitive" (Morini 2007), or "immaterial" (Hardt and Negri 2011). "Reproductive labor" remains, I think, the most inclusive and escapes many of the critiques lobbied against autonomists' "immaterial labor thesis." See, e.g., Caffentzis and Federici 2009, 126; Graeber 2011.
2. I am using queer theory in its capacity for "subjectless critique" (Eng, Halberstam, and Munoz 2005), rather than as a way to address the particular situation of queer identity.
3. This has been exceptionally clear in the Swedish and Canadian cases, in which the purchase of sexual services, rather than their sale, is criminalized. Such demand-centered policies reinforce the trope of sex-worker-as-victim and workers report that they have overwhelmingly negative impacts on their working conditions (Bernstein 2007, 148–55).

Works Cited

Ahmed, Sara. 2004. "Affective Economies." *Social Text* 22(2):117–39.

Berardi, Franco. 2009. *The Soul at Work: From Alienation to Autonomy.* Los Angeles: Semiotext(e).

———. 2012. *The Uprising: On Poetry and Finance.* Los Angeles: Semiotext(e).

Berg, Heather. Forthcoming. "(Re)Locating Labor in Feminist Discourses of Sex Work." *Feminist Studies.*

Bernstein, Elizabeth. 2007. *Temporarily Yours: Intimacy, Authenticity, and the Commerce of Sex.* Chicago: University of Chicago Press.

Boris, Eileen, and Jennifer Klein. 2012. *Caring for America: Home Health Workers in the Shadow of the Welfare State.* New York: Oxford University Press.

Caffentzis, George, and Silvia Federici. 2009. "Notes on the Edu-factory and Cognitive Capitalism." In *Toward a Global Autonomous University*, ed. Edu-factory Collective, 125–131. Brooklyn, NY: Autonomedia.

Cleaver, Harry. 2000. *Reading Capital Politically*. Edinburgh: AK Press; Leeds: Antithesus.

Cobble, Dorothy Sue. 2010. "More Intimate Unions." In *Intimate Labors: Cultures, Technologies, and the Politics of Care*, ed. Eileen Boris and Rhacel Salazar Parreñas. 280–296. Stanford, CA: Stanford Social Sciences.

Conrad, Ryan, and Eric Stanley, ed. 2010. *Against Equality*. Lewiston, ME: Against Equality Press.

Duggan, Lisa. 2006. "Queering the State." In *Sex Wars: Sexual Dissent and Political Culture*, ed. Lisa Duggan and Nan D. Hunter. New York: Routledge.

Edelman, Lee. 2004. *No Future: Queer Theory and the Death Drive*. Series Q. Durham: Duke University Press.

Eng, David, Judith Halberstam, and Jose Esteban Munoz. 2005. Introduction to *Social Text: What's Queer About Queer Studies Now?* 23(3–4 84–85):1–17. doi:10.1215/01642472-23-3-4_84-85-1.

Federici, Silvia. 1975. "Wages Against Housework." In *Revolution at Point Zero: Housework, Reproduction, and Feminist Struggle*. (15–22) Oakland, CA: PM Press; Brooklyn, NY: Common Notions; London: Autonomedia.

———. 2006. "Precarious Labor: A Feminist Viewpoint." *In the Middle of the Whirlwind* (blog). http://inthemiddleofthewhirlwind.wordpress.com/precarious-labor-a-feminist-viewpoint/.

———. 2008. "The Reproduction of Labor Power in the Global Economy." In *Revolution at Point Zero: Housework, Reproduction, and Feminist Struggle*. 91–110. Oakland, CA: PM Press; Brooklyn, NY: Common Notions; London: Autonomedia.

———. 2011. "Feminism and the Politics of the Commons." *Commoner: A Web Journal of Other Values*, January 24. http://www.commoner.org.uk/?p=113.

———. 2012. *Revolution at Point Zero: Housework, Reproduction, and Feminist Struggle*. Oakland, CA: PM Press; Brooklyn, NY: Common Notions; London: Autonomedia.

Gall, Gregor. 2012. *An Agency of Their Own: Sex Worker Union Organizing*. Winchester, UK: Zero Books.

Glenn, Evelyn Nakano. 2000. "Creating a Caring Society." *Contemporary Sociology* 29(1). 84–94.

Graeber, David. 2011. *Revolutions in Reverse*. New York: Minor Compositions.

Halberstam, Judith Jack. 2011. *The Queer Art of Failure*. Durham: Duke University Press.

Hardt, Michael, and Antonio Negri. 2011. *Commonwealth*. Cambridge, MA.: Belknap Press of Harvard University Press.

Hennessy, Rosemary. 2006. "Returning to Reproduction Queerly: Sex, Labor, Need." *Rethinking Marxism* 18(3): 387–95. doi:10.1080/08935690600748074.

Jeffreys, Sheila. 2009. *The Industrial Vagina: The Political Economy of the Global Sex Trade.* New York: Routledge.

Joseph, Miranda. 2002. *Against the Romance of Community.* Minneapolis: University of Minnesota Press.

Lazzarato, Maurizio. 2012. *The Making of the Indebted Man: An Essay on the Neoliberal Condition.* Trans. Joshua David Jordan. Semiotext(e) Intervention Series 13. Amsterdam: Semiotext(e).

Lotringer, Sylvére 2004. "Foreword: We, The Multitude." In *A Grammar of the Multitude: For an Analysis of Contemporary Forms of Life*, by Paolo Virno. 7–19. Los Angeles: Semiotext(e).

Mirha-Solil, Ross. 2007. "Dear John." In *Working Sex : Sex Workers Write About a Changing Industry*, ed. Annie Oakley. 211–218. Emeryville, CA: Seal Press.

Morini, Cristina. 2007. "The Feminization of Labour in Cognitive Capitalism." *Feminist Review* 87(1):40–59. doi:10.1057/palgrave.fr.9400367.

Morini, Christina, and Andrea Fumagalli. 2010. "Life Put to Work: Towards a Life Theory of Value." *Ephemera: Theory and Politics in Organization* 10(3). 234–252.

Pignarre, Philippe, and Isabelle Stengers. 2011. *Capitalist Sorcery: Breaking the Spell.* Trans. Andrew Goffey. New York: Palgrave Macmillan.

Pratt, Geraldine, and Philippine Women Centre of B.C. 2012. *Families Apart: Migrant Mothers and the Conflicts of Labor and Love.* Minneapolis: University of Minnesota Press.

Queen, Carol. 1997. "Sex Radical Politics, Sex-Positive Feminist Thought, and Whore Stigma." In *Whores and Other Feminists*, ed. Jill Nagle. 125–135. New York: Routledge.

Stanley, Eric. 2010. "Marriage Is Murder: On the Discursive Limits of Matrimony." In *Against Equality: Queer Critiques of Gay Marriage*, ed. Ryan Conrad, 15–20. Lewiston, ME: Against Equality Press.

Virno, Paolo. 2004. *A Grammar of the Multitude: For an Analysis of Contemporary Forms of Life.* Los Angeles: Semiotext(e).

Warner, Michael. 1999. *The Trouble with Normal: Sex, Politics, and the Ethics of Queer Life.* New York: Free Press.

Weeks, Kathi. 2011. *The Problem With Work: Feminism, Marxism, Antiwork Politics, and Postwork Imaginaries.* Durham: Duke University Press.

"Who We Are." 2013. National Domestic Workers Alliance. http://www.domesticworkers.org/who-we-are.

Global Warming Blues

Mariahadessa Ekere Tallie

The ocean had a laugh
when it saw the shore
I said the ocean had a big big laugh
when it saw the shore
it pranced on up the boardwalk
and pummeled my front door

There's no talking to the water
full of strength and salt
no, there's no bargaining with water
so full of strength and salt
I'm a Mama working two jobs
global warming ain't my fault

I said *Please water, I recycle*
got a garden full of greens
I said *looka here I compost*
got a garden full of greens
water say *big men drill and oil spill*
we both know what that means

 WSQ: Women's Studies Quarterly 42: 1 & 2 (Spring/Summer 2014)

now my town is just a river

bodies floatin, water's high

my town is just a river

but I'm too darn mad to cry

seem like for Big Men's livin

little folks have got to die

seems like for Big Men's livin
little folks have got to die

Mariahadessa Ekere Tallie is the author of *Karma's Footsteps* (Flipped Eye, 2011) and the poetry editor of the literary magazine *African Voices*. In 2013 she was one of five featured artists in Queens Art Express sponsored by the Queens Council on the Arts. Tallie's work and creative life are the subject of the short film "*I Leave My Colors Every-where*" which made its U.S debut at the Reel Sisters Film Festival in 2011. A student of herbalism and agriculture, Tallie was awarded a Queens Council on the Arts grant in 2010 for "*Osain's Children*," her work on herbalists of the African Diaspora.

PART IV. **CLASSIC REVISITED:** *BELOVED*

". . . whatever she saw go on in that barn"

Nell Painter

After many years as an academic historian, I undertook formal art study, earning a BFA from the Mason Gross School of the Arts of Rutgers University in 2009 and an MFA from the Rhode Island School of Design in 2011, both in painting. More recently I've been combining my old and new lives into artwork with significant subject matter as well as visual meaning.

I just now reread Toni Morrison's tough, magnificent novel *Beloved* for the first time in about a quarter century. It left me devastated by the sheer cruelty of slavery and the way it distorted humanity, even though as a historian, I was well acquainted with the institution's awfulness. I also saw in new ways Morrison's visual imagination, notably her insistence on the importance of color. Because this publication precludes the reproduction of my pieces in color, grisaille will have to represent the meaning of Morrison's investment in color, though I have reproduced some of the work's haunting lines of text.

Nell Painter (the artist formerly known as the historian Nell Irvin Painter)

WSQ: Women's Studies Quarterly 42: 1 & 2 (Spring/Summer 2014) © 2014 by Nell Painter. All rights reserved.

After Slavery

Patricia Ticineto Clough

That fugal, internal world theater that shows up for a minute serially—poor but extravagant, as opposed to frugal—is blackness, which must be understood in its ontological difference from black people who are, nevertheless, (under) privileged insofar as they are given (to) an understanding of it.

Fred Moten and Stefano Harney, *"Blackness and Governance"*

A man is no longer a man confined, but a man in debt.

Gilles Deleuze, Negotiations

Perhaps it is the blackness to which Moten and Harney point that permeates the life experiences that Toni Morrison's writings witness and to which she has given a quality of universality. It is, however, a universality from the (under)privileged perspective of those "who are owed, the ones who bear the trace of being owned" and who are in a world of poverty and extravagance, a world of "a debt unfairly imposed and untold wealth unfairly expropriated" (Moten and Harney 2011, 351). No less for Morrison than for Moten and Harney, blackness is an "*anoriginary* drive," a force that brings regulation into existence at the very same time that criminality, fugitivity, waste, and debt come into being. This is a regulation of populations, submitted to calculation, in a biopolitical governance about which we speak now but which has its roots in slavery.

After all, it is the slave trade, as Stephanie Smallword argues, that provides "not only a new economic moment for modern Western nation states but a new regime of calculation by which to measure and utilize human life" (qtd. in Ferguson 2012, 91). Africans were placed at the center of calculation in order to put to exchangeability the life capacities extracted from the species—through the extraction of living labor from slave populations. Drawing on Smallword's argument, Roderick Ferguson proposes that in the post–World War II years, this calculation for the exchangeability of physical capacities would come to an end as the site for calculation of life capacities shifted. With the entrance of *minorities* into the academy, their mental or intellectual as well as bodily capacities would be "evaluated in terms of their fitness for standards of excellence and merit" (2012, 91). While *excellence* promised a new beginning, it would, however, "betray its kinship to prior and emerging regimes of calculation and alienation" (92). *Minorities* would find themselves again and again to be those who bear the trace of being owned as they would come to bear an incredible amount of debt, circulating along with the drive to institutionality inhering in minority studies themselves, all part of a neoliberal biopolitical governance.

And over those decades of the postwar years, from the entrance of minority students into the academy to the establishment and institutionalization of minority studies, Toni Morrison's writings would hold up a mirror into which all are invited to gaze, shining a light on the "fugal, internal world theater" of poverty and extravagance. Whereas *The Bluest Eye* (Morrison 1970) reformulated the Dick and Jane primer to teach us how to read from an (under)privileged perspective, *Beloved* (1987) gave us an epic of magnificent survival—yes—but a cautionary tale as well. Morrison would ask us to be cautious in seeking answers to the very questions *Beloved* raises: How can the story of slavery be told? How can history be rewritten? How can you institutionalize a desire for recognition? How can the loss be mourned without one's turning to melancholy? How can the debt be calculated and paid?

While what is to be read—the content of *Beloved*—is a love story of mother and child, of man and woman, its form is the haunted realism of an impossible history. As Morrison puts it, "It was not a story to pass on" (1987, 274). Instead, it is a story in bits and pieces, not a unifying memory but the starts and stops of rememory, a reconstruction of a story that cannot be completely narrated, a story that instead makes visible the erasures, the forgetting, the disremembering. As such, is a history-with-holes, to use Fredric Jameson's terms, "a kind of bas-relief history in which only bodily manifestations are retained, such that we are ourselves inserted into it without even minimal distance" (1986, 321). We are released "to a present of uncodified intensities" (321) or incalculable affects offering an experience of something for the first time that at the same time seems to be already known, known before—the return of a repressed trauma.

This haunted realism, with its impossibility of meeting the demands of a crude empiricism, is announced with the arrival of Beloved herself, a ghostly figure of slavery and its aftermath:

> Everybody knew what she was called, but nobody anywhere knew her name. They forgot her like a bad dream. After they made up their tales, shaped and decorated them, those that saw her that day on the porch quickly and deliberately forgot her. It took longer for those who had spoken to her, lived with her, fallen in love with her, to forget, until they realized they couldn't remember or repeat a single thing she said, and began to believe that, other than what they themselves were thinking, she hadn't said anything at all. So in the end, they forgot her too. Remembering seemed unwise (Morrison 1987, 274).

But why does Beloved return from the dead, or refuse to be dead? Why is this story, about the enslavement of black men and women, also a story about a mother who, rather than being punished for appropriating godlike powers over life and death, is instead haunted by her own actions, drawing her to Beloved, to the ghost child and to the "join": "I want to join she whispers to me she whispers I reach for her chewing and swallowing she touches me she knows I want to join she chews and swallows me I am gone" (213). This ravenous ghost child would have the mother become a child, "in the chair licking her lips like a chastised child while Beloved ate up the mother's life, took it, swelled up with it, grew taller on it" (250).

There will be nothing left but Beloved and her hunger. The mother will come to despise herself for momentarily having trusted and surrendered to a man who finally would not understand, who could not see that killing the child was the mother's only way to save the child from the slave masters when they had come to take the child back into slavery. For the mother, the escape from slavery with her child had been "the only thing I had done on my own" (162). Yet the man would have her give up the ghost because of his own guilt for being seduced himself by the ghost, at least momentarily. In time, he comes to refuse the "join"; the mother cannot. Perhaps Morrison would have this mother stand against all the separations of mother and child during and after slavery, stand as long as she can between this world and some other, the world of ghost children that have been starved by slavery's rending the fabric of care.

But if Morrison finally would let the ghost child be delivered from the mother's house and would have the mother find some comfort in the return of the man in the wake of the ghost's departure, the story nonetheless resists a resolution; the very function of the family romance of providing a narrative closure is called into question, where a debt can neither be calculated nor paid. What remains is a profound loneliness that roams. "There is a loneliness that can be rocked. Arms crossed, knees drawn up; holding, holding on, this motion unlike a ship's, smoothes and contains the rocker. It's an inside kind—wrapped tight like a skin. Then there is a loneliness that roams. No rocking can hold it down. It is alive, on its own. A dry and spreading thing that makes the sound of one's own feet going seem to come from a far-off place" (274).

But is the ghost child still walking among us? Is the distinction between melancholy and mourning no less impossible, especially for those touched by being owned, and where the mother's milk drops on the baby's lips mixed with tears?[1] Or are we now all of an economy that binds by debt, when it is not physical capacities but psychic ones that are invested and circulated to produce a surplus value of affect? This is an economy that is *after economy*, as Randy Martin describes it in his discussion of derivatives, in that the political, usually excluded from economy, instead has been fully included, where political effectiveness is subjected to market measures. There is neither a social structure nor a social whole in the workings of a derivative logic in which "claims to integrate the wealthiest and poorest through lives directed by common principles of rationality and a shared promise of prosperity" have been unraveled (2013, 84). And if we are (and I do think we are) faced with a new regime of racism with a wider and deeper incurring of the debt of its costs, this regime too is after economy, in that there is no rationale or means for a just payment of racism's debt; there is no just retribution, only broken-up bits and pieces of debt packaged and circulated as attributes of derivatives. Yet this may be the very condition in which we can take direction from the works of Toni Morrison and Beloved, the ravenous ghost child. Recognizing all in debt, we might take the (under)privileged perspective and make it our task to find those ways that truly would put us after slavery.

Patricia Ticineto Clough is professor of sociology and women's studies at the Graduate Center and Queens College of the City University of New York. She is author of *Autoaffection: Unconscious Thought in the Age of Teletechnology* (2000); *Feminist Thought: Desire, Power, and Academic Discourse* (1994) and *The End(s) of Ethnography: From Realism to Social Criticism* (1998). Her forthcoming book is *The Ends of Measure*.

Note

1. I have paraphrased here from a longer quote: "The baby's lips are made moist by the mother's milk even while the mother's tears dampen them both. It is a confused joining as the good and the bad are internalized simultaneously into a combined experience that occurs prior to splitting . . . a whole object that is a product of the deadlines that was ingested together with life. . . . In this scenario, where the source of life is mixed with its failure to sustain liveliness . . . the closer one gets, the more alone one feels . . . the more of life, the more of death" (Gerson 2003). There is much more to say about the way *Beloved* addresses the issue of tearing apart the fabric of care that slavery instituted and the incalculable losses where the reproduction of mothering, while not impossible, is profoundly challenged (see Spillers 1987).

Works Cited

Deleuze, Gilles. 1997. *Negotiations, 1972–1990*. Trans. by Martin Joughin. New York: Columbia University Press.

Ferguson, Roderick. 2012. *The Reorder of Things: The University and Its Pedagogies of Difference*. Minneapolis: University of Minnesota Press.

Gerson, S. 2003. "The Enlivening Transference and the Shadow of Deadliness." Paper delivered to meetings of the Boston Psychoanalytic Society and Institute, 3 May.

Jameson, Fredric. 1986. "On Magic Realism in Film." . 12 (Winter): 301–326.

Martin, Randy. 2013. "After Economy." *Social Text* 114: 83–106.

Morrison, Toni. 1970. *The Bluest Eye*. New York: Washington Square.

———. 1987. *Beloved*. New York: Knopf.

Moten, Fred, and Stefano Harney. 2011. "Blackness and Governance." In *Beyond Biopolitics: Essays on the Governance of Life and Death*, ed. P. Clough and C. Willse, 351–61. Durham: Duke University Press.

Spillers, Hortense. 1987. "Mama's Baby, Papa's Maybe: An American Grammar Book." *Diacritics* 17(2):64–81.

The Debt of Memory: Reparations, Imagination, and History in Toni Morrison's *Beloved*

Richard Perez

This essay focuses on Toni Morrison's groundbreaking novel *Beloved* and examines the issue of reparations in economic, affective, and historical terms. *Beloved*, I claim, addresses these debts via fiction by delving into the recesses of traumatic memory. Debt is the overriding metaphor of our time, a quintessentially modernizing state and activity that weaves inequalities into the fabric and practice of capital. To incur debt is to enter into an interpolative arrangement in which capital confers recognition through repetitive consumption. Morrison's novel redirects our contemporary dependence on and understanding of debt from a tangible economic figure or amount to a cumulative colonial deficit spanning the space and time of slavery. In this sense, contemporary economic debt functions as a recurring sign in the *longue durée* of racial history, which calls for layered forms of reparations. When Morrison states, at the end of the novel, "This is not a story to pass on" (1987, 274), she asks the reader to confront the debt assumed by the traumas of slavery to enable us to transform this inheritance into a beloved future. To pass this story down is to forge a new repository of memory upon which a severely incurred debt—mnemonic, social, and material—can begin to be defrayed. Therefore fiction, for Morrison, compels the reader to reimagine a concealed past as a reparative starting point, which not only summons the ghastly foundations of the Americas but in so doing, initiates conversations surrounding what was lost, established, and still owed.

Indeed, the idea of reparations has seen various iterations since the end of slavery. Not only did President Lincoln favor some sort of reparations for newly freed slaves but several decades later, in 1915, Cornelius J.

 WSQ: Women's Studies Quarterly 42: 1 & 2 (Spring/Summer 2014)

Jones brought a lawsuit demanding sixty-eight million dollars in reparative compensation for unpaid slave labor. In 1944 Gunnar Myrdal, Swedish economist and Nobel laureate, in his book *An American Dilemma:
The Negro Problem and Modern Democracy*, argued for parcels of former
plantations to be made available to ex-slaves through manageable, long-
term installment plans. The call for reparations continued in the 1960s,
when black activist James Forman, in his controversial *Black Manifesto*,
boldly proposed five hundred million dollars in damages. Moreover, in
1972, in *The Case for Black Reparations*, Yale Law School professor Boris
Bittker asserted that a history of race-based discrimination from slavery
to Jim Crow, spanning over three centuries, caused undue social and economic injury to African Americans and suggested the creation of a program to distribute resources to America's black descendants of slaves.
Finally, in a more recent text, *The Debt: What America Owes to Blacks*, Randall Robinson makes the case for a national economic response that would
effectively close "the yawning gap between blacks and whites" (Robinson
2000, 204).[1] However, Robinson's argument marks a shift from a reduc-
tive, if necessary and just, economic discussion to a more wide-ranging
cultural, historic, and psychic understanding of debt.[2]

As he argues: "But only slavery, with its sadistic patience, asphyxiated
memory, and smothered cultures, has hulled empty a whole race of people
with inter-generational efficiency. Every artifact of the victims' past cultures, every custom, every ritual, every god, every language, every trace
element of a people's whole heredity identity, wrenched from them and
ground into a sharpe choking dust. It is a human rights crime without parallel in the modern world. For it produces its victims *ad infinitum*, long
after the active statge of the crime has ended" (Robinson 2000, 216). In
the absence of economic reparations, Robinson proposes a "black renais-
sance" (237–47), a dynamic return to knowledge, memory, and creativity
as a formula to halt the production of victims generated by the aftereffects
of slavery and colonialism. Thus, Robinson compels the reader to confront
the varying dimensions of debt as, on the one hand, the virulent conjunction of economic processes—centuries of forced and unpaid labor—and
on the other, the imposed erasure of memory and culture. The latter, for
Robinson, takes precedence in the refiguration of the modern black subject. For capitalism, in his estimation, makes a Circean offer of sorts, one
that dulls and transmogrifies the subject through "the memory-emptying
salve of contemporaneousness" to produce what he calls "history's amne-

siacs" (16). Capital, in essence, anesthetizes memory through a rationale of consumption, predicated on a myopic focus on the present and an incessant drive for instant gratification. Therefore, debt functions through a logic of addiction—inciting desire, maximizing pleasure, imparting recognition—in order to reduce the subject to a cycle of commodified dependency that overdetermines the present. In this sense, debt evacuates the subject by fixing his or her energies on an immediacy that disables the subject's sense of temporal depth and compromises his or her capacity to engage larger issues of history and ethics. Significantly, inscribed within the etymology of the word "debt" is this double enterprise as the Latin (*debere* and *dehabere*) means both "to owe" and "to keep away from." Hence, debt in capital signifies an attachment to deficit, a perverse habit, if you will, that works to distract and dispossess the subject by keeping him or her ensnared within the demands of the system. The question becomes, How can we calculate trauma and history into a just measure, which renders, if not an exact amount, then a certain revelatory content? In particular, what compensatory offers can fiction make to the (racialized) subject of capital to help assuage this predicament and open new avenues of psychic, social, and historic investment? Robinson cautions, "It would behoove African Americans to remember that history forgets, first, those who forget themselves" (231).

Morrison writes *Beloved* in this spirit, refiguring our modern notion of debt as a problem of cultural loss and forgetting. Morrison's fiction reorients the subject of capital from a hollow transactional mode of relation to an intersubjective engagement with temporal and spatial processes that provoke critical reflection. She therefore offers a fictional mode of reparation to help recover and reconstitute historical memory, altering the past into a transformative understanding of the present and a reenvisioned future. Specifically, *Beloved* retells the story of Margaret Garner, a runaway slave, who killed her daughter rather than relinquish her to slavery. What Morrison discovered, in the now famous newspaper article in which she found Garner's story, is a peculiar claim describing the child's death as the destruction of property and not murder. This legal distinction, Morrison understands, sits at the crux of American slavery. On the one hand, it defines the slave as the property of a master depriving her of her right to develop as what Colin Dayan calls a "thinking thing" (2011, 88). On the other hand, it demonstrates how a slave "guilty" of a crime "became a person," for "the crime proved consciousness, mind, and will" (89). Ironically, then, crime imparted recognition by illustrating the nuanced thought and affective processes of an action, thereby humanizing the slave even if the law held fast to a narrative of property.

This slippage between slave as utile object and mentally inert piece of property, capable, nevertheless, of conceiving and carrying out a crime, points to an uncanny gap in legal discourse through which Morrison reimagines the content of a black humanity. In killing her daughter, Garner carries out an enormously complex decision whose consequences affect, all at once, the life of her child, the law that opposes them, and the historical conditions of her time. Paradoxically, this extraordinary gesture—personal, social, and historical—demonstrates a level of ethical depth, displays Garner's substantive humanity, and serves as an incriminating comment on a society that would require such a decision in the first place. *Beloved* aims, in this sense, to redress the traumatic debt accrued by Garner's dispossessed humanity.[3] Significantly, the traumatic remainder of her decision does not annihilate Sethe (Garner); instead it sets off a process of traumatic self-discovery. By reaching into the archive and reconstructing Garner's story, then, Morrison recuperates her personhood and imbues her, via fiction, with a narrative afterlife for her extraordinary deed.

In an interview with *Essence* magazine, Morrison explains, "I'm trying to explore how a people—in this case one individual or a small group of individuals—absorbs and rejects information on a very personal level about something (slavery) that is undigestible and unabsorbable, completely" (qtd. in Taylor-Guthrie 1994, 235). Morrison's fictional project extends and expands the language of history by using the imagination as a vehicle to envision that "something" in our American past, "undigestible and unabsorbable," owed yet largely unaddressed. Yet how does a writer engage the story of American slavery in its staggering totality? Morrison approaches the problem metonymically, by focusing narrative attention on an exemplary event that impels the reader to reconceive not only what the life of a slave was like but also how those slaves, immediately following their freedom, worked through the traumatic remnants of their lives and histories. Therefore, Garner's story animates the lives of slaves lost in the oblivion of the archive. As Avery Gordon argues, "If the slave narrative was expected to speak for those who had no audible public voice and who had no legal access to writing or to personhood, then *Beloved* will not only retell the story of Margaret Garner, but will also imagine the life world of those with no names we remember, with no 'visible reason' for being in the archive. Morrison does not speak for them. She imagines them speaking their complex personhood as it negotiates the always coercive and subtle complexities of the hands of power" (1997, 150). This woman excavated in Morrison's archival research stands in for "sixty million and more" (Morrison 1987, epigraph); an exemplary account that grew into a "book idea." For the book idea gives fantastic form to a narrative inadequately told by the archive itself. In this sense, Morrison's novel functions as a reparative attempt to bridge the gap, to eschew "the memory-emptying salve of contemporaneousness" and rehouse a past rendered homeless by its exclusion from the official annals of history.

Significantly, the novel opens with an exact address to locate the reader in place and in an affective economy; Morrison writes that "124 was spiteful. Full of a baby's venom. The women in the house knew it and so did the children. For years each put up with the spite in his own way, but by 1873 Sethe and her daughter Denver were its only victims" (1987, 3). The novel immediately establishes a fraught relationship between the inhabitants of this new house and the venomous spirit that possesses it. The spirit, signified early in the novel by a searing "red and undulating light" (8), marks the residual presence of Beloved, Sethe's murdered child, foreshadowing the child's spectral return. Her "spite" concentrates on Sethe and Denver, "its only victims" and inheritors, in an attempt to reactivate memory, to unlock a traumatic knowledge located in the abyss of the dead. The horrific fact of Sethe's having murdered her daughter transfers narrative responsibility, a debt as memory, to Sethe, triggering an unending state of "Negro grief" (5). Thus, what is at stake for Sethe throughout the novel is the tension between a bare minimum of survival and the narrative demands of memory: a fact which permeates and distorts the very physical structure of the house, as if the intensity of the trauma curves the space it inhabits. From the onset of the novel, then, the house harbors several unresolved layers of signification: first, in relation to the death of Beloved; next, in negotiating the memory of slavery; and finally, in incorporating the past into a workable knowledge of the self that enables a livable present and more just future.

The extremity of Sethe's act expresses itself in spectral terms, a fever insisting on its narrative retelling so as to diffuse its brute force into legible marks and fragments. Interestingly, Derrida identifies "fever" as an element of the archive, produced by the violent discrepancy between the privileged and the socially dead, the institutionally housed and the nomads of history. According to Derrida, the archive contains a spectral malady or death drive, built up by unincorporated narratives, which push it toward its own destruction, inciting "memories of death" (1995, 11). Thus, the symbolic dimensions of the house, etymologically linked to the archive, establishes the individual subjectivity of lived experience in the present while serving as an architectural repository of history. It is in this double function of the house as metaphor of interior self and archival residence, subjective structure and historical receptacle, that Sethe must come to terms with the layers of her being. *Beloved* gives form to the story of this fever that lives both within Sethe and the historical memory of the house, in order to dramatize, through the imagination, the encounter between a mother and the child she murdered, the subject of slavery and history, a logic of debt and an ethical call for reparations.

Interestingly, the archival fever finds its material analogue in the scar on Sethe's back. Sethe receives her scar while pregnant, after she complains about a group of white men raping her and extracting her breast milk. This complaint against the white men incriminates her without redress. Sethe is beaten mercilessly with "cowhide" (17), which forms a gruesome scar reminiscent of a tree. The beating transmogrifies Sethe's back into a canvas upon which the image of American violence grafts itself. The scar presents a bodily imprint to be read in genealogical terms. For etched on the body, inscribed there for posterity to witness, experience, and decode, are the arabesque lines of racial injury, unspeakable indications of an aberrant design sitting at the heart of the nation's democratic experiment. Therefore, Sethe's back acts as a mute declaration of the inhumanity sitting at the foundation of a young country, while her stolen breast milk signifies the denial of futurity, a body nullified of its most elemental assets. This violence aims to convert blackness into a continuous signifier of social and historical debt—from the plantation to Jim Crow to the prison-industrial complex—that effectively forecloses the full purchase of freedom. What endures in this scar is the memory of slavery, traumatic images that require an "imaginative act" "to yield up a kind of truth"(Morrison 1990, 302). These images pass, via fiction, into memory and enable the reader to face the violent events and logic of the past.

Significantly, the image of an event persists in the space where it occurred, impressed there for all who travel through to experience, a kind of palimpsest of place where the past merges into the now through a convoluted process of rememory. Sethe describes her concept of rememory to Denver:

> "I was talking about time. It's so hard for me to believe in it. Some things go. Pass on. Some things just stay. I used to think it was my rememory. You know. Some things you forget. Other things you never do. But it's not. Places, places are still there. If a house burns down, it's gone, but the place—the picture of it—stays, and not just in my rememory, but out there, in the world. What I remember is a picture floating around out there outside my head. I mean, even if I don't think it, even if I die, the picture of what I did, or knew, or saw is still out there. Right in the place where it happened. . . . Someday you will be walking down the road and you hear something or see something going on. So clear. And you think it's you thinking it up. A thought picture. But no. It's when you bump into a rememory that belongs to someone else. Where I was before I came here, that place is real. It's never going away. Even if the whole farm—every tree and grass blade of it dies. The picture is still there and what's more, if you go there—you who was never there—if you go there and stand in the place where it was, it will happen again; it will be there for you, waiting for you" (1987, 35–36).

Sethe here explains a portentous and prophetic experience of time. She rejects time as something "to believe in," as a sequential structure organized around carefully chosen events, documents, and legal mandates meant to justify the universe of a racially ordered system. For Sethe the time-space of rememory consists of overlapping beings, a kind of sentient leftover, which leaves its contents inscribed in place. In this sense, rememory is not simply the result of the ability to remember but a collective "thought picture" of a different time that "belongs to someone else" and is seared into space by a lived intensity. In its remainder, rememory, "out there in the world," forms an extratextual archive "right there where it happened." So that "the picture of what I did, or knew, or saw is still out there" an experiential surplus informing all those it touches. The image or "picture" persists as if engraved within the atmosphere and made available to "you who was never there" as a phenomenon enmeshed within the fabric of the place that never ceases to exist—"if you go there and stand in the place where it was, it will happen again." Rememory, then, is not an accident but envelopes those who pass through its sphere of influence in active, "it will be there for you, waiting for you" spectral engagement. Rememory functions through neither a logic of debt nor simple vicarious acquisition. Rather, rememory names the traumatic substance of historical activity suffused into the atmosphere in the form of invisible pictures. Akin to dark matter in astrophysics, rememory describes an alternate dimension of reality, a space charged by dense layers of historical perception whose presence one feels, senses, and experiences. According to rememory, history, documented or not, awaits contact. For Morrison, contact occurs through the imagination, the organ in the mind most receptive to that "picture floating around out there outside my head." Imagination serves as a recuperative faculty filling in the deliberate gaps of history.

The racialized subject of capital, then, bereft of a place in the archives, rails against a history of imperialism through the imagination. The imagination invokes the murdered child in spectral form: "A fully dressed woman walked out of the water. She barely gained the dry bank of the stream before she sat down and leaned against the mulberry tree" (50). Beloved emerges from the "water" exhausted by the virulent forces of history. The water calls attention to the Black Atlantic, where slaves drowned, forming embodied artifacts. In order for Sethe to move forward she must reencounter Beloved, both as her daughter and an as emblem of the past. Through the encounter, Sethe faces the trauma of her personal and historical past to regain a personhood depleted by the violence of her life. It is not that Morrison creates a factual history that rivals the archives in what it gathers and remembers, but that she opens an alternative space where the "personhood" of the slave can speak and reemerge. If debt speaks to a lack in economic terms, in the imagination it designates a reparative potentiality through which history may be reached and refigured.

Morrison, in this vein, concludes her novel with a warning and an exhortation: "It was not a story to pass on." *Beloved*, in other words, is not a story about foundations and heroes but a traumatic narrative of the past, whose images reveal a "loneliness that roams" "disremembered and unaccounted for" (274) "like a bad dream" that forces a "remembering" otherwise. For Morrison, the archive of slavery is stored, produced, and kept alive by the workings of the imagination. Ultimately, alternative histories require a turn to fiction to give form to the traumatic voids of our past. Fiction directs us to those imaginative locations to witness the activity and negotiations of ghosts now outside the coercive partialities of power. There the imagination addresses historical debts with stories that repair what was forgotten so as to guarantee our futures.

Richard Perez is an assistant professor of English at John Jay College of Criminal Justice at the City University of New York and co-director of the U.S. Latino/a literature minor. He is co-editor of *Contemporary U.S. Latino/a Criticism* (2007) and *Moments of Magical Realism in U.S. Ethnic Literatures* (2012). His work has appeared in the *Centro Journal for Puerto Rican Studies*, *Latino Studies Journal*, and *MELUS Journal*. He is currently at work on a book titled *Towards a Negative Aesthetics: U.S. Latino/a Fiction and the Remaking of American Literature.*

Notes

1. Robinson's work contains a detailed overview of reparative literature.
2. Just to clarify, I am fully in favor of economic reparations.
3. For an interesting discussion on the relation of debt and dispossession, see Butler and Athanasiou 2013, 10–37.

Works Cited

Brogan, Kathleen. 1998. *Cultural Haunting: Ghosts and Ethnicity in Recent American Literature*. Charlottesville: University of Virginia.

Butler, Judith, and Athanasiou, Athena. 2013. *Dispossession: The Performative in the Political*. Cambridge, UK: Polity Press.

Dayan, Colin. 2011. *The Law Is a White Dog: How Legal Rituals Make and Unmake Persons*. Princeton: Princeton University Press, 2011.

Derrida, Jacques. 1995. *Archive Fever: A Freudian Impression*. Trans. Eric Prenowitz. Chicago: University of Chicago Press.

Gordon, Avery. 1997. *Ghostly Matters: Haunting and the Sociological Imagination*. Minneapolis: University of Minnesota Press.

Morrison, Toni. 1987. *Beloved*. New York: Knopf.

———. 1990. "The Site of Memory." In *Out There: Marginalization and Contemporary Cultures*, ed. Russell Ferguson, Martha Gever, Trinh T. Minh-ha, and Cornel West. Cambridge, MA: MIT Press, 299–324.

Robinson, Randall. 2000. *The Debt: What America Owes to Blacks*. New York: Plume.

Taylor-Guthrie, Danielle, ed. 1994. *Conversations with Toni Morrison*. Jackson: University of Mississippi Press.

"Unspeakable Things Unspoken": Reflections on Teaching *Beloved*

Barbara J. Webb

She said, that when the officers and slave-hunters came to the house in which they were concealed, she caught a shovel and struck two of her children on the head, and then took a knife and cut the throat of the third, and tried to kill the other,—that if they had given her time, would have killed them all.

P. S. Bassett, "A Visit to the Slave Mother Who Killed Her Child," 1856

A young escaped slave woman kills her baby girl and would have killed her other children if she had not been stopped. When I read the initial reviews of *Beloved,* Toni Morrison's 1987 novel, my own response was that this is not a story I wanted to read. Indeed it seemed "this was not a story to pass on." For me, after reading *Beloved* and especially after teaching it, the idea of stories that were not to be "passed on" took on a much more profound meaning about choices and responsibilities, the consequences of forgetting, and the need to come to terms with the past in the present so that such stories are not endlessly repeated. Also, we should not forget how controversial this novel was when it first appeared. Stanley Crouch denounced the novel as a melodramatic blackface holocaust story; it was not deemed worthy of the National Book Award, which led to forty-eight black writers and scholars signing a letter of protest in response to this lack of recognition. Although it went on to win the Pulitzer, *Beloved* remains on the banned books list in a number of U.S. school districts, presumably because of its depiction of brutality and sexual violence. Yet how else can such a story be told? After years of teaching this novel, it is ever more apparent to me not only what a literary achievement it is but also how important it has been for our rethinking of the history and legacy of slavery. It dares

WSQ: Women's Studies Quarterly 42: 1 & 2 (Spring/Summer 2014) © 2014 by Barbara J. Webb. All rights reserved.

to tell what many of us don't want to remember or know. Like Sethe, we are a people and a nation that still hasn't come to terms with the historical debt of slavery.

Beloved is a text that goes beyond statistics and ledger accounts and effectively imagines the profound psychological cost of slavery to the men, women, and children for whom no one was held accountable and for whom no debt is recognized. It not only belies the seemingly ever resurgent myth of slavery as a benign institution (Sweet Home) but also interrogates the deepest existential meaning of freedom (Denard 2008, 44–45). Teaching this novel in a class made up of a diverse group of students, of whom many are immigrants or children of immigrants, can create an underlying tension about issues of identity: belonging and not belonging, anger that is righteous or not so righteous. The subject matter of *Beloved* is emotionally charged, deliberately so. Some readers see themselves as outsiders; others lay claim to the text as part of their own personal history; many feel defensive about what they perceive as suggestions of racial complicity. For me as a native-born African American who spent her earliest years in the Jim Crow South, the classroom dynamics can be difficult to negotiate. Like Morrison's earlier novels, *Beloved* has personal resonance for me. It evokes a past that neither I nor my parents' generation experienced but that seemed to live on in the people and places we knew and had been told about. My great-grandmother was the daughter of parents born in slavery. She kept her Bible close but never went to church. As a child I wondered why, but never asked. What conflict did she feel about the power of salvation for descendants of slaves? Like Stamp Paid in *Beloved*, my great-grandfather changed his name, but in his case the new name was associated with a notorious outlaw, in an act of defiance by my great-grandfather against laws that were never intended to protect him or his family.

How then should I assume my own relationship to the text in the classroom? I cannot and would not want to pretend to have a false critical objectivity about the emotionally charged content of the novel, but I would want to leave space for each of the readers in the class to engage with the text, reflecting Morrison's own approach as a writer. Morrison is a great writer, but she's also a wonderful role model for good teaching. So I must perform the difficult dance of not claiming sole ownership and understanding of a historical experience with which I feel a deep personal identification. This is a story to be shared, even when the sharing is not comfortable.

Despite my surprise when in the early 1990s a colleague questioned whether Toni Morrison belonged in our department curriculum as a "major writer," I feel fortunate to have begun to read and teach the novels of Morrison before she became enshrined in the "canon" of American and world literature. Forgive me if I sound proprietary, but Morrison is a writer who literally and metaphorically struck home. Early on, she cautioned against the pitfalls of canonization as a potential process of erasure, yet another form of "silencing" for African American literature.

I've taught *Beloved* in a number of courses since its publication in 1987. The text appeared at the height of critical attention on the work of black women writers, which coincided with a renewed interest in the history of slavery. I taught a survey of African American literature called "Narratives of Liberation" that examined the quest for freedom, freedom as an existential category, from nineteenth-century slave narratives through the twentieth-century fiction of Hurston, Wright, Baldwin, Ellison, Margaret Walker, and Alice Walker, usually ending with Morrison's *Beloved*. Morrison's novel brought a renewed sense of urgency defining our personal and collective freedom in a period of post–civil rights disillusionment, and she accomplished this with a mastery of form and subject that indeed struck home. I've also taught *Beloved* in courses on black women writers, but probably the most successful of all has been my course "Toni Morrison and the African American Literary Tradition," which allowed my students and me to experience the development of Morrison's fiction and ideas about writing over a number of years and through several novels. We focused on the critical reception of her work, which in one way or another often seemed to spark controversy—is she a feminist or feminist enough? Is her work too political or not political enough? Does she sacrifice political consciousness for aesthetics? Does her work play into the discourse of black pathology?

What struck me most was the seriousness of student responses to Morrison's novels, the way students were often pushed beyond their comfort zones, challenged to think through their assumptions about blackness, about gender, about culture, about ethical dilemmas and choices—and this occurred whether they were white students or students of color, male or female, confident in their "Americanness" or not so much. *Beloved* was especially challenging not only because of its unconventional form but also because of its emotionally charged subject matter, intent on "ripping away the veil" of a brutal institution, acknowledging the damage done and the debt never paid. *Beloved* is one of only a few works of fiction that I have taught that not only provoked consciousness but also seemed to truly transform the consciousness of my students—even those who were initially resistant to it. In recent years some of the initial openness to Morrison seems to have waned—of course she still has her enthusiasts, but I think there has been what I would call a negative "canonization" effect, especially among graduate students—so much written about her work, not enough attention to the work itself. A text like *Beloved* requires slow reading, not fast consumption.

Beloved is especially important for its focus on the slave woman, the "property that reproduced itself without cost" (228). The other part of that story, however, is the fate of the male slave—not the heroic or triumphant slave of the nineteenth-century slave narratives but ordinary men like Morrison's Paul D, whose five attempts at escape fail. He is bought, sold, and resold—traded like any other financial instrument by a variety of owners: individual farmers, railroads, bank companies. One of the most powerful sections of the novel is the account of Paul D's ordeal in a prison camp in Alfred, Georgia, after his attempt to flee one of his new owners. The brutality and degradation of the chain gang or the labor camp foreshadowed the fate of all too many black men after emancipation—arbitrary arrest for vagrancy or minor offenses, forced labor in mining and construction. *Beloved*, like other Morrison novels, suggests meaningful parallels between the past and present.

In a 1987 interview, Morrison pointed out:

> There is no place you or I can go, to think about or not think about, to summon the presences of, or recollect the absences of slaves: nothing that reminds us of the ones who made the journey and of those who did not make it. There is no suitable memorial or plaque or wreath or wall or park or skyscraper. There's no 300 foot tower. There's no small bench by the road. There is not even a tree scored, an initial that I can visit or you can visit in Charleston or Savannah or New York or Providence or, better still, on the banks of the Mississippi. And because such a place does not exist (that I know of), the book [*Beloved*] had to (Denard 2008, 44–45).

Since then there have been many attempts to construct physical memorials, notably the Bench by the Road Project of the Toni Morrison Society. Ironically, the future National African American Museum for History and

Culture on the Mall in Washington, DC, plans to install a guard tower and prison cell from the notorious Louisiana State Penitentiary at Angola as one of the "memorials" of African American history. Some would argue that this prison memorial is not just a reminder of the past (the Jim Crow era from Reconstruction through the civil rights movement of the 1960s) but also what Michelle Alexander (2010) refers to, in her book on the mass incarceration of black men in the present, as "the new Jim Crow."[1]

Morrison's approach to narrative and history has produced considerable innovative cross-disciplinary interest in the academy. In my own teaching, I have been primarily interested in the questions she raises about the relationship between historiography and fiction and her insistence on the cognitive value of narrative. My students have always been drawn to these aspects of *Beloved*; it is a novel that makes them want to go back to the archives, to rethink traditional histories and the issue of black subjectivity in the past and present. A number of literary theorists and scholars in other fields have acknowledged the significance of *Beloved*, among them Homi Bhabha in *The Location of Culture*, Paul Gilroy in *Small Acts* and *The Black Atlantic*, and more recently, Ian Baucom in *Specters of the Atlantic* and Avery Gordon in *Ghostly Matters*. Both Baucom and Gordon recognize the cumulative effect of memory and time, so central to *Beloved*, as a radical reconceptualization of the relationship between past, present, and future (Baucom 2005, 34, 322–24, 329; Gordon 2008, 137–90, 207–8). The spectral presence of the "disremembered and the unaccounted for" still demands a reckoning in the present. Each new reading of *Beloved* in the classroom deepens our understanding of where we are and where we need to go.

Barbara J. Webb is an associate professor of English at Hunter College and the Graduate Center, City University of New York. She teaches African and African Diaspora literatures, with a special focus on women's studies and postcolonial studies.

Note

1. The Louisiana State Penitentiary was notorious for its brutal treatment of inmates. It was built on land that was originally a plantation called Angola, which was owned by Samuel James, a major in the Confederate Army (http://angolamuseum.org). See also Cohen 2013; Blackmon 2008; Alexander 2010.

Works Cited

Alexander, Michelle. 2010. *The New Jim Crow: Mass Incarceration in the Age of Colorblindness*. New York: New Press.

Bassett, P. S. 1856. "A Visit to the Slave Mother Who Killed Her Child." *American Baptist*, February 12. In *The Black Book*, ed. Harris Middleton, with the assistance of Morris Levitt, Roger Furman, and Ernest Smith, 10. New York: Random House, 1974.

Baucom, Ian. 2005. *Specters of the Atlantic: Finance Capital, Slavery, and the Philosophy of History*. Durham, N.C.: Duke University Press.

Blackmon, Douglas A. 2008. *Slavery by Another Name: The Re-enslavement of Black Americans from the Civil War to World War II*. New York: Random House.

Cohen, Patricia. 2013. "Tower and Cell, Signifying Much More Than a Prison." *New York Times*, July 9, C1.

Denard, Carolyn C., ed. 2008. *Toni Morrison: Conversations*. Jackson: University Press of Mississippi.

Gordon, Avery F. 2008. *Ghostly Matters: Haunting and the Sociological Imagination*. University of Minnesota Press.

Beloved Citizens: Toni Morrison's *Beloved*, Racial Inequality, and American Public Policy

Alex Zamalin

Toni Morrison's classic novel *Beloved* (1987) provides a lens through which to examine how social assistance shapes African American freedom. One dominant interpretation of the novel has been that it implicitly argues for the importance of recognizing the historical legacies of slavery upon African American lives. For example, James Berger claims that the novel counters 1980s neoconservative arguments of black cultural pathology by showing that "law and science, power and official knowledge continue to violate African American lives" (1996, 411). And George Shulman argues that the novel shows that addressing the historical legacies of racial exclusion must be an ongoing rather than temporary process, giving readers "the feeling of urgency and political necessity of a redemption people must seek but cannot guarantee, must not preclude but cannot possess" (2008, 202). These scholars point to the novel's central narrative, which depicts a postbellum community of ex-slaves in Cincinnati grappling with the traumatic legacy of slavery as it is embodied in an infant ghost named Beloved, who was murdered by her mother, Sethe, in an effort to save the child from enslavement.

What remains unexplored is how another narrative thread, in which the characters struggle to create a flourishing community during Reconstruction with few economic resources or opportunities, examines the effect of divergent models of social assistance on African American lives. As a work of literature rather than of political theory, *Beloved* does not provide direct arguments about politics. Furthermore, it does not directly advocate for certain public policies. But I suggest that it nonetheless examines how social assistance that is contingent upon work and adherence to normative

WSQ: Women's Studies Quarterly 42: 1 & 2 (Spring/Summer 2014) © 2014 by Alex Zamalin. All rights reserved.

moral standards reinforces African American marginalization, whereas unconditional social assistance has a greater potential to mitigate it. The novel thus offers important insights into the politics of debt: conditional social assistance is a further extension of the legacy of slavery because it makes African Americans indebted to American society for whatever aid they receive—aid often needed because of social conditions created by slavery. In contrast, the novel shows how unconditional social assistance, which imposes no debt upon recipients, can more effectively address the legacy of racial oppression. Over a quarter century after *Beloved*'s publication, these observations are valuable for conceptualizing the relationship between contemporary public assistance programs and racial inequality in the United States.

It is through the character of Edward Bodwin, a white former abolitionist, that Morrison most obviously dramatizes how conditional social assistance exacerbates African American marginalization. There is good reason to accept Berger's claim that Bodwin represents a tradition of postwar white liberalism that condescends toward African Americans, while providing them with jobs and housing (1996, 417). Berger suggests that Sethe's attack upon Bodwin at the novel's conclusion represents Morrison's repudiation of white liberal paternalism and her simultaneous acknowledgment that liberals' historic commitment to assisting African Americans nonetheless deserves respect. But a closer reading reveals that Morrison actually links Bodwin's assistance to his paternalistic attitude. What she shows is that his assistance actually tethers aid to work, available to recipients only on the condition that individuals adhere to moral standards of conduct that he defines. For these characters to receive assistance to help meet their most basic needs, Bodwin keeps them entirely dependent upon his authority and low-wage labor.

Morrison illustrates that Bodwin's type of aid effectively reproduces African American economic marginalization. Whereas Suggs performs certain domestic tasks for Bodwin in exchange for financial support, tasks such as cobbling, canning, and laundry and seamstress work, she dies with few assets and, on her deathbed, describes herself as nothing but "a nigger woman hauling shoes" (Morrison 1987, 179). And although Denver does nighttime domestic work for Bodwin, she seeks out extra opportunities to make money, still struggling to support herself and her destitute mother, Sethe: "She had heard about an afternoon job at the shirt factory. She hoped that with her night work at the Bodwins' and another one, she could put away something and help her mother too" (266). In this way, Morrison points to Bodwin's profit from the exchange of these women's labor for his aid. He benefits from their domestic work but undervalues it, so that Suggs and Denver spend hours improving Bodwin's domestic life only to struggle for financial stability and the free time to enrich their own lives.

Morrison also depicts Bodwin's mode of assistance as one that requires recipients to embody moral standards of conduct, thus making African Americans' socioeconomic security entirely contingent upon judgments they neither create nor control. In one passage we learn that Bodwin has told Sethe's mother-in-law, Baby Suggs, that her rent-free residence is contingent on self-discipline: "They would permit her to stay there. Provided she was clean. The past parcel of colored wasn't" (145). In another, Bodwin's decision to provide Sethe's daughter Denver with employment is presented as also requiring her to submit to a reeducation according to his sister's, and presumably his own, moral standards. Denver explains, "Miss Bodwin taught [me] stuff. . . . She says I might go to Oberlin. She's experimenting on me" (266). Bodwin's aid places the burden of proof on African Americans to show that they are "clean," a broad character trait that connotes sexual purity and honesty, as well as its more literal meaning of personal hygiene. And though African American women in the novel have no control over these standards, their living conditions are dependent upon their proper adherence to them, as determined by Bodwin and his sister. Morrison makes clear that their power of sovereign judgment is especially troubling because Bodwin sees deviance as integral to black culture: although believing in the equitable sanctity of humanity ("human life is holy, all of it" [290]), he also assumes that blackness is marked by dependency and laziness. This is made clear through a racist money box in Bodwin's home: a statue of a black boy with bulging eyes and a gaping mouth, bending toward its owner with excitement at being paid a pittance. The inscription on the statue reads, "At Yo Service" (255).

Bodwin's absolute power to define moral standards and assess adherence to those standards, alongside his assumption of African American deviance and inferiority, makes his aid fundamentally tenuous and unreliable. At the novel's conclusion, Sethe attempts to stab Bodwin with an ice pick as he arrives to pick Denver up for work. Bodwin interprets her action as governed by a pathological worldview, much as he views the black women gathered at Sethe's doorstop to exorcize Beloved from her home as driven by a pathological rage toward one another (a predictable collection of "colored women fighting," at a place "full of trouble" [264]). Bodwin fails to see that Sethe mistakenly stabs and identifies him as "schoolteacher," the vicious slaveholder whose prior arrival there prompted the infanticide around which the narrative revolves, or that this mistaken identity was partly a circumstantial outcome of her increased alienation as a black single mother who has just lost her low-wage job and savings. Morrison depicts Bodwin's inability to comprehend the world that Sethe inhabits as one that undervalues black women's work, a product of what Patricia Hill Collins calls "the interlocking systems of race, gender and class oppression" (1990, 77). All that Bodwin is able to see is Sethe's failure to fulfill the condition he has earlier articulated to Baby Suggs—cleanliness. His obliviousness has real consequences: Bodwin decides to sell 124 Bluestone, putting Sethe on the brink of homelessness. We may thus actually interpret Sethe's stabbing of Bodwin as the result of her fear that he has come to retrieve Denver to work for him. In Sethe's statement that Bodwin is "coming into her yard . . . coming for her best thing" (Morrison 1987, 262), "best thing" can be taken to mean Denver rather than Beloved.

Importantly, Morrison doesn't just implicitly criticize Bodwin's mode of assistance. She offers us an alternative, if neglected, model, symbolized through the activities of the black women in Beloved. Strikingly opposed to Bodwin's model, it embodies a feminist argument that all individuals are equally entitled to care. As Virginia Held writes of care ethics generally, "The central focus of the ethics of care is on the compelling moral salience of attending to and meeting the needs of the particular others for whom we take responsibility" (2006, 10). The description of Baby Suggs's generosity to all who enter her home reveals this ethic of care in noting that "124 had been a cheerful, buzzing house where Baby Suggs, holy, loved, cautioned, fed, chastised and soothed. Where not one but two pots simmered on the stove; where the lamp burned all night long. Strangers rested while children tried on their shoes. Messages were left there, for whoever needed them was sure to stop in one day soon" (Morrison 1987, 87). Without conditions or stipulations, Suggs offers individuals free emotional support, food, clothing, and shelter. That she does this even for strangers shows that her action is based on an ethical imperative rather than a rational calculation. Suggs provides care to all, whether it is costly, troublesome, or ultimately disadvantageous: like her home, her care is free and available to all.

That Morrison intends us to read Suggs's behavior as a potentially rep-licable model for social assistance is revealed when Denver approaches the black women of her community for aid. While Denver believes that "asking for help from strangers was worse than hunger" (248), the women recall Suggs's care-based assistance: "All of them knew her grandmother and some had even danced with her in the Clearing. Others remembered the days when 124 was a way station, the place they assembled to catch news, taste oxtail soup, leave their children, cut out a skirt" (249). Den-ver relies on Bodwin's assumption that all aid requires work and that she has no entitlement to care when she asks one of the women, Lady Jones, "Could she do chores in the morning?" (248). What Lady Jones makes clear is that Denver's request and her need are the only criteria for aid: "If you all need to eat until your mother is well, all you have to do is to say so" (248). Furthermore, rather than being dependent upon the judgment of a benefactor, Morrison emphasizes how the black women's assistance is available regardless of whether they believe they see failure of moral char-acter: "Some even laughed at Denver's clothes of a hussy, but it didn't stop them from caring whether she ate" (249).

Finally, Morrison's portrayal of care-based assistance ultimately rests on the assumption that all citizens are deserving of basic resources that liberate them from oppressive need. The black women eventually reflect on their decision to help Denver, describing one probable justification as simply that "when trouble rode bare back among them, quickly, easily they did what they could to trip him up" (249). In this way, they imply that the feeling of responsibility stemmed from a belief that they were obligated to minimize any obstacle to her freedom, a belief that parallels capabil-ity theorists' arguments that freedom is possible only after the establish-ment of basic necessities. Following Amartya Sen's claim that "[human] development consists of the removal of various types of unfreedom that leave people with little choice and little opportunity for exercising their reasoned agency" (1999, xii), Martha Nussbaum contends that the basic necessities that allow us to develop a sense of the good and engage in meaningful relationships include bodily health and integrity, emotions, and practical reason (1998, 41). The novel's black women provide Denver with these basics: not only food to maintain her bodily health, "some rice, four eggs and some tea" (Morrison 1987, 248), but also basic emotional support through weekly meetings to alleviate her distress. Denver eventu-ally learns that this is aid based on the responsibility to care, rather than on strategic interest, and that all it requires is a sincere expression of gratitude, a "Thank You" (249). It is precisely this sense of gratitude that is central to the conclusion of the novel: Sethe runs into the black women's arms and "loving faces" (260) as they exorcize Beloved, as well as the pain, hopelessness, and despair that the ghost has caused her.

Beloved does not make any direct arguments about what public policies can best facilitate racial justice. But the novel's insights can be instructive for understanding the possibilities of divergent models of social assistance. Acknowledging the problematic limitations of Bodwin's conditional model is especially relevant since the Personal Responsibility and Work Opportunity Reconciliation Act of 1996 transformed Aid to Families with Dependent Children (AFDC) into Temporary Assistance to Needy Families (TANF). AFDC was a federal entitlement program designed to give benefits to low-income households on the basis of need, but TANF makes aid contingent on the performance of wage labor and encourages states to use federal money to discourage out-of-wedlock births. Some states even make TANF eligibility contingent on mandatory drug testing or restrict it for those with drug felony convictions. All these factors show that TANF threatens to solidify the legacies of slavery and Jim Crow. In an obvious parallel to Bodwin's model, it makes African Americans' lives, including many African American single mothers' lives, dependent on minimal financial assistance tethered to low-paying jobs, reeducation into normative standards of family life, and a host of other conditions. For this reason, whether in discussions about welfare policy, affirmative action, or monetary reparations for unpaid black labor under slavery and Jim Crow, *Beloved* reveals the importance of unconditional forms of assistance for racial justice. As the title of the novel suggests, perhaps the crucial question that should motivate the distribution of resources to citizens is whether it enables them to "be loved."

Alex Zamalin is a PhD candidate in political science at the Graduate Center, City University of New York. His research focuses on African American political thought and American racial politics. He teaches at Hunter College.

Works Cited

Berger, James. 1996. "Ghosts of Liberalism: Morrison's Beloved and the Moynihan Report." *PMLA* 111(3): 408–20.

Collins, Patricia Hill. 1990. *Black Feminist Thought: Knowledge, Consciousness, and the Politics of Empowerment*. London: Routledge.

Held, Virginia. 2006. *The Ethics of Care*. Oxford: Oxford University Press.

Morrison, Toni. 1987. *Beloved*. New York: Alfred A. Knopf.

Nussbaum, Martha. 1998. *Sex and Social Justice*. Oxford: Oxford University Press.

Sen, Amartya. 1999. *Development as Freedom*. Oxford: Oxford University Press.

Shulman, George. 2008. *American Prophecy: Race and Redemption in American Political Culture*. Minneapolis: University of Minnesota Press.

PART V. **MORAL DEBT: DISLOCATION AND RESISTANCE**

Debt, the Precarious Grammar of Life, and Manjula Padmanabhan's *Harvest*

Jodi Kim

Life an' debt freedom not yet

—*Mutabaruka, "Life and Debt"*

What is a debt, anyway? A debt is just the perversion of a promise. It is a promise corrupted by both math and violence.

—*David Graeber,* Debt: The First 5,000 Years

In the first epigraph above, Jamaican artist Mutabaruka's pithy lyric captures freedom's antinomies by questioning freedom's content and temporality. To live a life excruciatingly tethered to debt is to live a conjunctional "life an' debt." [1] In Mutabaruka's formulation, life *and* debt are one and the same; debt owns your life, and in doing so, it owns your freedom. By taking residence as the content of formal freedom, debt works in this instance to vacate or evict the substantive meaning of freedom and to forestall the event and temporality of freedom as a "not yet." In this sense, we can speak of debt as a "shifting grammar of life" (Rajan 2006, 14) that perpetually recedes before our horizon into a future tense, a vanishing point through which a "not yet" freedom is perhaps glimpsed but always foreclosed. Haunting this vanishing point is the term that Mutabaruka self-consciously substitutes debt for: *death*. A life of debt *forecloses* an intimacy with freedom, which is to say that it *forces* an intimacy with forms of social and physical death. Debt, in other words, can be a death sentence, and while some might be able to have their sentences commuted and still live a social death, others experience a literal physical death flashing blindingly

WSQ: Women's Studies Quarterly 42: 1 & 2 (Spring/Summer 2014) © 2014 by Jodi Kim. All rights reserved.

forward, a fatal present tense. If, as David Graeber suggests, a debt is "just the perversion of a promise," a promise "corrupted by both math and violence," then who can have their debt/death sentences commuted, who can have their debts forgiven altogether, and who must fully repay their debts with interest (Graeber 2011, 391)? Within this economy, who must keep their promises? Mutabaruka, and his Jamaican nation, must do so; they must pay their promissory notes. The reason lies in the "math and violence" to which they have been subjected, a history of colonialism and racial chattel slavery succeeded by more recent forms of neocolonial domination and an international uneven division and proliferation not only of gendered racial labor but also of debt.

This continued corruption of the promise by math and violence perpetually keeps Mutabaruka's longing for freedom, the promise of freedom, in the future tense. His future tense grammar, as at once a specific temporality of freedom as well as a broader system of signification, calls to mind other similar grammars, such as that of Hortense Spillers. Tracing the total objectification of the captive body as flesh within the U.S. context of chattel slavery, she calls, and theorizes the symbolic order instantiated by the African slave trade as, an "American grammar." One of the distinctive features of this grammar is that it "remains grounded in the originating metaphors of captivity and mutilation so that it is as if neither time nor history, nor historiography and its topics, show movement, as the human subject is 'murdered' over and over again" (Spillers 2003, 208). This, as Saidiya Hartman writes, is the afterlife of slavery, an afterlife not only symbolic but also crushingly material (Hartman 2008). That is, formal emancipation for the enslaved in the United States represented not a radical rupture but rather a "nonevent." The whip of chattel slavery was replaced with the "burdened individuality of freedom," constituted by the tethers of liberalism: a guilty conscience, notions of responsibility modeled on contractual obligation, calculated reciprocity, and most importantly, indebtedness, since "debt played a central role in the creation of the servile, blameworthy, and guilty individual and in the reproduction and transformation of involuntary servitude" (Hartman 1997, 9). The *longue durée* of the "nonevent" of emancipation from a range of distinct yet related forms of unfreedom throughout the globe—whether racial chattel slavery, colonial subjugation, racial genocide, debt peonage, contract labor, apartheid, or incarceration—has produced and continues to produce increased levels of privation and debt, as well as greater vulnerability to being rendered surplus populations of essentially disposable lives. This is what we might call a precarious grammar of life.

I begin with these observations as a point of entry into this essay's analysis of the play *Harvest* (Padmanabhan 2003). In late 1995, Indian playwright Manjula Padmanabhan read the announcement for the Alexander S. Onassis Public Benefit Foundation International Play Competition. The theme for the competition was "the challenges facing humanity in the next [twenty-first] century" (4). Padmanabhan's play *Harvest*, completed and submitted the following year, was the winning entry.[2] This futuristic drama, set in 2010 Bombay, imagines a world in which a U.S.-based transnational corporation called InterPlanta Services sells its wealthy, aging, and sick clients not only organ transplants but also *whole-body* transplants. These bodies and body parts are purchased and harvested from impoverished, gendered racial residents in different parts of the world who are compelled to participate in this perverse economy because of debt and basic survival needs. That such a global industry could be legally sanctioned, economically profitable, and ethically unquestioned at a time that is not too distant from the time of *Harvest*'s actual writing would suggest that the "challenges facing humanity in the next century," a century we have now arrived at, are vexed and multifold. Not least among these challenges is the question of what constitutes "humanity"—or the very humanity of the human itself—in such a world.

In this essay, I analyze the ways in which *Harvest* makes a strategic intervention into the precarious grammar of life produced by the uneven distribution of debt and privation. While the play has been variously read as an allegory of globalization, neocolonialism, global capitalism, and disability (Gilbert 2006; Detsi-Diamanti 2002; Pravinchandra Laxmidas 2009; Davidson 2008), I read it more specifically as an allegory of gendered racial debt. I argue that *Harvest*, through the trope of transracial whole-body transplantation rendered as a dizzying series of gender and racial crossings, generates a conceptualization of gendered racial debt as a social relation, disciplinary regime, sleight of hand, and production of subjectivity. The aesthetic form this takes in the play is what I call a metadrama of surrogacy. In particular, *Harvest* generates a complex theory on the subjectivity of the indebted, one that goes beyond economistic and moralistic registers. It does so by highlighting the power of heterosexual and heteroreproductive desire in producing a relationship between time and gendered racial debt. This relationship forecloses alternative temporalities and futures by preempting the possibility of default. At the same time, precisely by gesturing to the multiple possibilities of gender and racial crossings, *Harvest* suggests how the debt relation ultimately attempts to enfold ever-larger segments of humanity into its economies and logics.

I analyze, moreover, the ways in which Padmanabhan's work imagines how the gendered racial subject represents not simply a site of relative vulnerability but also a locus of significant critique that calls for the abolition of gendered racial debt. The play suggests that impoverished and racialized women—through the commodification of their body parts as well as the affective and reproductive labor they are compelled to provide—at once register and thwart the regimes of gendered racial debt that would generate a precarious grammar of life. Indeed, Padmanabhan's imagining of a future without debt is rendered all the more urgent when we consider that the global organ trade and new biomedical technologies have made possible a shifting of the grammar of life to the future tense, or the chance at the indefinite extension of life, for those who can afford it. The condition of possibility for *this* future tense is another variety of future tense altogether—the one suggested by Mutabaruka in my opening discussion. That is, the indefinite extension of life as privilege is made possible by "life an' debt." Death for the former and something we might call freedom for the latter are both continually deferred. These are the distinct yet conjoined future tense grammars of life. What is at stake in these shifting *grammars* of life are the violent and uneven *valuations* of life, for in this distribution, whose lives are precisely denied an ongoing future tense? And in this uneven dispensation of indebtedness, what forms of sociality that exceed the brutal alchemy of math and violence are foreclosed?

Let us now turn to *Harvest*. In a series of surrogacies and substitutions that will be revealed as the play unfolds, Padmanabhan focuses initially on the male head of the household. Yet this focus soon takes a radical detour, as we shall see, so that the figure of the wife ultimately emerges as the subject that at once embodies and thwarts gendered racial debt. The play opens with Om Prakash, a twenty-year-old man who has just been laid off from his job as a clerk in Bombay, coming home to announce to his mother and wife, Jaya, that he has successfully obtained a new job. Before centering our analysis on Jaya, we shall linger for a moment with Om, as Padmanabhan's rendering of his character, and in particular the nature of his new job, sets into motion the economies of debt we are investigating. Om states excitedly, "We'll have more money than you and I have names for! Who'd believe there's so much money in the world?" (10). Yet what is this new job that pays so much? The Prakash family has the following exchange:

MA: Tell me again—all you have to do is sit at home and stay healthy?
OM: Not *sit* necessarily.
MA: And they'll pay you?
OM: Yes.
MA: Even if you do nothing but pick your nose all day?
OM: They'll pay me.
MA: And what about off-days?
OM: Well. *Every* day is off, in one sense.
JAYA: Why don't you tell her the truth?
MA: Isn't this the truth?
OM: Jaya—
JAYA: Tell her. Tell your mother what you've really done.
MA: Shoo! Don't speak to your husband in that voice.
OM: The walls are thin. Everyone can hear. When you talk like this.
JAYA: Everyone knows already! D'you think you're the only one with this
    job? D'you think people don't know what it means . . . when the guards
    come from the agency? All that remains to be known is which part of
    you's been given away. (19)

Ma is dumbfounded that Om's new high-paying job does not seem to require him to perform any actual work, or labor. How can it be that he will be getting paid even if he does nothing but "pick [his] nose all day"? At this point in the play, Ma does not know that Om's new job is this: he has sold, contractually promised, his organs to a U.S.-based transnational corporation named InterPlanta Services, whose rich clients seek to purchase everlasting life through multiple, successive whole-body transplants. Her confusion registers the sedimented ways in which we have come to understand the relationship between labor and money, or more generally the creation of value. The Marxian insight that labor is the source of the creation of value—the labor theory of value—has increasingly been complicated by contemporary developments. Writing on the transition from feudalism to capitalism and the invention of wage labor, Marx observed that, "these newly freed men became sellers of themselves, only after they had been robbed of their own means of production, and all the guarantees of existence afforded by old feudal arrangements" (1977, 875). When Marx wrote that "these newly freed men became sellers of themselves," he meant the sellers of their labor power, and he could not have imagined how developments in the life sciences would one day make it possible for people to sell their literal biological selves—their body parts and organs.

Padmanabhan stages a critical and strategic intervention by imagining a not too distant future when the human organ's reduction to the predatory tendencies of capital would be a legally sanctioned global industry. Upon Om's successful "selection" and signing of the contract, InterPlanta "guards" barge into the Prakashes' small apartment to sanitize it and install the necessary devices, including a "Conduct Module" and multicolored pellets that will now be the family's sole food source. The Prakashes are subjected to a disciplinary regime, a care of the self that will ensure the harvesting of healthy organs. The Contact Module, a white faceted globe that hangs from the ceiling, is a high-tech device that makes it possible for Om (the "donor") to see and speak with Ginni (the "receiver"). In essence, it is a surveillance mechanism that allows Ginni to monitor the family's every move. The Contact Module is also a pedagogical tool through which Ginni imperiously instructs the family on the proper protocols of personal hygiene and care of the self. After all, she would not want to receive diseased, infected, or unhealthy organs. Unsurprisingly, Ginni is a wealthy American, a young, beautiful, white woman whose health ailments remain undisclosed until the end of the play.

While Om signed away his body parts in order to avoid the debt that comes with unemployment, the terms of his contract with InterPlanta Services ironically enter him into an economy of debt. That is, InterPlanta and Ginni have made an initial capital and infrastructural investment in Om and his family by transforming their apartment and outfitting it with modern-day conveniences such as a toilet. Yet, when Om signed the contract, he was not immediately required to "donate" any of his organs. Indeed, InterPlanta does not inform him which of his organs he will ultimately need to donate, or when. Within this contractual economy, Om is effectively compelled to promise all his organs. Because he is an impoverished subject and the male head of his household, this is one kind of gendered racial debt that he is obligated to repay. He literally owes his life. The value of his promise derives not from a speculative bet on something that might be produced or invented in the future but from the commodification of the very material, organic matter of his life itself as it exists now. Om's debt, as a gendered racial debt, is one that will *not* be rolled over indefinitely or forgiven and therefore demands to be repaid to InterPlanta and Ginni.[3] While he hopes for a delay in the first donation he will have to make, Jaya reminds him, "But in the end it would always come to this—the bill collector at the door" (51).

In reminding us that the arrival of the bill collector is an inevitability, Padmanabhan's Jaya reveals how a debt relation functions. More specifically, she apprehends the relationship between debt and time. The debtor-creditor relationship is not simply governed through the borrowing and lending of money but is animated and enforced by an already existing asymmetry in power relations. As such, debt indexes not only the state and sum of money owed but also a broader social relation structured by violent disciplinary protocols compelling the indebted to conduct themselves in a manner that will maximize the likelihood of repayment. In this sense, to be indebted is not simply to owe money. It is to inhabit a subjectivity that robs one of the possibility of having multiple futures, multiple ways of conducting oneself and being in the world. This, then, is the relationship between debt and time; debt neutralizes time so that it conforms to the homogenous time of repayment (Lazzarato 2012, 45). In *Harvest*, by having Jaya be the acerbic voice of reason, Padmanabhan provides a political diagnosis of the violence of this debt relation, particularly for gendered racial subjects. Yet ultimately, as we shall see, Jaya is the figure of resistance who will throw into question the asymmetries of power subtending this relation.

Writing on the ascendance of neoliberalism and the debt economy since the 1970s, and following Nietzsche and Deleuze and Guattari on debt, Maurizio Lazzarato observes, "The credit relation does not mobilize physical and intellectual abilities as labor does . . . [Rather, the relation mobilizes] the morality of the debtor, his mode of existence (his 'ethos'). The importance of the debt economy lies in the fact that it appropriates and exploits both chronological labor time and *action*, non-chronological time, time as choice, decision, a wager on what will happen and on the forces (trust, desire, courage, etc.) that make choice, decision, and action possible" (2012, 55; emphasis in the original). In choosing an impoverished Indian household as the figure of debt, and a blond, white American woman as the bearer of credit, Padmanabhan makes possible an extension of Lazzarato's general observations on debt to a specific analysis of what I have been calling gendered racial debt. To make an obvious point, we know by now that the debtor-creditor relation does not follow a vulgar color line. That is, to be white is not necessarily to be a creditor, and to be a gendered racial subject is not necessarily to be a debtor. The point, rather, as revealed by a work like *Harvest*, is that the contemporary debtor-creditor relation at once relies upon and invents anew what I have called the *longue durée* of the "nonevent" of emancipation from a range of distinct yet related forms of unfreedom experienced disproportionately by gendered racial subjects throughout the globe. *Harvest* suggests that in this, our era of late-capitalism, the bill collector will always still come for impoverished, gendered racial subjects like Om and Jaya.

In our presumed moment of formal emancipation, decolonization, and post–civil rights, what does the intersection of race, gender, and class signify? *Harvest* dramatizes how impoverished, gendered racial bodies are disproportionately rendered the raw material of neoliberal rationalities such as structures of nonrenewable debt and technologies of surveillance and incarceration. Indeed, Padmanabhan figures Om's contractual obligation, one he entered into "freely" and for which he is being paid handsomely, as a form of incarceration leading to the death penalty. The InterPlanta office is described as a prison cage, with "iron bars, snaking around and around. And everywhere there were guards" (10). Om explains, "We were standing all together in that line. And the line went on and on ... not just on one floor, but slanting up, forever. All in iron bars and grilles. It was like being in a cage shaped like a tunnel" (11). It is as if Om has entered a modern-day debtor's prison. His home also becomes a claustrophobic prison, with the constant monitoring by Ginni and InterPlanta that he and his family undergo through the Contact Module as a literal technology of surveillance. Indeed, Jeetu, Om's brother, calls the home a "fancy prison" (56).

Om subsists within, and has been the prey of, a violent regime of value in which, on the one hand, his life is reduced to *zoe* and, on the other, he must perform a kind of affective labor for Ginni each time they interact through the Contact Module. Om is literally being expended by Ginni in her (re)production of herself. The violence of this transaction is occluded through the mechanism of formal legality— the contract Om has signed is legal. He is legally bound to die a death by slow degrees. This elision of violence is further achieved through his affective labor. Here, *Harvest* deploys a metadrama of surrogacy. In this instance, surrogacy operates as a mode of substitution on various registers. Through the Contact Module, Om's and Ginni's virtual images stand in as substitutes for their physical bodies, and this will in turn mediate the forthcoming transplantation/substitution of body parts. Ginni beams herself into the Prakash household not only to surveil the family but also to seduce and interpellate Om. In other words, ensuring his cooperation is her way of insuring her major purchase. Whether or not Om is seduced by Ginni's blond Western beauty—and more broadly by the heteronormative romance plot on which her strategy depends—he must act as if he is. This is the metadramatic element of the play: we see Om performing for Ginni. And this performance of sycophantic adoration and unquestioning cooperation is affective labor that is integral to the whole transaction. Indeed, Padmanabhan's complex imagining of the debt relation—mediated by surveillance technology and animated by the force of heterosexual desire—lays bare and further complicates the economy governing many global service industries. An unevenness of economic and gendered racial power between client and worker means that much of the labor that is involved is affective. Even if the job itself does not necessarily entail the worker's making the client feel better, the worker is compelled to perform the affective labor of acting as if his or her job makes him or her happy, as if the worker is happy to serve. This is another kind of surrogacy, an affective surrogacy. In Om's case, he must literally perform his affective labor for the camera (the Contact Module) and substitute eager cooperation for whatever feelings he might have—of fear, dread, or regret—about owing his life to Ginni.

Whereas Om has thus been effectively interpellated by Ginni, Jaya refuses to succumb. In figuring Jaya as the voice and embodiment of resistance, Padmanabhan gestures to gendered racial debt as engendering one debt relation that not so much begs a bailout or forgiveness but rather demands an abolition of the debt relation altogether. Toward the end of *Harvest*, it is revealed that Ginni was just simply "a computer-animated wetdream," a fictive computer-generated image, and that she is really Virgil, an aging man who has already undergone four body transplants in the span of fifty years. This is yet another layer of the metadrama of surrogacy; substituting Ginni for Virgil, and Virgil's performance as Ginni, seem to accelerate Om's death sentence. To add another twist to the story, when the InterPlanta guards come for Om so that he can make his first "donation," they take Om's brother Jeetu instead, seemingly by mistake and with no protest from Om. It turns out that Virgil wanted Jeetu's body, and not Om's, all along, so that he could seduce Jaya, who was once Jeetu's (her brother-in-law's) lover. Virgil explains:

VIRGIL: We look for young men's bodies to live in and young women's
  bodies in which to sow their children—

JAYA: What about your own!

VIRGIL: We lost the art of having children.

JAYA: How can it be?

VIRGIL: We began to love longer and longer. And healthier each generation. And more demanding. . . . Soon there was competition between
  one generation and the next—old against young, parent against child.
  We older ones had the advantage of experience. We prevailed. But our
  victory was bitter. We secured Paradise at the cost of birds and flowers,
  bees and snakes. So we designed this programme. We support poorer
  sections of the world, while gaining fresh bodies for ourselves.

JAYA: And it works? You live forever?

VIRGIL: Not everyone can take it. We fixed the car, but not the driver. I'm
  one of the stubborn ones. This is my fourth body in fifty years.

JAYA: Fourth!

VIRGIL: Two were not successful. It hasn't been easy, Zhaya. I won't hide
  that from you. But so long as I can afford to keep trying—I will. (86)

Here, Padmanabhan reveals why Virgil (with Jeetu's body) wants to seduce
Jaya. Hers is the "young woman's body in which [he wants] to sow [his]
children." Yet he does not want to risk his health by traveling to the Third
World, so he asks Jaya to undergo artificial insemination. In the absence of
physical contact, the seduction ploy is still important to Virgil because he
wants to interpellate Jaya as an eager gestational surrogate, just as he (as
Ginni) had interpellated Om.

Harvest sets these economies of heteronormative and heteroreproductive desire into motion, but the question of their ultimate fulfillment is
left ambiguous. First, we are led to believe that Om, the male head of the
household, is the principal character. But it turns out that he is neither the
organ donor nor the potential gestational surrogate; he is simply the vehicle or dupe through which the organ donations and potential surrogacy
occur. For reproductive purposes, it turns out that Jeetu's body, that of a
homeless sex worker, is more valuable than Om's presumably clean and
healthy body. And finally, Jaya, the cheating wife who seems to have very
little power in the household except to criticize acerbically her husband's
decision, actually turns out to be the voice of political critique and agent
of resistance. From the very beginning, she demonstrates a clear under-

standing of what Om has done. She does not wish to be a "widow by slow degrees" (21), and she realizes that Om has offered himself up, as a living sacrifice of sorts, to Ginni as a piece of meat. Ginni will consume him as she would a piece of chicken for dinner. Through Jaya's protestations, *Harvest* dramatizes how impoverished households are compelled to engage in transactions that precipitate a precarious grammar of life, ironically and precisely so that those families can keep on living. As Brett Neilson and Ned Rossiter (2005) argue, contemporary forms of precarity go beyond questions of access to jobs, housing, food, security, and the like. Precarity also indexes a beleaguered sociality whose affective dimensions cannot be underestimated.

By the time Virgil reveals his master plan, sociality within the Prakash family itself has become frayed. Jaya is effectively alone. Her relationship with Om was already precarious and fraught, and it is rendered more so when Ginni/Virgil enters the dynamic. She does not get along with her mother-in-law at all. Indeed, by the end of the play, Ma detaches herself from any semblance of sociality and kinship at all by literally attaching herself to a "SuperDeluxe VideoCouch model XL 5000" with "seven hundred and fifty video channels from all over the world" and "full-body processing capacities" (77). She becomes the ultimate couch potato; the video couch becomes the surrogate for actual human interaction and sociality. And Jeetu, the one person for whom Jaya has affection, has been cannibalized by Virgil and will die in the near future. And because the Prakash family members have effectively been rendered prisoners within their own home, sociality between them and anyone else becomes virtually impossible. This is another sense in which they experience a precarious grammar of life.

Padmanabhan's most pointed intervention in *Harvest* comes toward the end of her play, when it becomes unlikely that Jaya will ultimately surrender to this precarious grammar. That is, it is not certain that she will pay the gendered racial debt that she uniquely shoulders by bearing Virgil's child. Unlike Jeetu, she would not be giving up her body parts by being a gestational surrogate. She would, however, be providing crucial affective and reproductive labor. Here, Padmanabhan is shedding critical light on an "international womb boom" in which racialized women, particularly in India, are increasingly being hired as gestational surrogates for infertile white couples. In this process, the surrogate is radically instrumentalized as a "Womb for Rent" (DasGupta 2010). Padmanabhan writes against this. She has Jaya resisting Virgil by attempting to negotiate the terms of the transaction, by insisting that he come to India rather than having her undergo artificial insemination: "Look, I've understood you now. I know you're stronger than me, you're richer than me. But if you want me, you must risk your skin to get me. Even though it's really Jeetu's skin—I want you to risk it!" (89). By insisting that Virgil take on some risk, Jaya attempts to reverse the dominant economy in which impoverished and gendered racial subjects are compelled to be the bearers of risk, to pay for the speculative practices of finance capitalists. In other words, she is insisting that Virgil and his like also have a debt to pay. Indeed, by what means have he and his kind come into their wealth?

Padmanabhan stages a powerful intervention into the debtor-creditor relation by calling it out as a sleight of hand. In asking Virgil to take on risk, Jaya is lifting the veil. The historical flow of wealth into Europe and the United States has been made possible by the violent theft, plunder, and expropriation of land, resources, labor, and captive human bodies. Indeed, as Frantz Fanon writes, "Europe is the literal creation of the Third World." As such, moral reparations are not enough. Rather, "we will not accept aid for the underdeveloped countries as 'charity.' Such aid must be considered the final stage of dual consciousness—the consciousness of the colonized that *it is their due* and the consciousness of the capitalist powers that effectively *they must pay up*" (2004, 58, 59; emphasis in the original). That is, Europe and the United States owe a huge debt to the world that created them. Yet various calls for economic reparations, particularly for slavery, have gone unheeded. Forms of economic and humanitarian aid given to formally postcolonial nations elide the very reasons why such aid is required in the first place, namely, a protracted history of colonialism and continued neocolonial domination. The afterlife of colonial plunder persists through the neocolonial policies, of, for example, institutions like the IMF and World Bank. The purported mission of these institutions is to alleviate poverty, yet the loans they provide are at high interest rates with attendant structural adjustment policies that putatively "support" the so-called developing world, but actually function to sink that world further into debt. In this way, the debtor-creditor relation is a sleight of hand, a role reversal in which the actual debtors have transmogrified into creditors, and vice versa.[3] This, too, is a metadrama of surrogacy, a violent substitution and crossing whose dramatis personae are as yet unable to make real promises.

Harvest calls for another kind of structural adjustment policy altogether. While Virgil describes the InterPlanta program as a "win-win situation" in which clients like himself are a source of "support" for "poorer sections of the world while gaining fresh bodies for [them]selves," Jaya's resistance makes visible how the scheme is a unidirectional extractive enterprise. In dramatizing the question of risk and demanding a reversal in the directionality of risk, Padmanabhan not only unveils the debtor-creditor relation as a sleight of hand but also imagines a different economy of debt altogether. This goes beyond a call for debt forgiveness. Fred Moten and Stefano Harney call for the inhabitation of "bad debt"—"the debt that cannot be repaid . . . the black debt, the queer debt, the criminal debt"—as a fugitive public (2010, 1). In the fugitive public, there are no creditors; it is a refuge where the debtor seeks other debtors, offers and acquires debt, and can owe more. It is the place, in other words, where debt, the promise, has not been "corrupted by both math and violence." This debt without a creditor gestures to an alternative social relation and economy and refuses quid pro quo calculations of reciprocity. Indeed, if debt differently conceptualized in nonmonetizable terms is a lateral form of reciprocity and obligation, it is the very thing that makes sociality possible. Yet its monetization, or its corruption by both math and violence, has converted that sociality into social hierarchy.

In *Harvest*, Padmanabhan asks how we might be able to break out of this violent cycle. She portrays Jaya's attempting to break out by enacting the ultimate refusal—killing herself—should the InterPlanta guards try to compel her to undergo the artificial insemination procedure. She tells Virgil, "I'll die knowing that you, who live only to win, will have lost to a poor, weak and helpless woman. And I'll get more pleasure out of that first moment of death than I've had my entire life so far! . . . And in the meantime, I want you to practice saying my name correctly. It's Jaya—'J' as in justice, 'J' as in jam" (91). As she recounts, the perverse economy of gendered racial debt means that her life is not really hers anymore. She claims the only thing she actually owns: "The only thing I have which is really mine now is my death" (90). This is the precarious grammar of life—when one's sole possession becomes one's own death. What greater perversion of a promise than the leveraged promise of one's own death? Yet Jaya attempts to upturn the gendered racial debt by withholding, through an act of revolutionary suicide, that which will enable Virgil's future tense grammar of life. In critically situating Jaya's life and death in this way, Padmanabhan's work asks us to consider the threat of suicide, or the threat of default, as a placeholder of sorts until "'J' as in justice" can be realized. What might this justice look like? When this justice arrives, the bill collector will never arrive because there will be no bill collectors. This justice, in other words, is the abolition of debt altogether.

Thus, by the end of the play, we have been confronted with multiple and dizzying gender and racial crossings. Padmanabhan dramatically deploys these crossings, I argue, in order to amplify, critique, and imagine alternatives to the ways in which the debt relation at once relies upon and produces a certain kind of subjectivity, on the one hand, and also presumes a fiction of equality or fungibility, on the other. After all, Virgil could have appeared as Virgil, gone straight for Jeetu's body, and revealed Jaya's use-value as a gestational surrogate right away. Why the subterfuge and vertiginous rerouting of these plans through gender and racial crossings? In terms of the production of subjectivity, the debt relation relies on the acts of borrowing and repayment/reimbursement as a twinned exercise. While individuals are compelled to borrow for a variety of reasons—usually impoverishment, sometimes hyperconsumption, and at other times predatory lending practices—what compels them to pay back what they owe, or at least to make an attempt at it? To be a good debtor implies a certain subjectivity. In *Harvest*, that subjectivity comes in the form of heterosexual desire. Padmanabhan displays how Om is compelled to repay the debt, in this case his very life, because he is seduced by Virgil qua Ginni. This instance of gender crossing is strategically deployed to interpellate Om via not only his heterosexual desire but also an interracial desire whose privileged object is whiteness. Heterosexual desire is also harnessed as a site of interpellation with Virgil's instance of racial crossing. The desire for a transracial whole-body transplant is itself a case of racial crossing, a particularly disturbing and cannibalistic one given the asymmetries of power involved. Yet instead of choosing Om's body, as we are initially led to believe, Virgil has strategically chosen Jeetu's body because he, and not his brother, Om, is the object of Jaya's heterosexual desire.

Padmanabhan's deployment of these crossings complicates existing understandings of the subjectivity of the indebted. It has been generally understood, particularly within European critical thought, that this subjectivity is constituted by a morality and ethics of guilt.[4] Within this scheme, it is guilt that demands and compels repayment. Yet what Padmanabhan's aesthetic of the metadrama of surrogacy suggests, particularly through the matrix of gender and racial crossings or substitutions and the focus on the politics of heterosexual desire, is that a theory of the subjectivity of the indebted also needs to take into account the affective dimensions of desire. If a consuming desire can catalyze the act of borrowing, in the sense that one desires to own, for instance, a SuperDeluxe Video-Couch model XL 5000, desire can also compel repayment. What does it mean, then, that desire emerges in *Harvest* specifically as heterosexual desire and is marshaled to ensure heteroreproductive futurity? If, as I have argued, gendered racial debt as a violent social relation produces a precarious grammar of life for the Prakashes of the world and an ever-extending future tense grammar of life for the Virgils of that same world, then the question of temporality and futurity becomes all the more pressing. *Harvest's* complex dramatization of how the power of heterosexual desire is strategically harnessed both to compel repayment of debt and to attempt to ensure heteroreproductive futurity complicates the notion that debt neutralizes time. While it is true, on the one hand, that debt forecloses the possibility of proliferating, heterogeneous, and unpredictable futures and times by violently forcing them to conform to a single, predictable payback time, what this violent preemption of default ensures, on the other hand, is continued social reproduction. A vital component of social reproduction, of course, is heteroreproductivity and its norms. Padmanabhan's work thus generates a conceptualization of the subjectivity of the indebted that complicates and revises economistic and moralistic understandings by highlighting the nexus of race, gender, and sexuality in the formation of desire. Her dramatic intervention, moreover, in making heteroreproductive desire visible through the characterization of Virgil, generates a critique of that desire via Jaya's resistance and throws into doubt the question of its ultimate fulfillment.

In terms of the presumption of equivalence and fungibility, Virgil's ability to engage in gender and racial crossings would seem to suggest that genders are interchangeable just as races are. Yet what affords Virgil the ability to do this? The obvious answer, of course, is that it is the power of his wealth as well as his race and gender privilege as a white male. He can escape or cross the very mortality of his body, yet the Prakashes are crushingly trapped in the precarity of theirs. That is, the existence of formal equality and political rights obscures the extent to which the exchange relation, and in particular the debt relation, already implies an asymmetry of power. What Padmanabhan has Virgil call the "win-win situation" of the exchange relation, in this instance the buying and selling of bodies as organic biological material, is meant to highlight the very absurdity of the presumption or fiction of equivalence driving the logic of exchange. Conditioned as it is by the profoundly uneven distribution of power, wealth, and resources wrought by global capitalism and its imbrication with race and gender, the exchange relation as a presumed lateral form measured by the universal equivalent called money belies the very *nonequivalence* of the transaction. In this sense, *Harvest* mocks the very notion that an equitable win-win situation can emerge from the exchange relation between Virgil and the Prakashes.

Harvest thus takes up the challenge of grappling with the Onassis Foundation International Play Competition's theme of "the challenges facing humanity in the next [twenty-first] century" by critically dramatizing the problem of human organ trafficking but also by linking it to and anticipating the global debt crisis that has transpired more recently. While since the 1970s the idea of a debt crisis has tended to be conflated with Third World debt, it has become increasingly obvious in the more recent historical conjuncture that the "Third World" is not the only site that is vulnerable to debt regimes. Indeed, the recent emergence of the sovereign debt crisis in Onassis's own Greece is but only one example of this. Yet in examining debt at the more intimate scale of an impoverished household in India, Padmanabhan crafts a powerful drama that illuminates the human cost of debt as a violent social relation. Crucially, her work suggests that while vulnerability to debt is no longer specifically a "Third World" problem, the distribution of that vulnerability and the ways it is lived, felt, and embodied remain as yet uneven. More crucially still, the play imagines alternatives to the different grammars of life produced by this unevenness by offering a complex rendering of the subjectivity of the indebted and allowing us to see the debtor-creditor relation as a sleight of hand.

In this way, as an allegory of multiple gendered racial economies of debt and the different grammars of life it produces, *Harvest* lays bare the stubborn persistence of the "nonevent" of emancipation. It reveals how debt's deferral of freedom engenders a precarious grammar of life. The play provides a social autopsy of a global social formation whose death-worlds metastasize alarmingly before our eyes. Yet this, too, is a sort of vanishing point, because the precarious grammar of life is a banality that resists critical apprehension. This is to speak about an ever-growing grave of disposable bodies, a mortuary of the living dead. However, it is the living dead who are compelled to incubate, through their labors at once affective and reproductive, through their bodies at once performative and fleshly, the promise of everlasting life for the Virgils of this world. *Harvest* imagines, finally, what it would mean to refuse these labors and withhold these bodies and bodily capacities. That is, what would it mean to abolish the debt relation altogether?

Jodi Kim is associate professor of ethnic studies at the University of California, Riverside. She is the author of *Ends of Empire: Asian American Critique and the Cold War*, published by the University of Minnesota Press in its Critical American Studies series in 2010. Her articles have appeared in journals such as *American Quarterly*, *MELUS*, and the *Journal of Asian American Studies*.

Notes

1. Mutabaruka's song is featured on the soundtrack of a 2001 Canadian documentary of the same title, *Life and Debt*, directed by Stephanie Black. This work provides a compelling account of the devastating effects of World Bank, IMF, and "free trade" policies on Jamaica.
2. The play premiered in Athens in 1999, in Greek, at the Karolous Theatre. It has been broadcast on the BBC World Service and adapted into a film, titled *Deham* (Body), by Indian director Govind Nihalani.
3. The United States replaced the gold standard with a transformed U.S. Treasury bill, a government-issued debt, as an international monetary standard. Essentially, what this has meant since the early 1970s is that foreign banks with a surplus of dollars can no longer exchange them for gold. Rather, the banks must purchase U.S. Treasury bonds, i.e., U.S. Treasury debt, thereby extending a continuous loan to the United States.
4. See, for example, Lazzarato (2012), who traces debt, morality, and guilt through figures such as Nietzsche, Deleuze and Guattari, and Marx.

Works Cited

DasGupta, Sayantani. 2010. "(Re)conceiving the Surrogate: Maternity, Race, and Reproductive Technologies in Alfonso Cuarón's *Children of Men*." In *Prescribing Gender in Medicine and Narrative*, ed. Marcelline Block and Angela Laflen, 178–211. Newcastle, UK: Cambridge Scholars.

Davidson, Michael. 2008. *Concerto for the Left Hand: Disability and the Defamiliar Body*. Ann Arbor: University of Michigan Press.

Detsi-Diamanti, Zoe. 2002. "Bio-slavery, or the Cannibalistic Quest for

Longevity: Harvesting for Human Organs in Manjula Padmanabhan's Futuristic Drama." In *Biotechnological and Medical Themes in Science Fiction*, ed. Domna Pastourmatzi. 111–127. Thessaloníki, Greece: University Studio Press.

Fanon, Frantz. 2004. *The Wretched of the Earth*. New York: Grove Press.

Gilbert, Helen. 2006. "Manjula Padmanabhan's *Harvest*: Global Technoscapes and the International Trade in Human Body Organs." *Contemporary Theatre Review* 16(1):123–30.

Graeber, David. 2011. *Debt: The First 5,000 Years*. New York: Melville House.

Hartman, Saidiya V. 2008. *Lose Your Mother: A Journey Along the Atlantic Slave Route*. New York: Farrar, Straus, and Giroux.

Hartman, Saidiya V. 1997. *Scenes of Subjection: Terror, Slavery, and Self-Making in Nineteenth-Century America*. New York: Oxford University Press.

Lazzarato, Maurizio. 2012. *The Making of the Indebted Man: An Essay on the Neoliberal Condition*. Los Angeles: Semiotext(e).

Marx, Karl. 1977. *Capital: A Critique of Political Economy*. Vol. 1. New York: Vintage Books.

Moten, Fred, and Stefano Harney. 2010. "Debt and Study." *e-flux journal* 14: 1–5.

Mutabaruka. 2002. "Life and Debt." In *Life Squared*. Heartbeat/Pgd. CD.

Neilson, Brett, and Ned Rossiter. 2005. "From Precarity to Precariousness and Back Again: Labour, Life, and Unstable Networks." *Fibreculture Journal* 5. http://five.fibreculturejournal.org/fcj-022-from-precarity-to-precariousness-and-back-again-labour-life-and-unstable-networks/.

Padmanabhan, Manjula. 2003. *Harvest*. London: Aurora Metro Press.

Pravinchandra Laxmidas, Shital. 2009. "Inhuman Transactions? Representing the Commodification of Human Body Parts." PhD diss., Cornell University.

Rajan, Kaushik Sunder. 2006. *Biocapital: The Constitution of Postgenomic Life*. Durham: Duke University Press.

Spillers, Hortense J. 2003. "Mama's Baby, Papa's Maybe: An American Grammar Book." In *Black, White, and in Color: Essays on American Literature and Culture*. 203–229. Chicago: University of Chicago Press.

Fine in High Summer Sudden When

Shane McCrae

As Conrad Barbed

the inventor of barbed wire

Recounted to his

daily   / Hourly in his later years

Biographer it was a fine

day a fine afternoon a walk

fine in high summer sudden when

He realized

No injury no threat

of injury could prevent him

from risking his soft pink

WSQ: Women's Studies Quarterly 42: 1 & 2 (Spring/Summer 2014) © 2014 by Shane McCrae. All rights reserved.

Hands in the thorns of the wild blackberry bushes
along the lane   / And just like that

he understood

his cousin Igor's favorite maxim

Where there is suffering

there is money to be made

Was wrong

Where there is suffering

he leaned   recounting close *already*

The money has been made

Shane McCrae is the author of *Mule*, *Blood*, and three chapbooks—most recently, *Non-fiction*, which won the Black Lawrence Press Black River Chapbook Competition. His poems have appeared, or are forthcoming, in *The Best American Poetry*, the *American Poetry Review*, *Fence*, *Washington Square*, and elsewhere, and he has received a Whiting Writer's Award and a fellowship from the National Endowment for the Arts. He teaches in the brief-residency MFA program at Spalding University.

Illiberal Promises: Two Texts on Immigration and Moral Debt

Mimi Thi Nguyen's *The Gift of Freedom: War, Debt, and Other Refugee Passages*. Durham: Duke University Press, 2012.

Lisa Marie Cacho's *Social Death: Racialized Rightlessness and the Criminalization of the Unprotected*. New York: New York University Press, 2012.

Nicholas Gamso

As of this writing, a new immigration bill promising undocumented migrants a "pathway to citizenship" has made its way through key votes in both houses of the U.S. Congress, its success enabled by an amendment to spend as much as forty-six million dollars militarizing the U.S.-Mexico border. President Barack Obama, who has in five years overseen the deportation of more undocumented immigrants than any other U.S. president, plans to sign the bill into law later this year, authorizing the expansion of the border patrol to forty thousand agents, the construction of a seven-hundred-mile border fence, and the use of unmanned drones to police the sky over the Rio Grande (Cowen and Ferraro 2013). And all at a time when the rate of immigration from Mexico is not increasing, but remains steady (D'Vera et al. 2012).

One lesson of this irrational political dealing, these solutions without a problem, is clear: the rhetoric of our lawmakers, the volley of media cliché and political scheming, grows denser and more complicated all the time. In exchange for the illusion of progress and humanitarian goodwill, the Obama administration will preside over an elaborate, wasteful, and oppressive infrastructure, lining the pockets of security contractors while substantiating our mass media's most paranoid fantasies. The effects of what seems to be mere political negotiation are to be material and corporeal; every assault and trauma, every suicide in an immigrant detention center or along a stretch of border fence will reveal that even the rhetoric of immigration can be a force of life and death.

Two recent books address this convergence of mind, body, and the political: Mimi Thi Nguyen's *The Gift of Freedom: War, Debt, and Other Ref-*

WSQ: Women's Studies Quarterly 42: 1 & 2 (Spring/Summer 2014) © 2014 by Nicholas Gamso. All rights reserved.

ugee Passages and Lisa Marie Cacho's *Social Death: Racialized Rightlessness and the Criminalization of the Unprotected.* These works treat amnesty and immigration as discursive technologies of liberal governance, the "freedom" that, as Foucault says, is "never anything other . . . than a relation between the governors and the governed" ([1978–79] 2010, 63). Nguyen and Cacho push strongly at narratives and images that constitute and enhance such technologies, those that claim to "win hearts and minds" and provide a "pathway to citizenship," and see in this elaborate system the workings of permanent moral debt.

Nguyen applies theories of the gift and reciprocity—articulated by Mauss, Derrida, and Bourdieu—to the U.S. government's frequent "humanitarian" military interventions during the cold war. The United States provided sanctuary to refugees from the decolonizing global South, who were in turn obliged to make a pledge of service not unlike forms of debt bondage in the colonial era; in addition to labor and civil and military service, refugees from Vietnam and elsewhere were and are expected to express loyalty to the United States, its strategic international programs, and its regimes of development and Westernization. Nguyen pursues what supposedly constitutes the gift—"pipe dreams, bogus concepts, and moral luck" (24)—but spends more time working on the terms of reciprocity, which often mask the imbalance of power wherein "liberalism creates the conditions under which one is free to be free" (73). Nguyen finds varied narratives of freedom and reciprocity in media scripts, in speeches by politicians, generals, and analysts concerning the United States' brutal, ten-year war in Vietnam. She sees these narratives recast and contested in the works of present-day artists and filmmakers in Vietnam and among its diaspora.

Throughout her analysis, Nguyen emphasizes the enduring demands of war images, their silent imperatives, what she calls the "imperial forms and forces that endure beyond the cessation of military intervention and occupation" (27). She discusses depictions of refugee camps in Timothy Linh Bui's film *Green Dragon*, arguing against the imperial tendency to pathologize the stateless, to diagnose them with what she calls "the refugee condition." Here she borrows from postcolonialists Johannes Fabian and Dipesh Chakrabarty to discuss the temporality of the refugee, the way the refugee is depicted as backward and wanting, and the terms by which he or she can be afforded access to any number of modernizing and developmental institutions.

Nguyen also, in a discerning treatment of the image and what she calls "the apparent non-coincidence between pain and beauty" (97), recounts the afterlife of one of the war's most iconic and troubling photographs: that of nine-year-old Phan Thi Kim Phúc, naked, crying, running down a road in Trang Bang with American soldiers sauntering behind her. Nguyen sees the picture as a "war frame," a limited view of the conflict in Vietnam and its sanctioned reactions—liberal empathy, realist derision—and as a central referent for the theater of reconciliation to follow. Nguyen notes that two decades after the famous picture was taken, Kim Phúc appeared in a *Los Angeles Times Magazine* feature titled "The Girl in the Photograph"; lovely and charming in her adulthood, Kim Phúc has reemerged in the form of the refugee saved, beatified, at peace: a "politics of beauty" establishes and sustains "the politics of life" (99).

Nguyen's book is tremendously convincing. Her use of familiar theories by Foucault and Derrida, augmented by major writings on postcolonialism and contemporary critical race theory, is ambitious but soundly conceived and refreshingly well written. This book should prove instructive to scholars in areas where writerly sensitivity—generous engagement with ambiguous texts and the confidence to ask speculative, even oblique questions—is perhaps not as lauded as it should be. As we pursue interdisciplinary questions, those that derive from the entrenchment of knowledge systems but also the extant social conditions we wish to subvert, we would do well to follow Nguyen's lead, looking beyond the immediate discourse, the shallow optics of mass mediation, and finding in culture the ambivalences and tensions that can't be spoken outright. This is perhaps what she means when she says that she is interested in uncovering not "the analytics of truth" but an "ontology of ourselves," and when she warns against "compulsive interiorization, a wish for a metaphysics of voice or a kind of nature, whether attached to a condition (being a refugee) or another presence (a self)" (27).

Whomever "we" are, as theorists of postcolonialism have long cautioned, is likely already to be the subject of so much truth talk and so much theory. Critics should think twice about the cultures of scholarly self-possession that prescribe their interest in the self—singular or collective—as if it were necessarily a reservoir of limitless depth or of resistance. If we are to pursue the opportunities afforded by critical divination, we must also consider seriously the limits imposed on even what we think of as critical thinking by the diffuse regimes of language and metaphor in which we work, limits imposed by everyone and also by no one in particular.

This concern animates Lisa Marie Cacho's *Social Death*, a book that applies a similar theory of freedom and moral reciprocity to contemporary U.S. law, politics, and media, structures of knowledge and influence that stage liberalism's many ruses. Cacho's book may operate as a significant supplement to Nguyen's because it clarifies the ugliest but most insidious terms of liberal reciprocity. The immigrants and minorities who supposedly benefit from U.S. liberal democracy are not expected merely to praise the state or to engage in the kind of obsequious political theater that has long sustained imperial ideologies. They are expected also to participate in a race for minority recognition. Pitted against one another, they are compelled to rehearse and proliferate stereotypes, to pathologize groups, to refer to dehumanizing social categories, and to do so with guileless affect. They become complicit in a bureaucracy of language and power, of violence, that knows no end.

Cacho adopts the concept of "social death" from sociologist Orlando Patterson's well-known work *Slavery and Social Death* (1985). Patterson used the term to describe the imperative of loyalty that accompanied nineteenth-century slave liberation; because slaves owned no property that could be exchanged for their freedom—of course, they were themselves the property—their reciprocity took the form of commitment and enthusiastic gratitude. For the most part, Cacho puts Patterson's thesis to good use, parsing political rhetoric and arrogant statements about crime, poverty, race—and in particular immigrants and the undocumented—in the mainstream U.S. press and especially in "official" discourses of the law and state. She writes about the ratification and strategic misuse of California's Proposition 21, which allows suspects to be prosecuted as gang members purely on the basis of association and increases penalties for juvenile offenders; attempts by mainstream media to tokenize and immobilize the often undocumented residents of low-income minority communities; the rhetoric of good and evil deployed by the George W. Bush administration after September 11, 2001, to underwrite the invasions of Iraq and Afghanistan; and in a final chapter, the story of Brandon Jesse Martinez, her own cousin, no stranger to the inequities of the criminal justice system, who died in a car wreck in 2000.

What characterizes most of these case studies are the imperatives of what Cacho and others call "comparative racialization." Here Cacho explains the significance of racial antagonisms that are more complicated, that trouble and in fact exploit traditional, dualistic formulations of race and of nationality—black-white, alien-citizen, et cetera: "Represented as if in constant conflict, aggrieved groups are placed within different racialized binaries and value hierarchies that overlap and intersect in a way that essentially hides, disguises, and displaces American racism, stabilizing rather than subverting practices and processes of criminalization" (13). The limits of our language, the limits even of our thinking, are so clearly defined that any attempt to defend or promote a community and certainly to depict it as more patriotic or deserving than another, is, as Cacho likes to say, "always already" racist, grounded in a system of value designations that can render a subject or a whole group socially and civically dead. Terms such as "illegal alien" and "terrorist" do the work of attaching essential criminality to specific racial corollaries; these in turn become incorporated in U.S. imperial moralism, legitimizing the state's heady but banal platitudes about "spreading democracy," the "American dream," and so on. In the nation of immigrants and individualists, any expressions of one's own value must also be a denigration of another's.

This set of expectations is complicated further when one considers the noncitizen, the extralegal, the refugee, the figure who is constructed discursively to serve as the civic order's constitutive other, what the Italian philosopher Giorgio Agamben (1998) calls "homo sacer." Cacho, who does not cite Agamben's influential theory, is more interested in how this liberal sleight of hand is manifest, recurrent, diffuse, but stable in the bureaucratic overlay of law and discourse. Here she quotes Hannah Arendt's deceptively simple assessment of rightlessness: "'Their plight is not that they are not equal before the law, but that no law exists for them'" (82). This thinking, which approaches the question of legal equity from the outside, is the basis of Cacho's most insightful arguments: her analysis of the U.S. criminal justice system, its strategic failures and lacunae, and the cynical manner in which politicians, jurists, lawyers, and the press deploy and misuse laws that were purportedly enacted to redress one form of racism or another. For Cacho, it is this bureaucratic ruse that establishes limits to any serious legal or even discursive recourse, and is indeed what allows her to declare (as early as the introduction) that there is "no way out" of liberal modernity's many discursive demands (17).

Readers may be frustrated by this apparent resignation and by Cacho's reluctance to hold anybody accountable for the system she describes, her insistence that "assigning and allocating culpability are not what's at stake" (82). She argues instead that because some illegal immigrants lack social and monetary resources—and are in the most literal sense without any rights—they have no choice but to exist as the products of representation or, on the other hand, to be "rendered illegible" (63). And though this assessment strikes me as a useful rejoinder to those methodologies that deterministically name an enemy, it nevertheless poses some problems: Cacho ends up accepting media bromides as evidence of a general sentiment, or as she suggests more than once, for an "ideology." In these sections, Cacho emphasizes the passivity of audiences and the moral and intellectual poverty of realpolitik. At times, Cacho's analysis feels like a litany of complaints (which even the back cover describes as "relentless"): when an immigrant rights activist says, "I am not a criminal. . . . We are workers, mothers, and human beings," she is accused of "unintentionally reify[ing]" the family (132); when a commentator discusses poverty and violence in low-income communities, he is automatically "pathologiz[ing]" their residents (83); even the father of a slain soldier, one who was granted citizenship in exchange for dying in Afghanistan, is chastised for promoting U.S. hegemony (110).

I wondered reading this last example why Cacho's should be the definitive interpretation of such a gesture, and why we should not dwell instead on the distressing tension that emerges when a man mourning his son's death is forced to bow before an empire and to smile while he does so. There are of course many writings that express all the things that her examples do not and cannot. Cacho might have pursued interviews; she might have done some ethnographic work in legal and activist communities or among the undocumented themselves; or she might have included writings that quarrel with the distant presumptions of her own "social death" thesis, essays and letters by death row inmates or undocumented workers or others whose acquaintance with the justice system and all its inequities are sure to be as intimate as Cacho's. Her final chapter is something of an antidote; she not only parses the newspaper articles about her cousin's death—articles loyal to the scripts Cacho criticizes—but also keeps a record of alternative and unofficial memorials, those that seem not to be sanctioned by public discourse but that are nevertheless felt. Despite some reservations, it seems to me that Cacho is basically right in her assessment of death and devaluation, especially under the slanted promises of liberal democracy and national consciousness.

Together, Cacho's and Nguyen's works might help us think about the darker relationship between difference and its mediation—and what this relationship has to do with life and death. Their texts provide, in other words, a profound way to think about freedom, whether in its Foucauldian valences—a mere technology of relation—or as something to which many people aspire honestly, to which they devote their bodies, and, to borrow that cold war cliché, their hearts and minds. The violence that accompanies liberal expansion does not, to my mind, quell the seriousness of these expressions or the authenticity of these feelings but, on the contrary, gives them depth and obliges provocative and generous criticism; when one remembers that a half million people are held in a network of immigrant detention centers throughout the United States, the critical obligations of honesty and of the truth are clarified and the obligation to *imagine* is illuminated.

Nicholas Gamso is a doctoral candidate at the City University of New York. He teaches writing and literature at Queens College.

Works Cited

Agamben, Giorgio. 1998. *Homo Sacer: Sovereign Power and Bare Life*. Trans. Daniel Heller-Roazen. Palo Alto: Stanford University Press.

Cohn, D'Vera, Ana Gonzalez-Barrera, and Jeffrey Passel. 2012. "Net Migration from Mexico Falls to Zero—and Perhaps Less." Pew Research Hispanic Trends Project, April 23.

Cowen, Richard, and Thomas Ferraro. 2013. "Immigration Bill Passes Key Test in Senate." Reuters, June 24. http://www.reuters.com/article/2013/06/24/us-usa-immigration-idUSBRE95N1EB20130624.

Foucault, Michel. (1978–79) 2010. *The Birth of Biopolitics: Lectures at the College de France*. Trans. Graham Burchell. London: Palgrave.

Patterson, Orlando. 1985. *Slavery and Social Death: A Comparative Study*. Cambridge, MA: Harvard University Press.

Twenty-First-Century Debt Collectors: Idle No More Combats a Five-Hundred-Year-Old Debt

Amanda Morris

Self-determination. Survival. Sovereignty. These are the principles driving the Idle No More movement and the ideas that have consistently driven Indigenous peoples in North America to fight against their colonizers' destructive designs on their bodies, lands, and spirits. From the genocidal actions of Manifest Destiny and residential boarding schools to Sand Creek, Wounded Knee, and reservations, the governments of the United States and Canada have persistently colonized the Indigenous peoples of this continent in word and deed. Idle No More is an ongoing grassroots effort created by four First Nations women in Canada that has attracted global attention and support. On its website, the group calls for the repeal of provisions in Bill C-45, which became law in 2013, "(including changes to the Indian Act and Navigable Waters Act, which infringe on environmental protections, Aboriginal and Treaty rights) and abandon all pending legislation which does the same." In cooperation with Defenders of the Land, this growing Indigenous network also calls on Canada to increase proportional representation with regard to "all legislation concerning collective rights and environmental protections"; to live up to the United Nations Declaration on the Rights of Indigenous Peoples and to "respect the right of Indigenous peoples to say no to development on their territory"; and to "officially repudiate the racist Doctrine of Discovery and the Doctrine of Terra Nullius and abandon their use to justify the seizure of Indigenous Nations' lands and wealth" (Idle No More 2013). The "vision" of Idle No More seems simple: "Idle No More calls on all people to join in a peaceful revolution, to honour Indigenous sovereignty, and to protect the land and water." However, peaceful revolution is a complicated goal

 WSQ: Women's Studies Quarterly 42: 1 & 2 (Spring/Summer 2014)

Idle No More by Kevin Konnyu.

that requires an understanding of why these women were motivated to act in November 2012.

Indigenous women lead their communities with visionary leadership skills; deep cultural knowledge; and a central focus on spiritual faith, honesty, and integrity. As they have since before the European invasion, Indigenous women are responsible for the health of their communities and have always taken this role seriously. Under continued assault from external and male-dominated political forces, such as the Indian Act, Indigenous women need to possess and exercise forms of political empowerment to maintain and improve the day-to-day lives of their people. Idle No More presents an Indigenous vision of politics that surpasses the control that state sovereignty has over contemporary Aboriginal life. The women leading Idle No More are twenty-first-century debt collectors who have created an attention-grabbing model for decolonial Indigenous feminism that builds upon a rich history of Indigenous resistance to colonial control over land, culture, and lives: a movement that empowers Indigenous women on the path to achieving social justice for Indigenous nations. As other contemporary movements respond and react to injustice and the trampling of rights through street protests and occupation of public spaces, the Idle No More movement is trying to shift the contemporary discourses of rights, sovereignty, and nationhood by arguing that it is Indigenous women who ought to ultimately hold the political power of Indigenous nations, or at the very least have an equal seat at the debate table. According to Leanne Simpson in *Dancing on Our Turtle's Back: Stories of Nishnaabeg Re-creation, Resurgence and a New Emergence*, "Western-based social movement theory has failed to recognize the broader contextualizations of resistance within Indigenous thought, while also ignoring the contestation of colonialism as a starting point. . . . Part of being Indigenous in the 21st century is that regardless of where or how we have grown up, we've all been bathed in a vat of cognitive imperialism, perpetuating the idea that Indigenous Peoples were not, and are not, thinking peoples—an insidious mechanism to promote neo-assimilation and obfuscate the historic atrocities of colonialism" (2011, 32). In this respect, Indigenous nationhood entails a fundamentally different understanding of political power than that seen in Western European–style politics. Cheryl Suzack (Anishinaabe), editor and contributor to *Indigenous Women and Feminism: Politics, Activism, Culture*, uses several important legal cases from Canada to locate her examination of Aboriginal women in legal and political contexts in her chapter "Emotion Before the Law." Underlying every turn of her argument is Canada's Indian Act of 1876, which Suzack calls "an instrument of bureaucratic regulation" with a "dehumanizing structure, engendering consequential emotional, social, and political effects" that heavily affect Aboriginal women, including through such outcomes as "gendered and racialized status categories" and the "continuing disempowerment of Aboriginal women" (129). According to Suzack, new knowledge gained from these struggles should lead not only to questions about disempowerment, injustice, and politics, but also to activism by and for Aboriginal women as a "politically important and inclusive feminist goal" (142).

A central aspect of decolonization involves the gendering of indigenous issues. Linda Tuhuwai Smith writes, "Colonization is recognized as having had a destructive effect on indigenous gender relations. . . . Family organization, child rearing, political and spiritual life, work and social activities were all disordered by a colonial system which positioned its own women as the property of men with roles which were primarily domestic" (1999, 151). This gendered positioning is quite in opposition to the traditional roles that Indigenous women often hold in their nations, from leadership positions and the acceptance of the spiritual significance of women, to their "full participation in many aspects of political decision making and marked gender separations which were complementary in order to maintain harmony and stability" (152). As a result, Indigenous women "hold an analysis of colonialism as a central tenet of an indigenous feminism," including a return to this more traditional, fully inclusive, and powerful role in First Nations societies. Pamela Palmater is a prime example of the influential political female leadership so often found in Indigenous societies, as is Idle No More collectively, much to the irritation of Western expectations and the colonial project.

Idle No More exposes the problems with the legal and political relationship between First Nations and the Canadian government specifically, and Indigenous peoples and colonialist governments generally. The movement was originally motivated by the existence and implementation of Bill C-45, another in a long line of omnibus budget bills that amends the Indian Act, which is widely considered by many Indigenous peoples to be an exclusionary, assimilationist, and deeply discriminatory piece of legislation that is particularly hard on Indigenous women. Mi'kmaq woman, lawyer, and spokesperson for Idle No More Pamela Palmater shares her personal experience with the Indian Act in *Beyond Blood: Rethinking Indigenous Identity*. She writes about how her identity is heavily reliant on connections to ancestors, traditional territories, shared languages, histories, customs, and practices in the home community. This knowledge and understanding stands in stark contrast to the limiting parameters of the Indian Act, which she analyzes in terms of denial and exclusion for herself and others. Palmater writes, "The Indian Act and its membership provisions have kept me from enjoying both the legal identity of 'Indian' and membership in my band. As a result, I have not had the same access to elders and cultural practices as those who have been legally recognized as Mi'kmaq" (2011, 13). She writes about "injustices forced on Indigenous peoples by colonial and modern governments" as causing "the worst kind of sickness: our own people are now perpetrating the same injustices imposed by governments" (14). These injustices are written into the Indian Act and continue to be addressed by Indigenous activists looking to improve and change the language of the act and the resultant outcomes. One such exclusionary provision is the second-generation cutoff rule, "which stipulates that two successive generations of an Indian parenting with a non-Indian will result in no status for their descendents" (19).

Many bands in Canada make membership decisions based upon the Indian Act and its amendments, such as Bill C-31, which amended the Indian Act in 1985 to include specific degrees of birth descent to determine who might be recognized as a status Indian. Palmater explains, "One generation of marrying out equals 50 percent notional Indian blood quantum, two generations equals 25 percent, and so on" (29). The results can be devastating to First Nations families. The lack of status and membership suffered by those falling outside of this second-generation cutoff means that Palmater, whose grandmother married a non-Indian, will be able to live on her home reserve of Eel River Bar First Nation in New Brunswick, but her children will not be permitted the same right. Thanks to Bill C-31 amendments, Palmater will also be able to vote in reserve elections, participate in her band's governance activities such as land claim negotiations, receive benefits and treaty entitlements, and have regular access to elders and community based mentors, but her children will not. And so, while this reconciliation embedded in Indian Act amendments does improve access and opportunity for some Indigenous peoples, many others are still left out. Bill C-45 is the most recent legislation to further amend the Indian Act, and this time it involves sovereignty and treaty rights.

In January 2013, Pam Palmater spoke to the CBC's (Canadian Broadcasting Corporation's) Brent Brambury on his show, *Day 6*, about the particulars of C-45, how it might affect Indigenous peoples in Canada, and why Idle No More has expanded its protests to include funding cuts to First Nations peoples and other federal legislation that undermines treaty rights, particularly land use. One amendment to the Indian Act through C-45 drastically reduces the number of band members needed to surrender reserve lands to the federal government or a corporation for leasing purposes. The Indian Act originally required a majority of band member electors to vote to surrender land absolutely or conditionally; now, after C-45 passed in December 2012, a simple majority of whoever shows up to vote is necessary. Prior to December 2012, a majority of the electorate had to vote and a majority of that group had to vote in favor of surrender. According to Palmater, now five people could vote in favor of surrendering reserve lands. In her radio interview, Palmater (2013) explains,

> Say you had a First Nation of 5,000 band members and there's a small contingency who wanted to make a deal with Enbridge to have a pipeline go across the community and a majority didn't want that. You could

now set up a vote to surrender a piece of the reserve land to allow a pipeline to go through by those handful of people. . . . What you have to understand is that many First Nations in this country resist the paternalistic control of Indian Affairs over their communities and they refuse to participate in referendums held by Indian Affairs held on their territories. . . . So this can be extremely divisive and even destructive of reserve lands.

As a result, treaty rights are being violated by C-45 because the reserve lands were set aside for the exclusive use and benefit of band members only, "so the concept of surrendering those lands conditionally or unconditionally is something that takes away from the collective use and benefit . . . especially if the integrity is not maintained. At a minimum, it requires the consent of First Nations to agree to this legislative change, and that's a legal requirement by the Supreme Court of Canada," according to Palmater (2013). These unilateral changes to the legal functioning and decision making of First Nations were made without their consent, and so Idle No More continues to fight against this abrogation of treaty rights with protests and road blockades across Canada. Indigenous women's voices matter to official conversations about the legal, financial, and political standing of First Nations communities because their actions directly affect the functioning, survival, and future of their communities. Pam Palmater is one among many Indigenous feminists who are taking the lead in this fight to restore and maintain what equity for band members has been established by the Canadian Constitution, as well as the beneficial amendments to the Indian Act through the decades.

As an exemplar of Indigenous feminist activism, Idle No More makes the voices and concerns of Indigenous women central to its platform and protests. From land use and treaty rights for current and future generations to contesting colonial domination over bodies, actions, and identities, First Nations women now have a larger and more media-intensive platform from which to act. Idle No More provides a more public stage for the anticolonial arguments that have been made for years but that have fallen on deaf ears. Aboriginal feminism merges feminism with anticolonialism "to show how Aboriginal peoples, and in particular Aboriginal women, are affected by colonialism and by patriarchy. It takes account of how both racism and sexism fuse when brought to bear on Aboriginal women" (Green 2007, 23). With its focus on the C-45 amendments to the Indian Act, the defunding of First Nations, and the changes to the Navigable Waters Act, Idle No More presents an Indigenous feminist alternative to this patriarchal deconstruction of a healthy society by asking the government to reverse course and respect the sovereignty and treaty rights of First Nations. One valuable planned strategic initiative of this decolonial Indigenous feminist movement is its use of social media and online platforms to generate support and gain participants. Although online environments can often be hotbeds of racist and sexist expression, when the women of Idle No More use these tools, they are challenging patriarchal forms of expression and accepted attitudes of oppression. Building feminist solidarity in order to challenge patriarchal colonization makes Idle No More unique in the contemporary current of social justice movements.

In late January 2013, Navajo media consultant Pamela J. Peters and Lakota human relations professional Shawn Imitates-Dog, organized an Idle No More round dance rally in Los Angeles in reaction to a poorly organized, much smaller, and less effective Idle No More rally they attended where the central message of sovereignty and Indigenous rights to protect water, air, and land for future generations seemed lost. The women successfully reached out to their communities through Facebook, email, and media alerts, resulting in about three hundred attendees at their Idle No More rally. Shawn spoke to Indian Country Today Media Network (2013) reporter Rob Schmidt and expressed relief, "'Thank God for social media. . . . I don't know how AIM [American Indian Movement] did it back in the '70s" (qtd. in Schmidt 2013). When these Indigenous women took action, their communities and non-Native allies responded and joined in, this is a microcosm of the broader movement. One rally attendee, Shauna Baker, Stellat'en First Nation, commented on the non-Native presence: "It was amazing to see so many non-Natives at The Grove to support the Idle No More movement. . . . It just goes to show that we are all human and this isn't just a Native issue. It's about human rights" (qtd. in Schmidt 2013).

The Indigenous rights revolution and its feminist human rights core attract supporters daily. The Idle No More website exhorts visitors to "take action near you" with a list of upcoming protests to choose from in such different locations as Pacific Oil Conference and Trade Show in Los Angeles in September 2013 and the Canada We Want three-day summit in Calgary in October and November 2013. Anyone interested in supporting or participating in the movement can follow #IdleNoMore on Twitter; like the group's Facebook page; or receive email updates about events, protests, and other activities through the official website. By using these social media platforms to communicate ideas, generate support, and gain allies, Idle No More steps outside the boundaries of corporate-owned media in order to control its message and presentation. Although the movement has received serious media attention, most mainstream attention has been quite negative.

A review of headlines from December 2012 and January 2013 featuring stories about Idle No More tells readers more than the facts: these headlines reflect or refute Western expectations, suggesting how readers should interpret this movement, its participants, and its objectives, as well as how to feel about it. Regardless of the media outlet, the messages are crystal clear:

> "Idle No More: Canadian Union of Postal Workers Honors Attawapiskat Chief's Strong Stand Against the Country's 'Moral Bankruptcy'"

> "Idle No More's Thunder Heard Through Walls of Prime Minister's Office"

> "Idle No More Movement Led by Aboriginal Women"

> "Harper, Atleo to Meet as Militants Threaten Economy"

> "Charges Considered After Idle No More Protest Shuts Down City Bridge (with video)"

> "'Idle No More' March in Missoula Draws Attention to Aboriginal Rights"

The first three headlines hail from Indigenous journalistic outlets: Indian Country Today Media Network ("Idle No More" 2013), Aboriginal People's Television Network ("Idle No More's Thunder" 2013), and the First Perspective (Plecash 2013). Use of the empowering terms "honors," "strong stand against," "moral bankruptcy," "thunder," and "aboriginal women" respect Indigenous sovereignty and support the aims of the movement. The second set of three headlines provides a much different perspective, seemingly in support of a colonial agenda: *Calgary Sun* (Akin 2013), *Calgary Herald* (Howell and Cuthbertson 2012), and the *Missoulian* (Briggeman 2013). The language change is significant, shifting in both word choice and tone: "militants," "threaten," "charges," "shut down," and "draws attention," the last being the most benign of the mainstream list. Noticeably absent is coverage of this movement by any of the United States' largest media outlets: silence thunders across our media streams. Silence and dismissive language, both powerful, are weapons of colonizing governments and sympathetic, if ignorant, press media.

In the first set of headlines, written by journalists for Indigenous press outlets, the silence is broken by the decolonizing word choices and front-page presence of the stories. In fact, in all Indigenous journalistic outlets, the Idle No More movement story takes a dominant stance and is center stage in January 2013. In places like the *Washington Post*, the movement received three brief stories in January, written not by *Post* reporters, but retrieved from the Associated Press wire and used as back-end filler. These peoples and their legal, political, and sovereignty rights issues are present in this land, and yet the *Post* and the *New York Times* and every other major mainstream media outlet in the United States remain silent and complicit in their colonizing agenda and, by default, not supportive of Indigenous efforts to reclaim sovereignty.

In Canada, where the most damning and robust headlines are found, major media outlets are as attentive as their Indigenous counterparts, only much more negative and less supportive. Readers could recognize the phrase "as militants threaten economy" as a reification of their own mis-guided beliefs that First Nations peoples are to blame for Canada's eco-nomic slump. This systematic messaging that pits non-Native Canadian citizens against their Aboriginal neighbors serves to divide and conquer. By keeping these two groups at odds with language, story placement, or silence, the government's agenda of colonization may continue unabated and unchallenged.

One significant strategy used by Idle No More is the use of social media to challenge and change perceptions of the group in the broader conversa-tion, but also to share the facts of its platform and inspire action. On the Idle No More Facebook page, which has almost 114,000 followers as of September 2013, one commenter states, "I am an ally, it is not my call to tell people who are oppressed how they should fight their oppressor. . . . Men tried to do the same thing to us when we fought for equal rights and to stop violence against women many years ago. . . . The women across the nation do not need our help making decisions, if they do, they will ask for it." And a re-tweet from @WilderUtopia on the #IdleNoMore Twitter feed on September 4, 2013, states, "Love the 'Grand Mother's Rising Up' ban-ners—so beautiful & reminder about sacred role of Indigenous women!"

Idle No More is peopled with Indigenous women whose stories of determination, strength, hope, love, and resilience resonate with non-Native women because of the widespread experience of domination by any group who takes without considering the damage done by thoughtless seizing of rights, of bodies, of land, of minds and spirits.

In *Reinventing the Enemy's Language: Contemporary Native Women's Writings of North America*, a collection edited by Joy Harjo and Gloria Bird, the introduction declares, "It is through writing in the colonizers' languages that our lands have been stolen, children taken away. We have often been betrayed by those who first learned to write and to speak the language of the occupier of our lands. Yet to speak well in our communities in whatever form is still respected" (1997, 20). Indeed, to "speak well" and share stories of experience in order to generate support for a movement focused on improving sovereignty and self-determination for Indigenous peoples is precisely what the women leaders and allies of Idle No More are doing. From journalism and (re)visioned traditions of activism, to the potent rise of impassioned youth voices on Facebook and Twitter, Indigenous women are using every tool at their disposal to decolonize lands and minds, to leverage themselves against the equity stolen years ago in order to collect their rights and assert Indigenous nationhood.

The theory of decolonization also resonates from the heart of the Idle No More movement as it seeks to shift deeply embedded attitudes about Indigenous sovereignty and rights. Linda Tuhiwai Smith writes in her groundbreaking *Decolonizing Methodologies: Research and Indigenous Peoples*, "Indigenous peoples across the world have other stories to tell which not only question the assumed nature of those ideals and the practices that they generate, but also serve to tell an alternative story: the history of Western research through the eyes of the colonized" (1999, 2). While her purpose in this book is to counter the research methods and stories collected and told by non-Indigenous scholars, her underlying goal of creating a decolonizing framework as "part of a much larger intent" is highly relevant to the Idle No More movement. The women who started this movement were not looking to simply deconstruct the dominant story and the text of Canada's most recent legislative insult; they want to overturn entrenched attitudes and take action that leads to real change within their communities. These Indigenous women deserve tangible support so that Canadian and American colonizing debt may be diminished.[1]

Smith believes that Indigenous peoples' survival relies on contexts and environments, rather than "some active beneficence of our Earth Mother. We had to know to survive. We had to work out ways of knowing, we had to predict, to learn and reflect, we had to preserve and protect, we had to defend and attack, we had to be mobile, we had to have social systems which enabled us to do these things. We still have to do these things" (13). Such ideas and practices resound in the words and actions of those participating in the Idle No More movement: a powerful reminder that decolonization is an enduring concern for all Indigenous peoples living in a colonized state. For Smith, a decolonial action is similar to either the "writing back" or the "talking back" tradition "that characterizes much of the post-colonial or anti-colonial literature" and requires a disruption of the assumed positional superiority of Western knowledge through "indigenous methodologies [that are] a mix of existing methodological approaches and indigenous practices" (143). For instance, Smith lists twenty-five Indigenous projects that disrupt Western-centric assumptions and place Indigenous knowledge and practices at the forefront of both intellectual and practical action. Themes for these projects run the gamut from cultural survival and self-determination to social justice, healing, and reclamation. Idle No More as a movement naturally uses many of Smith's listed themes and practices because it is an Indigenous revolution of the mind, spirit, voice, and land designed to (re)frame the discussion of Indigenous peoples' rights.

Fighting back and dismantling the colonial debt requires more than words: this project also requires the persuasive power of physical action and the (re)visioning of traditions. Indeed, when considering the objectives and goals of Idle No More, it is the women who are asserting Indigenous nationhood with every blockade, dance, demonstration, and protest. Dance as resistance to governmental tyranny with five-hundred-year-old roots may be the most innovative development of the Idle No More movement. Dancing as protest and dancing flash mobs are not new to our modern era, but the use of the specific Indigenous ceremonial round dance as protest action delivered via flash mob and promoted on social media is decidedly new and innovative as a strategy designed to capture the world's imagination and attention. The result of this visual and performance tactic is often the creation of support for the Idle No More cause within Indigenous communities and without. The *Vancouver Sun* reported in January that one rally participant, thirty-two-year-old Lorelei Williams from the Skatin Nation, and her seven-year-old daughter held a sign that read,

"When sleeping women wake, mountains move." Another popular phrase making the meme rounds on the web is a Cheyenne proverb: "A nation is not conquered until the hearts of its women are on the ground." Both the sign and the proverb reflect the current reality for Indigenous women—they have been pushed far enough by the colonial agenda and are pushing back, inspiring their nations and allies to follow and reconcile the debt. In Thomas King's (2012) CBC interview about his new book, *The Inconvenient Indian*, he says, "When you have this long history of injustice, at some point that bill's going to have to be paid." As an inspirational protest action against the legislative injustices perpetrated by colonial governments on Indigenous nations, the round dance was likely chosen because of its inclusive nature. According to the Centre for Aboriginal Culture and Education (2013), "This dance was a healing ceremony that became a social dance for Aboriginal people and is held in the winter season. . . . We join hands in a circle and dance around the drummers and singers. The beat of the drum is like the heartbeat of the community, and everyone moves as one. It's a dance for everyone: children, friends, families, youth and Elders." Clearly, the choice of dance for these protest rallies was a wise selection on the part of the organizers.

However, not all Indigenous peoples are enthusiastic about Idle No More. For instance, Taiaiake Alfred, a prominent Mohawk nationalist and professor in Indigenous governance at the University of Victoria, suggests that Idle No More hasn't gone far enough to achieve the goals of freedom, sovereignty, and land occupation and use. During an interview with Indigenous Waves radio in February 2013, Alfred called the movement a first step toward changing Indigenous complacency:

> What we need to do to achieve our goals is to find a way to put ourselves back on our land because that was the first and ongoing objective of colonization—to remove us from our territory. Everything else flows from that. The ill health, the cultural confusion, the spiritual alienation and everything that those things produce come from one place, and that place is the removal of our people from a life lived in their territory. . . . If that's the source of the discontent, and I think there's ample evidence for that, I think that has to be the primary goal. The awakening of Idle No More has to be followed with a movement to re-occupy our territories . . . sacred places, ceremonially, physically for use in terms of self-sufficiency, and just being there and not surrendering that space to people who would imagine that we are a memory.

Alfred further asserts that Indigenous nations should not be negotiating with the Canadian government on its terms but should be reasserting nationhood in more proactive ways. Alfred's perception of Idle No More is a critical expansion of the movement's goals but seems incompatible with the goals of one of its founders, Sylvia McAdam. In June 2013, McAdam spoke about the current status and future of Idle No More with Indigenous Waves radio from the Thirteenth Annual United Nations Permanent Forum on Indigenous Issues in New York City. While Alfred sees Idle No More as a first step that doesn't go far enough in its activism, McAdam seems confident that the movement's focus on improving dialogue and using protests, roadblocks, and meetings to pressure the Canadian government to stop ignoring treaty rights, in addition to ceasing its permission of land and water contamination, is enough for now. According to McAdam, human rights violations by multinational corporations as they relate to land use are a concern for Indigenous peoples worldwide and are not just restricted to Canada. In this respect, McAdam argues that Idle No More has been an inspiration in the global fight around loss of land, language, and Indigenous cultures. Asserting that it is important for Indigenous voices to be heard, and acknowledging the inspiration of the UN's permanent forum, she said, "It's important that the international community know that Canada is not implementing nor honoring the treaties they made with Indigenous peoples. We need to bring back that level of nation to nation dialogue. It can't be just a rhetoric any more, and that's what Idle No More is about, we need to bring that discussion back to what it truly should have been when we took treaty, and that's nation to nation." She further suggests that the devastation to land and water would not have occurred had Indigenous nations remained in a nation-to-nation relationship with Canada.

Envisioning a new future for Indigenous peoples requires not only resistance but also hope and compromise. "I'm always hopeful. There's always hope. The reality is that we can't keep going the way we're going," McAdam said in her Indigenous Waves radio interview. After three months of sustained activism, Idle No More achieved a small modicum of success when a Declaration of Commitment was written by the Assembly of First Nations chiefs and signed by the Native Women's Association of Canada, the Liberal Party of Canada Parliamentary Caucus, and the New Democratic Party National Caucus (Rickert 2013). The commitment states, "We solemnly commit to undertake political, spiritual and all other advocacy efforts to implement a renewed First Nations–Crown relationship where inherent Treaty and non-Treaty Rights are recognized, honored and fully implemented as they should be, within the next five years" (Rickert 2013). Some of the specific efforts include immediate meetings to discuss the treaty relationship between First Nations, Canada, and the British Crown and mandates to enforce existing treaties on a nation-by-nation basis and ensure that "all federal legislation has the free, prior and informed consent of First Nations where inherent and Treaty rights are affected or impacted" (Rickert 2013).

This document is a successful result of Indigenous women's collective activism on behalf of their nations. Also as of this writing, Idle No More continues to maintain its significance in the broader fight for Indigenous sovereignty rights. Social media platforms such as Facebook and Twitter have been instrumental in spreading the word, generating support, and creating global Idle No More activism days such as January 28, 2013, when "more than 40 Idle No More events took place worldwide . . . in an unprecedented showing of indigenous solidarity," including flash mob dances and other actions in such disparate places as Ottawa, Halifax, Chapel Hill, Minneapolis, Paris, and London (Bernd 2013). According to Taiaiake Alfred (2013), these protests are not as effective as direct action to reoccupy lands, to stop negotiating with the Canadian government on the government's terms, and to more forcefully confront the government's assimilationist agenda. Euro-American governments are notorious for writing things down and then either not following through on the written promises or just blatantly ignoring the documents, so Alfred's criticism of the movement is a valid one. However, Idle No More is laying the tracks for a future fight, a fight that cannot occur without these foundational moves. The problem with Alfred's criticism is that he seems to expect Indigenous nations to be ready right now for such a tangible active battle that will restore land to the First Nations. As long as Idle No More doesn't allow the patriarchal system to quash its purpose and continues asserting that indigenous sovereignty exists and must be respected as an equal player, then Alfred may get his wish at some future point. But as of right now, Idle No More still has work to do to build the solidarity that will allow such direct action to be effective.

As resistance to the colonized state swells, Linda Tuhiwai Smith's

Indigenous project of "Envisioning" takes center stage. Envisioning is "a strategy which asks that people imagine a future, that they rise above present day situations which are generally depressing, dream a new dream and set a new vision. The confidence of knowing that we have survived and can only go forward provides some impetus to a process of envisioning" (Smith 1999, 152). Global indigenous activism is on the rise once more, but the road to honoring Indigenous existence, treaties, and contemporary reality remains long and arduous. Idle No More seems poised to enact real change in relation to how the Canadian government works with First Nations groups. This colonial debt is due; it is time to (re)vision political empowerment for Indigenous women and their nations. The governments and many citizens of the United States and Canada have been made financially wealthy through the theft of the greatest Indigenous asset of all: land. As a result of this asset seizure long ago, colonial cultures have been rendered morally and ethically bankrupt. The Idle No More movement inspires change and suggests ways and means to cancel this bankruptcy: Americans and Canadians owe these Nations our allegiance and assistance to convince these governments to reconsider the original treaty obligations; to remunerate individual Nations for the tangible theft of land, water, and mineral resources through retroactive revenue-sharing programs with government and private industries that are developing resources on this continent; and to acknowledge, speak out about, and teach others about this terrible debt. In this way, women of the Westernized nations of the United States and Canada might help the Indigenous women of the continent gain back their lands, homes, hearts, and spirits. That which was taken away must be returned. Idle No More persuades us to act.

Amanda Morris is an assistant professor of multiethnic rhetorics at Kutztown University in Pennsylvania. Her teaching and research agenda focuses on contemporary Indigenous rhetorics.

Note

1. To vision a future in which the colonization debt has been diminished, visit the Museum of the American Indian in Washington, DC; listen to Stream 6 on NativeRadio.com; and watch films produced by Native directors and writers, which can be found at the American Indian Film Institute (http://aifisf.com/).

Works Cited

Akin, David. 2013. "Harper, Atleo to Meet as Militants Threaten Economy." *Calgary Sun*. January 10. http://www.calgarysun.com/2013/01/10/gg-to-meet-with-chiefs-friday-after-manitoba-leaders-threaten-to-boycott-talks.

Alfred, Taiaiake. 2013. Interview with Susan Blight. Indigenous Waves Radio. CUIT-FM, February 27. http://indigenouswaves.com/2013/02/27/taiaiake-alfred-returns-to-indigenous-waves-to-discuss-idle-no-more-wasase-indigenous-nationhood-and-more/.

Bernd, Candice. 2013. "Idle No More: From Grassroots to Global Movement." Truthout. http://truth-out.org/news/item/14165-idle-no-more-from-grassroots-to-global-movement.

Briggeman, Kim. 2013. "'Idle No More' March in Missoula Draws Attention to Aboriginal Rights." *Missoulian*. http://missoulian.com/news/local/idle-no-more-march-in-missoula-draws-attention-to-aboriginal/article_5225cd1e-5c52-11e2-9b07-0019bb2963f4.html.

Centre for Aboriginal Culture and Education. 2013. http://www1.carleton.ca/aboriginal/.

Green, Joyce. 2007. "Taking Account of Aboriginal Feminism." In *Making Space for Indigenous Feminism*, ed. Joyce Green. Nova Scotia, Canada: Fernwood. 20-32.

Harjo, Joy, and Gloria Bird, eds. 1997. *Reinventing the Enemy's Language: Contemporary Native Women's Writings of North America*. New York: W.W. Norton.

Howell, Trevor, and Richard Cuthbertson. 2012. "Charges Considered after Idle No More Protest Shuts Down Bridge." *Calgary Herald*. http://www.calgaryherald.com/life/Charges+considered+after+Idle+More+protest+shuts+down+city+bridge+with+video/7812320/story.html.

Idle No More. 2013. http://idlenomore.ca/.

"Idle No More." 2013. Indian Country Today Media Network. http://indiancountrytodaymedianetwork.com/story/idle-no-more.

"Idle No More's Thunder Heard Through Walls of Prime Minister's Office." 2013. APTN National News. APTN (Aboriginal People's Television Network). http://aptn.ca/pages/news/2013/01/11/protest-dying-down-as-harper-says-hell-stay-for-entire-meeting-with-fn-leaders/.

King, Thomas. 2012. "Thomas King on *The Inconvenient Indian*." Interview with Brent Bambury. CBC Books, November 23. http://www.cbc.ca/books/2012/11/thomas-king-on-the-inconvenient-indian.html.

McAdam, Sylvia. 2013. Interview with Susan Blight. Indigenous Waves Radio. CUIT-FM, June 3. http://indigenouswaves.com/2013/06/03/sylvia-mcadam-the-united-nations-permanent-forum-on-indigenous-issues/.

Palmater, Pamela. 2011. *Beyond Blood: Rethinking Indigenous Identity*. Saskatoon, Canada: Purich.

———. 2013. Interview with Brent Brambury. *Day 6*. CBC Radio, January 4.

Plecash, Chris. 2013. "Idle No More Movement Led by Aboriginal Women." First Perspective. http://www.hilltimes.com/news/politics/2013/01/14/idle-no-more-movement-led-by-aboriginal-women/33300

Rickert, Levi. 2013. "This Declaration Leads Chief Spence to End Her Hunger Strike." Native News Network. http://www.nativenewsnetwork.com/declaration-leads-chief-spence-to-end-her-hunger-strike.html.

Schmidt, Rob. 2013. "Idle No More, Hollywood Style." Indian Country Today Media Network. http://indiancountrytodaymedianetwork.com/2013/01/28/idle-no-more-hollywood-style-147286.

Simpson, Leanne. 2011. *Dancing on Our Turtle's Back: Stories of Nishnaabeg Re-creation, Resurgence, and a New Emergence*. Winnipeg, Canada: Arbeiter.

Smith, Linda Tuhiwai. 1999. *Decolonizing Methodologies: Research and Indigenous Peoples*. New York: St. Martin's Press.

Suzack, Cheryl. 2010. "Emotion Before the Law." In *Indigenous Women and Feminism: Politics, Activism, Culture*, ed. Cheryl Suzack, Shari M. Huhndorf, Jeanne Perreault, and Jean Barman. Vancouver: University of British Columbia Press. 126–143.

PART VI. **DEBT'S BODY: AESTHETICS AND AFFECT**

Speculative Technologies: Debt, Love, and Divination in a Transnationalizing Market

Larisa Jasarevic

Four young women with love on their mind are waiting to learn about their future. It's a summer afternoon in a neighborhood of Tuzla, a city in northeastern Bosnia. The waiting room is filled with old sofas, well loved and bent out of shape by a history of bodies getting comfortable, and the table in the middle is crowded with cups, upturned messily and leaking coffee tails. The mood is as inviting as the open seats: expectant, pleasurable, excited by the stories women share of previous visits. New arrivals are instructed on what to expect. One by one, women take their dry coffee cups to Zlata in the adjacent room. Coffee mud has painted the insides of turned cups with an intricate, biographically significant landscape, but Zlata apparently "reads" beyond the phenomenal, grasping what Jacques Derrida calls the very "possibility of an event dawning" (2005, 3).

Coffee mud is an appropriately murky medium for grasping what is not (yet), whatever may come to be under the circumstances of habitual uncertainty. The women are living in a precarious, transforming economy, where the market has been exploding since the end of socialism and the 1990s war, drawing masses into the business of trade and consumption. Thus inflated, the economy has been weathering a prolonged shortage of capital since the turn of the millennium. The popular market economy—everyday household provisioning and small entrepreneurship—is sustained by debt: informal lending and borrowing between intimates, kin, and clients and formal bank and microcredit loans. The clientele of Zlata, a coffee cup reader with a fabulous reputation for accuracy and reasonable price, however, are primarily concerned with forecasts for love affairs, illicit passions, urgent or wilting desires, marriage prospects, and such. A

WSQ: Women's Studies Quarterly 42: 1 & 2 (Spring/Summer 2014) © 2014 by Larisa Jasarevic. All rights reserved.

divining session just as often yields business advice, as the women at Zla-ta's take it for granted that love and money, market and passion, longing and owing, in short, economic and affective relations are contiguous and intersecting.

Zlata's vision is up to date on Bosnia's economic trends. I have been casually visiting Zlata since 2006. In 2011, I found the cups much larger and the scope of her vision extended to keep up with the migration of economic opportunities, from regional, largely informal market trade to more transnational pursuits of fortune with American defense contractors (KBR and Fluor International) in Afghanistan and Iraq. Among those who seek her out—and recently, for reasons left unexplained, Zlata has received only women—many work for or are applying to Fluor International or else dating, desiring, marrying, and otherwise caring for men employed or seeking employment in Afghanistan and Iraq. A young woman, anxious about her protracted engagement, walked out of Zlata's room with assur-ances about the date for her wedding and, just as exciting, news of her future husband's job offer in Afghanistan. A later arrival, a mature woman and seasoned trader named Besima, has been visiting eagerly for several weeks, expecting an interview with a Fluor recruiter and, with perhaps more impatience, wondering about the twists and turns of a love affair emerging online.

Speculations

This is an essay about love, divination, and the debt market. Divination and debt are, clearly, speculative forms, while love, broadly speaking, is a central concern to both divining and debt enterprises in ways that are less obvious and locally specific. This text too is part speculative, part ethnographic. Starting with messy, abundant evidence that local practice effectively interlaces with the affective and economic, I ask what one spec-ulative technology—forecasting the future from coffee mud—can tell us about another: contracting and extending debts.

If technologies, with a nod to Foucault (Martin, Gutman, and Hutton 1988, 17–19), could be thought of as matrices of practical reason, con-cerned with production, efficacy, and care of self and others, then thinking debt via an extended detour of divination and love explores speculation in a different mood. First, this is not the "scheming and projecting" of the financial speculator, the classic figure, whether in economic history (see Sombart [1915] 1967) or in contemporary critiques and media exposés of "casino capitalism." Rather, what we see here are strategies of different experts in forward thinking and acting: diviners and ordinary people practicing everyday economics, which in Bosnia, more often than not, translates into working on deferral, accounting with promises and negative numbers. I am primarily concerned here with the problem of time, which defines debt universally in relation to deferral and projection, and the specific, divergent, but intersecting temporalities of informal and formal debts that underwrite the local market. Second, I bring attention to the matters of love and intimacy as they figure in debt practices, everywhere, and in Bosnia specifically. Because informal loans in Bosnia are giftlike insofar as they are given without interest, counting on the generosity of a lender who cannot easily turn you down and to whom you thus owe more than money and goods can repay—gratitude, loyalty, affection—they urge attention to the economies of care and affect. Divination is similarly concerned with love, which, in Bosnia, is a more thoroughly, if counterintuitively, bodily affair.

"Love is chemistry," a boutique owner in the city of Tuzla tells me over coffee, clarifying that it is "something that happens in your organism so that the soul falls madly for someone." Love, through this logic, is a biochemical process, instigated by an accidental event that implicates one's organic and metaphysical nature in an exceptional, affective, and mental state of disorder. If this woman's definition makes a muddle of conceptual domains, rather than sorting out molecular from physical body, social relations from metaphysical assumptions, it is no more "confused" than Aristotle's biological notion of the soul or, more recently, Jean-Luc Nancy's (2008) poststructurally phenomenological rendering of the psyche, self, or soul as a form of tangible-intangible extension inseparable from the body. "The body's simply a soul," Nancy writes, suggesting that the physical and the incorporeal are interlaced to the point that they are indistinguishably distinct, predicated on each other's difference and intersections (144, 152–53). In short, philosophical imagination as well as vernacular common sense in Bosnia provide us with an image of the body that is a far cry from the crude, and amply critiqued, duality of material and psychological that underpins biomedical science and (still) some social scientific studies and informs a series of affiliated distinctions between symbolic and material, subjective and objective, represented and real, none of which would help us explore how "love" relates to the practical matters of debt and divination.

Owing Time: Elastic

Debt is essentially defined by time. *Pace* Derrida, who has critiqued the possibility of giving time, arguing that time *is* (not): not something one can have, give, or take. Sound business logic, however, has advertised the claim that time is money—disposable and potentially profitable—and ordinary experience proves that our time *is*: claimed, overextended, stolen, even (or especially) if we are employed for a wage. Market debt is made through the exchange of something (commodity, money, hype) for promises of later returns. Debt is, therefore, a gift, or a loan, of time that lubricates the generation and circulation of values in the meantime. It is marked at once by suspension and anticipation, by necessary deferral and eager or anxious forward looking. As such, debt is speculative. It counts on the future, optimistically, anxiously, or doubtfully, and leans heavily on insurance, social or institutional, that delivers the projected incomes, or else. In financial markets, speculation is professionally fine-tuned with debt instruments that turn deferral into money, at the going rates of interest (plus hidden fees and interest on interest). This helps lenders accumulate profit under the contemporary conditions that make us preferred customers for as long as we are revolving our balance from one month to the next while reliably paying the minimum monthly balance that includes interest and fees.

The most popular and efficient way of buying and selling in Bosnia is by means of debt, *na dug* in the colloquial. The end of the 1990s war expanded trading and consuming efforts to the point that everyone "from doctors to doormen," as one trader put it, was buying and selling across the proliferating sites of the market: outdoor stalls, curbside or door-to-door sales, secondhand stores and stands, an excessive number of neighborhood shops, and pharmacies. Small shop owners stay in business by running open tabs for loyal customers and themselves purchase wholesale goods from long-term suppliers on informal credit. Traders also borrow funds from each other to meet due payments, make purchases for cash, or invest in repairs. Those with tabs in the neighborhood store are likely to be multiply indebted—to vendors in marketplaces, to boutique owners, to a herbalist and pharmacist—and to juggle repayment time lines in the most creative ways, given that outstanding debts well exceed the monthly incomes, pensions, or fortunes that people gather by whatever means. And everyone leans on friends and family to obtain money for everyday pleasures and emergencies, from vacations to medical bills.

Returns of informal loans are loosely arranged and negotiable. Time lent is erratic, contingent on chance windfalls or losses of either party that affect the possibility of the debtor's speedy return or the lender's impatience. A shopkeeper gently reminds a customer with a lengthy tab with a simple, unfinished "Dear lady, did you forget . . . ?" telling her apologetically about the costly repairs of the store refrigerator and the impending microcredit installment. Time is elastic, subject to intervention and negotiation. Significantly, it doesn't appreciate interest, it is not monetized, but it effectively appreciates the obligations and passions that relate the giver and the taker. It doesn't so much "flow" as spatialize: plotted onto daily routines and recurrent schedules and habitually opened to accidents and delays, time takes place around other people and events. Time here is an extension: it is irreducibly relational and biographical.

Formal loans, by contrast, are inflexible, contracted with a stipulated repayment plan from banks, whose stringent borrowing procedures make them inaccessible to the informally employed masses and to microcredit organizations (MCOs), which serve clients outside the banking system with easy loans at steep interest rates. Fixed on the calendar, institutional lending presumes a flow of abstract time and reliable incomes and spells out consequences for default. "The due date is inscribed in our heads," says one shop owner of her microloan.

In practice, the two forms of debt intersect. Because the funds borrowed from banks and MCOs are invested in the same popular economy of deferral, repayment time lines can be met only by means of vigorous, last-minute personal borrowing, negotiated settlements of open tabs, or some stroke of luck that so often in Bosnia delivers, just in the nick of time and against the odds, some unexpected cash. My interlocutors often spoke of such mysterious mobilities of money as related to fortune, or *nafaka*, which eludes simple bookkeeping. And just as well it does, for many Bosnians who profess living on *nafaka* are aware that in an economy marked by gross unemployment (estimated at from 40 to 60 percent), GDP per capita at 50 percent of the southeast European average, and incomes of half of the prewar figure (Pugh 2005, 453; Stites et al. 2005, 52), living decently is impossible without the miraculous tendencies of fortune to come from nowhere obvious and, equally mysterious and generative, other people's generosity (see Jasarevic, forthcoming).

Looking Forward

Divination iconically concerns speculation, a forward-looking curiosity, tinkering with the very nature of time as an object of everyday experience and knowledge. Modern time is an abstraction that is calculated with mathematical and geographic precision; a resource allocated according to the principles of efficiency; a value that registers socially necessary rates of productivity and rates of profitability that the market will bear; a mode, compressed and sped up to maximize transformation of information into capital, particularly in financial markets. Modern management of time presumes a linear flow from known past to uncertain but predictable future and has developed a portfolio of realist forecasting genres that aim to evaluate, calculate, and mitigate chance. The modern notion of uncertain but predictable future cultivates a particular kind of optimism in its subjects, encouraging them to think ahead and budget time accordingly and prudently. It disciplines them with the ambition to "take control" of their lives, inspires them with time-sensitive adult objectives (dream job, marriage and family, mortgage), advertises happy retirement scenarios, and hides death out of view—we don't talk about that—in the domain of ever more advanced old age, that is, nothing to worry about, anytime soon. Under the conditions of neoliberalism, borrowing rather than saving has become the primary financial instrument for provisioning a future, optimistically and anxiously. This is as true in North America, where consumer credit is financing the bankrupt dream of affluence and fringe banking appreciates the racialized gap between the rich and the poor, as it is in the urban slums of Chile, where residents exchange personal loans and run on department store credit to weather spells of unemployment and medical crisis, to care for the relatives, and to invest in homes (see Williams 2004; Manning 2000; Han 2012).

Anthropologists have been increasingly interested in the ways the future (value) is known and capitalized in advance in the biomedical, (post)genomic, and pharmaceutical markets (Rajan 2006; Lakoff 2008). Lakoff, for instance, writes about future orientations in the climate of present uncertainty and, more specifically, about the recent shift in U.S.

national security planning for public health responses to an imminent bio-security threat. He picks up Niklas Luhman's proposition that in modernity, the future presents itself as knowable by modern means of divination, which are precise, expert calculations of probability that aim not for certain prognosis but for "provisional foresight," a competent understanding of present conditions and options. Thus, the present is oriented toward managing risks and making decisions as well as adjustments to a future that turns out otherwise. In the meantime, the professionalization of forecasting is highly effective insofar as it shapes public policies and imaginaries and creates financial capital out of hype and anticipation.

While Luhman, and Lakoff after him, emphasize the distinctly modern, nonteleological concepts of the future's informing the contemporary market, ethnographies outside the Euro-American context show that divination is more often than not a tentative vision, groping for what is contingent and changeable. As Evans-Pritchard ([1937] 1976) has shown in his classic work on Azande oracles, people count on an uncertain present and future that are radically susceptible to practical and magical manipulations. Diviners practice special insight into what is possible, desirable, or inauspicious and earn their reputation with a record of accuracy and soundness of advice on how to avert or court certain outcomes. Furthermore, divination outside or at the fringes of "the West" is not premodern but contemporary and highly conversant with various modernizing projects, from colonial to socialist to developmental. James Smith, for instance, describes how divination manages ecological and social crisis, prescribing ritual intervention and innovation in southern Kenya, marked by the history of development discourses and projects, while Laurel Kendall finds South Korean contemporary economies informed by both International Monetary Fund (IMF) and shamanic insights and rites, guiding entrepreneurial and fiscal behavior (Smith 2008; Kendall 2009; see also Langwick 2011 and Holbaad 2012).

Unlike professional market prophecies, other forms of forecast are concerned not with mass phenomena and abstractions (population, trends, averages) but with specific, biographical events. Moreover, divinatory practices do not recognize the universal validity of abstract, homogenous, empty time or the utility of statistical calculations of precedents, odds, and chances for lending insight into someone's particular circumstances. This is not just a matter of non-Western cosmologies producing time as an enchanted relation with myriad specific and unknown forces, but a knowledge born from the quotidian obviousness of our singularity. The anomalous in the midst of the common and recurrent provokes, unapologetically, the classic question "Why me?" that Azande asked at the sight of misfortune and Evans-Pritchard placed outside the domain of social scientific inquiry.

The 1990s have taught Bosnians that life does not go according to anyone's plan. Anxieties about poor health and premature death, as well as permanent economic crises since the peace have disturbed the socialist-modern expectation of the "normal," orderly life course closely tied to the expectations of productivity, relative plenty, and comfortable retirement, courtesy of the state. The local verb for popular forms of divining from coffee cups, cards, and beans (more rarely from sieves or spoons) is *ogledati* (from *ogledalo*, "mirror," and *gledati*, "to watch, gaze"), but Zlata, the future reader reputedly sees not with her eyes, and reads more than the signs, which form a rather limited vocabulary. Hers is a sensuous, prospective vision, which I read with a cue from Derrida's (2005) exploration of the nature of knowledge that is prephenomenal, that precedes the event, and so is prior to sensation and yet engages senses in perception of both the visible and the intangible, which reside in the same form. As in the encounter between two pairs of staring eyes, a more subtle exchange of gazes ensues, so that vision grasps not only what is visible and seen (retina) but also what sees, and is intangible and intuited (the gaze). In other words, divining begins with the presumed entanglement of the phenomenal and metaphysical that underwrites all material life and recruits expert senses and sensibilities that are adequate to the task of catching the "possibility of an event dawning."

Zlata has been glimpsing the prospect of an appointment in Afghanistan for Besima, the client I found in Zlata's waiting room, who visits frequently because of work and a love affair. Employment opportunities with American defense contractors have been presenting themselves to Bosnians since 1995, when the American contingent of NATO deployed to implement military provisions of the Dayton Peace Agreement, which concluded the war. KBR (Brown & Root at the time), which staffed the Bosnian mission for the U.S. Army, began recruiting local support staff to aid the American military in Afghanistan and Iraq. The appeal of working for the American military in conflict zones was not immediate but grew over time as the formal economy continued to stagnate and informal economies expanded to breaking point. Transnational employment with KBR and Fluor International has been generally, though anecdotally, evident in the country since 2006, most obviously in the investment of newly made wealth in apartments, vehicles, small businesses, and sophisticated consumption habits. While the new migrants are typically skilled and semiskilled workers—car mechanics, cooks, or electricians—among them are also other, perhaps surprising types: university professors and students; various professionals dissatisfied with local opportunities; and young or single mothers, ambitious on behalf of their children, whom they leave in the care of sometimes disapproving husbands, mothers, and mothers-in-law.

Besima twice has come close to deployment in Afghanistan in the past two years and although she has not heard from the recruiters in a while, Zlata has not been wrong so far. "This woman sees," Besima tells me, reviewing for my sake specific evidence of Zlata's accuracy, focusing mostly on details of Besima's love history—the marriage on the rocks, reunion following a separation, and minute details of her current infatuation, all of which Zlata previewed. Besima herself is not desperate to go, she says. She made a fortune in the informal trade, built a house, and saved enough money to get her daughter started on a career after university.

Specifics of Besima's economic and affective circumstances—her *nafaka*—are rendered discernible during a divination session. *Nafaka* is one's biographical specificity that orients one in the world, a world populated by multiple forces, material and metaphysical, human and nonhuman. *Nafaka* in a debt economy foregrounds the relational nature of each singular being—the elasticity of time is predicated on, and engenders, a specific, and changing, form of existence (being worried, taken care of, overextended, obliged, bankrupt)—and is at once inseparable from the metaphysics of Being and Time and from historical conditions. In short, *nafaka* teases both historical and speculative imagination.

Equally legible in a coffee-painted landscape, for Zlata, are Besima's *nafaka* and the more general economic trends in Bosnia that shifted from the informal commodity to transnational labor markets. In the late 1990s Besima joined the masses that tried their luck at the largest regional open market, called Arizona. As the profits at Arizona began to slump, Besima turned to the traveling trade, procuring goods from Turkey and Hungary for boutiques in the region. Since I finished a year of ethnographic residence in Bosnia in 2007, my interlocutors in the marketplaces, pharmacies, street stalls, boutiques, and grocery stores have been complaining bitterly about slackening demand, growing competition, and the exhausted and exhausting informal debt economy. Many market pioneers, like Besima, started exploring other income opportunities, whether as sales representatives of local companies or as migrant workers in the ex-Yugoslav region or farther into Europe and beyond. In 2011 Besima told me, "All of us here are now seized by a fever, a fever called Afghanistan."

Zlata's expertise in the concealed, vague, half-said, otherwise meant, and inconstant—qualities common to both professional and intimate matters—seems highly appropriate for the occluded and precarious nature of the transnational outsourcing economy. When it comes to American defense contractors, occasional corruption scandals are only the most obvious proof of popular suspicion that the apparent transparency of the online application is part of a more obscure and haphazard hiring process. Furthermore, jobs held in Afghanistan or Iraq are reportedly easily lost as a result of the smallest missteps; frequent operational restructuring; or the subversive efforts of one's colleagues, not infrequently impelled by means of sorcery, contracted out to the specialists back in Bosnia. In other words, the transnational labor market suggests a topography of purportedly obvious materials and signs (online application or terms and conditions of labor contract) and a multitude of concealed and erratic processes and dynamics (preferential hiring, cost-cutting strategies, scandals and missteps, collegiate sorcery). And the more Zlata emphasizes the limits of how much she knows, the more she is recruited by clients who would like her to try to find out life's possible turns and accidents. After all, she is the closest they can get to appreciating the secret workings of the American defense economy, her reputation is impressive, and the price is right.

Besima was unusually patient compared with other Iraq-Afghanistan job seekers throughout the ex-Yugoslav region, with whom she communicates daily via a web forum and on whose behalf she submits application materials and résumés in person to the Fluor International recruitment office (an option much preferred to that of applying online). It was through this online forum that she met her current romantic interest, Besima confides to me while we are waiting, though love, she says, was the last thing she had in mind, settled as she was in a comfortable marriage.

"Solves, Very Effectively, Love Sorrows and Financial Problems"

Love and money intersect with and through the body. Zlata's clients took it for granted that prospects of libidinal and professional ambitions were equally legible in the cup. Remember the waiting room. The anxious nurse wondered about her prolonged engagement and, in addition to a wedding update, received news of her future husband's transnational employment offer. Seeking a job in Afghanistan, Besima inconveniently fell in love and relied on Zlata to foresee the outcomes of her joint pursuits. Moreover, what a fortune reader intuits and perceives is the pairing of domains that are always already critically related. When Besima diagnoses a "mass fever called Afghanistan," she speaks not merely metaphorically but from the local vantage point that tends to foreground the body as the primary, visceral, and experiential ground that registers interactions with income, wealth, and money. All three—love, money, body—are compound "objects," materially weighty and consequential, historically produced and socially productive, and teeming with subtle, intangible, mysterious energies and qualities, unprovable and all the more obstinate inasmuch as they exceed attempts to record, predict, or explain them, using properly scientific instruments, whether psychological, political-economic, or bio-medical (see Farquhar n.d.; Stengers 2003). Thus, the prospect of fortune is presumed to be embodied—it concerns one's bodily habits; alters the routines of sleeping, eating, thinking, and fantasizing; and shapes one's moods, dispositions, and relations. Similarly, financial misfortunes bear on the bodily being and this local medical fact is very much advertised in the thriving market for various therapeutic remedies for both health and wealth. *Aura* is a popular monthly magazine on health and fortune. A hybrid of news, testimonials, and ads on anything from clinical and alternative medicine to popular science, divination, and magic that circulates widely (though many Bosnians are skeptical), *Aura* advertises a herbal tonic supplement, Revita, as "the best friend of a private businessman." The etiological assumption here is that business is personal: it literally depends on one's bodily performance and tendencies, vigor, composure, and endurance that can be cultivated. And business compromises health and body, which thus have to be cared for and protected.

Adding to the popular sense that body and being are at stake in the precarious new economic conditions is the growing visibility of the love magic market. Because most Bosnians aspire to cosmopolitan modernity built around the conceptual scaffolding of scientific reason and economic rationality, the contemporary salience of "magic" is shocking and not something one can easily appreciate initially or an appropriate topic to discuss in the official public sphere, except in a learned tone of disbelief and denunciation. But careful ethnographic attention to medical concerns and practices in the region has shown magic to be readily available and its effects regularly feared and treated (Jasarevic, forthcoming). Magic in action is typically messy, leaving plenty of room for doubt, second-guessing, or reinterpretation, inviting at once faith and skepticism and evoking the inconclusive authority of experience. In Bosnia, one may have grounds to suspect sorcery in cases in which one is in love beyond measure, has been left inexplicably, has left another but then became ill or began pining after one's ex, or has become stubbornly involved with someone whom one's friends and family find a strange match or when one's formerly affectionate lover or spouse turns cold. But love magic may also be blamed for recurrent business failures and misguided investments, for money mysteriously vanishing, for debtors' repeated defaulting, for pernicious generosity toward lovers, other intimates, or acquaintances. Like sorcery in general, it brings about side effects that biomedicine treats as anatomical, biochemical, or neurological disorders. Love magic acts on the victim's body to compel, to charm, and to affect desires, habits, and dispositions, as well as to alter material circumstances, because the target of a libidinal-magical act is understood to be either someone's fortune or someone's heart.

Aura advertises the competence of a piously veiled Sabina Medina to treat a long list of health problems, beginning with rheumatism and headaches, and adds the assurance that the healer, "very effectively, solves love troubles and financial problems." Articles in *Aura* busily pair love and finance and associate health complaints with both. This is a locally specific assumption rather than a universal characteristic of magical thinking, as is obvious from a cursory look at the magic in "the West," say, in the online spell boutique of Lady Shadow that rehearses typically bourgeois norms and sensibilities. For example, Lady Shadow's website quotes, separately, prices for love magic (from a simple intervention for £150 to a fancy package of ten spells for £1,050, amounts that the displayed currency converter icon readily translates to US$231.04 and US$1,617.18, respectively) and for the comparatively inexpensive money spells (£100).

Men and women working in Iraq and Afghanistan, as well as locally employed doctors and entrepreneurs, are said to be particularly vulnerable to love magic. Part of Zlata's talent is to conclusively "see" the traces of sorcery in a tangle of signs that may just as well be the result of ordinary contingencies, a change of heart, a charming distraction, and so on.

Love and Debt, Everywhere

Love magic exercises influence at a distance with principles of sympathetic resonance and contiguity that find no recognition in Newtonian laws of action and causation. Divination also extends beyond the immediate—the subject "present" in the body, his or her predetermined future inscribed in the cup—to "look," with a nonsensuous sense, at the potentiality of an event arising. Neither love magic nor divination requires the physical presence of the subject in order to "work" or "read" him or her: it is sufficient that the party contracting services at a distance renders the target palpable via desirous, social, familial, legal, and affective relations. Multiplicitous, messily entangled social beings are not discrete physical entities. Therefore, while Zlata sees only women, all the women's relations are subject to her purview: women here mediate men's access to knowledge of the future. Multiply so, considering that Zlata not only sees far ahead but also advises on the best course of action in the meantime. In addition to a wedding date and the future husband's job announcement, the young nurse I met in the waiting room received advice on how to persuade the reluctant man to accept his job offer. Similarly, when it comes to the treatment of love magic, women, the primary caregivers in Bosnia, tend to meddle more frequently in the business of others—enchanted, denying a problem, refusing a cure—and recruit expert help on their behalf, often without their knowledge. Divination and magic traffic in secrets of more than one kind.

The logic of extension in place of presence, I want to suggest, is equally at play in quotidian attachments formed through love and debt. Giving-taking regularly indebts for as long as what is given is surplus, exceeds the possibility of an equivalent, or of an accounting, which happens all the time if what is given is love and time, for instance. If you receive plenty of something that is unique, you can reciprocate in kind but not quite in exact quantity, although people register sacrifices and shortages. Some surpluses cannot be tallied, not least because it would be inappropriate to try. Imagine your mother presenting you with a bill for a nine-month uterus rental, or your parents adding up the cost of all the Band-Aids they placed on your bruised, bleeding knees, or your lover submitting a neat account of all the passionate exchanges undertaken, coming up with a negative balance. All intimate relations are marked by unreckoned surpluses of such kinds.

Love: when you receive and take all that you have not asked for, when whatever you give in turn does not and is not supposed to make you even. Daily exchanges everywhere produce such unevenness that goes unnamed as either "gift" or "commodity" debt but is recognized as generous or obliging, taken for granted, enjoyed or unappreciated, abused, and responded to ambivalently or accordingly. In some ethnographic contexts, such excess is brought to bear on the market, spontaneously or deliberately, as a public subscription to a moral economy of good measure in response to the logic of capital that aspires to reduce all encounters to the exchange of equivalents or monetary instruments that bring about debt at the current rate of interest (see Thompson 1991; Klima 2008; Taussig 1980). And ethnographers of care have documented instances in which neighbors and family lavish tender gifts or loans of credit instruments on loved ones in trouble, even when it costs them dearly (see Han 2012). But even the North American market, a model of the capitalist logic of exchange, continually sneaks affective surpluses into our strictly business transactions: Nutsonline, a family-owned store selling snacks and supplements, tirelessly reminds me, in words emitting from cute cartoon characters printed on every bag, that I am welcome to their family, which has kept the business going since the 1920s, "because we care." Nutsonline cares for me more than I can pay and they probably hope I've noticed. It somehow matters that I'm more than a customer and they are more than shrewd businesspeople. This is counterpoint to the other, brutally honest tendency to couch all appeals in the language of the purely economic rationality of a taxpayer, a citizen, a consumer, as when the city of Chicago in the spring of 2012 labeled trees around the city with the announcement "This tree gives back $___ worth of benefits to our environment," each blank filled in with the exact calculation of each tree's contribution, predicated on age, size, and type, to carbon reduction, cooling effects, and the management of water systems.

In Bosnia, the ties between love and debt are only more exaggerated because informal lending, presuming intimacy and gifting sensibilities, is sited squarely within the market. Even formal loans are more readily available with the help of friends, colleagues, and family whom one persuades to act as cosignees. In the back room of a pharmacy one day I saw a medical doctor, an energetic, persuasive woman, rush a pharmacist into cosigning a bank loan without so much as giving him the time to read the legal document or ask about her repayment plans. He showed discomfort in his typically understated way, laughing quickly at his own half joke: "I will not be repaying this on my own, will I?" The pharmacist had every reason to be nervous; the region in 2006 was full of stories of bank borrowers' defaulting and their betrayal of those intimates they'd recruited for cosigning. Nevertheless, the expectation that one cannot refuse a loan (or a cosigning) request, just as one cannot withhold a gift when a gift is due or ask for its return at will, is powerfully effective against the common sense that would recommend caution or denial.

Nor do expectations and claims attenuate with the distance that transnational employment puts between Bosnia and workers in Afghanistan and Iraq. Many workers have accepted an oversees assignment because of accumulated formal and informal debts, their own or their loved ones', and many more still are lending, borrowing, or giving money to those whom they want to help, treat well, or cannot refuse. I am told of a woman in her thirties who worked at an army camp in Afghanistan to settle her outstanding debts—to a bank for a car repayment; to multiple parties her parents owed money to when her parents' business went bankrupt; to her best friend, who financed her postgraduate education. A man in his late thirties has been working in Afghanistan for years, seven days a week, twelve hours a day, and has complained to his friends: his wife spends lavishly; his family and in-laws borrow his money to invest in business or to make ends meet, promising to repay him one fine day. He apparently has no heart to tell his wife how difficult life at the army base is for him and that he would rather quit. A woman in her twenties has been supporting her mother, younger brother, and older sister for almost a decade and reportedly became upset with her mother, who once withdrew 500 BAM (some three hundred dollars) from the woman's account, to which the mother has access, without asking, because she decided to purchase an irresistible handbag.

Irresistibly Indebted

We live in times of unprecedented global indebtedness. The Third World debt has long been displaced from the media by ever new debt crises, Cyprus being only the latest. If capital and its money form are always speculative, forwarding an advance on account of future value (Marx [1867] 2003, 106–24; Harvey 1982, 239–63), contemporary debt instruments are recklessly proliferating, perversely profitable for some and loaded with growing costs for others. And yet debt cannot be reduced to a single, all-too-familiar market form any more than market speculation can be an authoritative guide to the range of forward visions and nature of temporality. We live in debt, obliging and obliged, and this fact should make us wonder about complicated relationships made through uneven exchanges that cannot be voiced in the question "How much do I owe you?" In Bosnia, informal debts are intimate but squarely within the market, whether local or transnational, and the predicaments of an economy so thoroughly extended and personal concern for anyone who arrives at Zlata's, create a murky surface for reading. Stakes are high, as is made clear if once more we flip through *Aura*. Its crowded pages turn to the rhythm of unfailing optimism about the effectiveness of featured experts for love, business, and health matters. But the overall mood of the magazine is nervous, as the articles—featuring ordinary-looking, common-sense-speaking people against the backdrop of plain Bosnian homes—suggest a treacherous world of intimate betrayals.

Larisa Jasarevic is a senior lecturer in the International Studies Program at the University of Chicago. Her book manuscript on bodily experience and economies of debt in post-socialist Bosnia is currently in preparation with Indiana University Press.

Works Cited

Derrida, Jacques. 2005. *On Touching—Jean-Luc Nancy*. Stanford: Stanford University Press.

Evans-Pritchard, Edward. (1937) 1976. *Witchcraft, Oracles, and Magic Among the Azande*. Oxford: Clarendon Press.

Farquhar, Judith. n.d. "Metaphysics at the Bedside." In *Concept and Convention: Historical Epistemology of Chinese Medicine*, ed. Howard Chiang. Manchester: Manchester University Press.

Han, Clara. 2012. *Life in Debt: Times of Care and Violence in Neoliberal Chile*. Berkeley and Los Angeles: University of California Press.

Harvey, David. 1982. *Limits to Capital*. New York: Verso.

Holbaad, Martin. 2012. *Truth in Motion: The Recursive Anthropology of Cuban Divination*. Chicago: University of Chicago Press.

Jasarevic, Larisa. Forthcoming. *Intimate Debt: Health, Wealth, and Embodied Experience in the Bosnian Market*. Bloomington: Indiana University Press.

Kendall, Laurel. 2009. *Shamans, Nostalgias, and the IMF: South Korean Popular Religion in Motion*. Honolulu: University of Hawai'i Press.

Klima, Alan. 2008. "Thai Love Thai: Financing Emotions in Post-crash Thailand."

In *The Anthropology of Globalization: A Reader*, ed. Jonathan Xavier Inda and Renato Rosaldo (121–37). Oxford, UK: Blackwell.

Lakoff, Andrew. 2008. "The Generic Biothreat; or, How We Became Unprepared." *Cultural Anthropology* 23(3):399–428.

Langwick, Stacey. 2011. *Bodies, Politics, and African Healing: The Matter of Maladies in Tanzania*. Bloomington: Indiana University Press.

Martin, Luther, Huck Gutman, and Patrick Hutton. 1988. *Technologies of the Self: A Seminar with Michel Foucault*. Amherst: The University of Massachusetts Press.

Manning, Robert. 2000. *Credit Card Nation: The Consequences of America's Addiction to Credit*. New York: Basic Books.

Nancy, Jean-Luc. 2008. *Corpus*. New York: Fordham University Press

Marx, Karl. (1867) 2003. *Capital: A Critique of Political Economy*. Vol. 1. London: Lawrence & Wishart.

Pugh, Michael. 2005. "Transformation in the Bosnian Political Economy since Dayton. *International Peacekeeping* 12(3): 448–462.

Rajan, Kaushik Sunder. 2006. *Biocapital: The Constitution of Postgenomic Life*. Durham: Duke University Press.

Smith, James Howard. 2008. *Bewitching Development: Witchcraft and the Reinvention of Development in Neoliberal Kenya*. Chicago: University of Chicago Press.

Sombart, Werner. (1915) 1967. *The Quintessence of Capitalism: A Study of the History and Psychology of the Modern Business Man*. New York: H. Fertig.

Stengers, Isabelle. 2003. "The Doctor and the Charlatan." *Cultural Studies Review* 9(2):11–37.

Stites Elizabeth, Sue Lautze, Dyan Mazurana, and Alma Anic. 2005. *Coping with War, Coping with Peace: Livelihood Adaptation in Bosnia-Herzegovina, 1989–2004*. Feinstein International Famine Center (FIFC), Friedman School of Nutrition Policy and Science, Tufts University, and Mercy Corps International. http://reliefweb.int/sites/reliefweb.int/files/resources/98 E8BFFC00C9FB83C1257019003774D3-FIFC%20MCI%20Bosnia%20 Livelihoods%20Study.pdf

Taussig, Michael. 1980. *The Devil and Commodity Fetishism in South America*. Chapel Hill: University of North Carolina Press.

Thompson, E. P. 1991. *Customs in Common: Studies in Traditional Popular Culture*. New York: New Press.

Williams, Brett. 2004. *Debt for Sale: A Social History of the Credit Trap*. Philadelphia: University of Pennsylvania Press.

"Even a Freak Like You Would Be Safe in Tel Aviv": Transgender Subjects, Wounded Attachments, and the Zionist Economy of Gratitude

Saffo Papantonopoulou

*what are you?? if your not a male or a female, perhaps something in between?? then
can you explain to me your ridiculous & ignorant hate against the only country
in the Middle-East that someone like you could live a peaceful life, almost without
prejudice, having the law on your side, and also having the same rights as a male or
female heterosexual??? because darling, someone like you would be strung up by yr
pigtails and stoned to death, tortured or imprisoned, in any of those "peace loving"
"democratic" non-judgemental" [sic] Muslim countries that surround Israel!!*
　　　　　　　　　　　　　　　　　　　　—YouTube comment directed at me

*There is something about anger that is akin to this gift exchange. Once anger is given
to you, it is passed along as quickly as possible. . . . There in the street, as the army fired
over our heads, but also at us, the first impulse was to return the gift of death straight
back to the original donor, with no lapse in time. But, in that case, you would be killed.
So you pass it along, and it just leaps out, somewhere else and at another time. . . .
There were a lot of people who returned to their everyday life unable to control their
anger, and exploded into senseless rage at the slightest trifles for months afterwards.*
　　　　　　　　　　—Alan Klima, The Funeral Casino: Meditation, Massacre,
　　　　　　　　　　　　　　　　and Exchange with the Dead in Thailand

In 2007, the Israeli foreign ministry officially launched a campaign called Brand Israel. With professional corporate PR firms hired to revitalize the apartheid state's international image, a total of almost $20 million was set aside for Israeli state propaganda in that year alone.[1] This rebranding campaign, which persists today, has consisted of multiple different tactics. The tactic that has received perhaps the most attention, and the one

 WSQ: Women's Studies Quarterly 42: 1 & 2 (Spring/Summer 2014)

with which I am the most concerned here, is what has been dubbed by Palestine solidarity activists as "pinkwashing" (Schulman 2011). Haneen Maikey, cofounder of the queer Palestinian organization Al Qaws, defines pinkwashing as "the cynical use of gay rights by the Israeli government . . . in order to divert attention from Israeli . . . occupation and apartheid, by promoting itself as a progressive country that respects gay rights, and, on the contrary, portraying Palestinian society and Palestinians as homophobic" (Maikey 2013). Jasbir Puar (2007) coined the term "homonationalism" to refer to this process. Since the launch of Brand Israel, there has been a proliferation of activist organizing around pinkwashing. In 2013, much of this activist and academic work culminated in a conference, titled "Homonationalism and Pinkwashing," held at the City University of New York Graduate Center in April 2013. Both Maikey and Puar were keynote speakers at this conference.

While much of this work so far has focused on the cynical deployment of cisgender queer subjectivities, the question I want to pose, then, is *where, in the age of neoliberalism and homonationalism, is the transgender subject relative to colonial economies of gratitude?* Ironically, to the extent to which this question is beginning to be addressed within the academy, responses to pinkwashing as it relates to transgender subjectivities and politics have followed the gradual "inclusion" of transgender subjects into homonationalism. During her keynote speech at the conference, Jasbir Puar raised the question of a rise, in recent years, of a trans version of homonationalism, citing the example of U.S. vice president Joseph Biden's statement that transgender issues are "the civil rights issue of our time." A question I raised to Puar during the Q&A session, and one that remains an issue, is the question of the incitement to discourse—the "call and response" that Puar describes between pinkwashing and the queer response to pinkwashing. Is this the moment, now, when transgender subjectivities can be discussed in relationship to pinkwashing and homonationalism? Did transgender subjects have to wait to be invoked by Joseph Biden into another wave of homonationalism before we could theorize our relationship to it? This call-and-response is particularly troubling, as it seems to reenact the same narrative as the historical development of trans theory within the Western academy—"First there was women's studies, then queer studies, then trans studies" gets replaced by "First there was colonial feminism, then there was pinkwashing/homonationalism, then there was trans-homonationalism."[2] This call-and-response is troubling in another way. During her keynote speech, Haneen Maikey critiqued activists who took part in the first official U.S. LGBT delegation to Palestine (many of whom, including Jasbir Puar and Sarah Schulman, were in the audience) for their complicity in the "tension between LGBT solidarity with Palestine and the focus on . . . Palestinian queer lives" (Maikey 2013). Is an attempt to narrate transgender experiences of pinkwashing complicit in this same dynamic? Although not much can be done about the historical context of this essay, it is my hope, however, that through deploying an autoethnographic approach the present essay may indirectly address some of these questions.

In his ethnography of death and political violence in Thailand, Alan Klima paraphrases Marcel Mauss in arguing that "the giver [of the gift] has a hold over the receiver because the thing given away always contains within it a bit of the giver, the 'spirit of the gift'" (Klima 2002, 240). He ties this to neoliberalism and U.S. military "aid" to the Thai dictatorship: "Development loans, aid grants, military aid, machine guns, . . . 'advisors,' spies, counterinsurgency expertise, . . . American anthropologists . . . —these gifts the military rulers were more than happy to receive. . . . Every Thai connected through this gift economy to the juntas was, in turn, connected to the U.S. gift" (58). Klima connects this to the "gift of death" given by the Thai military to protesters during the 1992 Black May massacre, as quoted above. He goes on to elaborate on Derrida's critique of Mauss: "The idea of a pure gift between people seems . . . impossible to conceive. . . . In the way that Jacques Derrida writes of the impossible language of giving, once the recognition of the gift event occurs, the gift is annulled, most of all by its *noble identification.* Once a gift has been identified as such it cannot help but enter the circle of debt in which it ceases to truly be a gift, freely given" (246; emphasis mine). Rather than focus, as Derrida does, on the impossibility of a "pure gift" (which Klima argues is besides the point, for all gifts exist in this cycle of debt), I want to focus on the politics of this "noble identification." When does a gift get called a gift and why? In other words, how does transgender "safety" become a gift given by the West/Israel?

In the YouTube comment quoted at the beginning of this essay, the absent Palestinian becomes a site onto which queerphobic Zionists may project their queerphobic fantasies. These projections accomplish several things. They allow the queerphobic Zionist to live out his own queerphobic fantasy while simultaneously deploying a pretext of caring about queer people, in order to posit himself as the savior of victimized queers. They also posit the West as a point of origin for queerness. Zionists love to ask me, "How would you fare in Gaza?" to which I love to respond, "How would I get to Gaza?" This first question, like many transphobic heckles that I have received from Zionists, is an Althusserian hail. According to Althusser (1971), the hail serves to interpolate the individual into the subject, to bring the individual into ideology. The noble identification of "gay friendly" Tel Aviv's gift to all queers is a hail—an interpolation of the transgender body into an always already indebted subject position, one enmeshed in a "cycle of debt." Under the Zionist economy of gratitude, the transgender subject is perpetually indebted to capitalism and the West for allowing her to exist. The properly delimited space for the transgender subject within this ideology is essentially one confined to an apoliticized space of pride parades and gay bars, but never the front lines of an anti-imperial or anticolonial project. It is a queer/transphobic assault against those visibly queer bodies who refuse to be properly disciplined neoliberal queer consumers—and transgender bodies are often the most visibly queer bodies and hence the ones singled out for attack. As one cannot return the gift to the one who gave it (in this case because the Zionist disidentified from his own queerphobia), the transgender subject is forced to pass it along—to Palestinians. Hence, the queerphobic Zionist can pass the gift of his racist colonial phobia as well as his queerphobia on to the transgender subject. The projection allows the Zionist to disidentify from the transphobia inherent in his hail. This is particularly important, since it is precisely the violent transphobia—"what *are* you?"—that is an *incitement to vulnerability*. I am supposed to feel vulnerable, afraid, attacked by this hail, in order that I may pass on that gift of death to the supposedly transphobic Palestinian.

Economies of gratitude (Hochschild and Machung 1989) are marketplaces where material capital is exchanged with affective/moral capital. The fact that the Israeli state has provided a multimillion-dollar market for professional corporate PR companies to discursively project Israel onto a moral high ground over Palestinians demonstrates that economies of gratitude are very much material realities. The Zionist economy of gratitude and its incitement to vulnerability are actually a reformulation of an older dialectic of Jewish suffering/Jewish virility inherent to Zionism—what I term the Sabra-Holocaust dialectic. Zionism has historically fluctuated between deploying notions of universal, transhistorical Jewish suffering and trauma, and the muscular, masculine virility of the Sabra (Shalit 1994). Zionism has depended on deploying a narrative of victimization—from the Holocaust to suicide bombing—in order to legitimate its colonial violence against Palestinians. This leads to the almost laughable situation of Israel projecting itself as victim as it rains down white phosphorus over the Gaza Strip.

The Zionist victim narrative is consistent with Wendy Brown's (1993) reading of Nietzsche's (unfortunately named) notion of "slave morality": Israel, according to Zionist self-fashioning, embodies Nietzsche's notion of the "triumph of the weak as weak." But furthermore, while Jewish and Israeli trauma is mobilized into a colonial narrative, Palestinian trauma is simply not allowed to exist, as Palestinians are, within the Zionist narrative, senseless terrorists without history or subjectivity. The deployment of vulnerability in Israel works as a mimesis to tell Israelis, "Remember that you are vulnerable," while it works to tell Palestinians, "Remember that you are less than human." This mobilization of trauma is projected back in time, turning Jewish history into a "morbidly selective 'tracing the dots' from pogrom to pogrom" (Shohat 2006, 213). This is counterposed to the rupture provided by the virility of the Sabra—only the Israeli nation-state and its militaristic dreams of security can save Jews from this history of endless suffering. We can read the shift deployed by Brand Israel as a reformulation of the Sabra-Holocaust dialectic. According to a 2005 article in the *Jewish Daily Forward*, the "new approach to Israeli image control" was to cultivate an image of Israel as a place "where there are cool, hip people," without mentioning "the conflict" (Popper 2005). In other words, military prowess would be replaced by chic, neoliberal capital. Sabra virility has given way to market virility, and queers are caught between a dialectic of "gay friendly" Tel Aviv and the specter of a pervasive, global queerphobia.

Transgender pinkwashing and the Holocaust-Sabra dialectic are both emblematic of what Wendy Brown (1993) termed the politics of "wounded attachments." Brown identifies the production of an "incitement to resentment" through a *renaturalization* of capitalism that can be said to have marked progressive discourse since the 1970s." Brown ascribes this to the growth of "class resentment without . . . class analysis" that has typified the dematerialization of identity politics. This process is at work more generally, since, using Nietzsche's concept of resentment, class resentment "like all resentments, retains the real or imagined holdings of its reviled subject." In other words, the wounded subject holds on to the very violent structures that produced it in the first place. Brown turns away from Foucault, reading Nietzsche's "diagnosis of the culture of modernity as the triumph of 'slave morality'" as explaining how liberalism has brought about this proliferation of resentment. What she leaves out, however, are the various ways in which these proliferated resentments can become organized and directed by an affective economy such as Brand Israel. In other words, economies of gratitude and incitements to vulnerability seek to align "proper" ways of expressing one's righteous indignation and trauma in the service of capital and the state.

One of the sites of tension with members of the U.S. LGBT delegation to Palestine that Maikey referenced during her keynote was a conflict over the question of activists being "out" in Palestine. Part of Maikey's point was that the "coming-out narrative" is a Western narrative, and one needs to be aware of one's privilege in such a context. I agree; however, I would counterpose the point that the coming-out narrative is also a cisgender narrative. What does it mean for a transgender person to *not* be "out"? "Out"ness is a complicated question for transgender subjects. It is not simply a matter of whom one sleeps with or forms relationships with, but a matter of one's both intimate and public relationship with one's own body. And it is a question of *gender ontology*. In order to address this question, I wish to switch tone, toward the personal/autoethnographic—focusing on my own "coming out" as transgender. As I hope will be apparent, this is necessary in order to outline some of the specificities of the transgender subject and its relation to pinkwashing.

My own personal relationship with transgender pinkwashing is perhaps best exemplified by a former friend—let me refer to him as X—whose own articulation of a transgender identity was foundational to my eventual "coming out" as transgender. I met X in the early 2000s. X's fear for his family in Israel, as well as his pain and frustration of having had to fight so much to assert his right to be a man—*ontologically, not referentially*—coalesced to produce the first version of pinkwashing I ever encountered. Long before I learned the term "pinkwashing" or had a political vocabulary to respond to it, he told me stories about queer and trans Palestinians "fleeing" to Tel Aviv and Jerusalem—consolidating many fears around the phobogenic object of the Palestinian. X would often deploy the trauma that he had experienced—both as a trans person and as someone with family in Israel—to silence any articulation of a transgender politics that is anticapitalist, antimilitarist, or anti-Zionist. I am particularly struck, for instance, by an argument we once had over Amanda Simpson, the first transgender presidential appointee in the United States and former project designer for U.S. military contractor Raytheon. X insinuated that any trans person who articulated a politics critical of transgender celebrations of people such as Simpson were privileged and did not understand what it is to struggle to find employment as a trans person. This deployment perfectly represents Brown's notion of "class resentment without class analysis," as the exclusive focus of X's political project was always based around responding to present pain—through, for instance, a precise and transcendent definition of gender terminology, and the ever-elusive search for "safety"—and resenting those who advocated a more systemic transformative politics as inherently privileged.

Having first learned of the term "transgender" from X, as well as a series of encounters with mostly binary-identified trans men (trans men who identify solidly within the gender binary, as men), I began a difficult process of interrogating my own relationship to my body and what gender meant to me. Having felt that the subject position of the "transgender," which, by that time in the early 2000s metropolitan United States had already become firmly entrenched as a discourse, did not seem to completely fit with me, I felt ambivalent. Further contributing to my ambivalence was my, at that time, total commitment to a certain tyrannical articulation of identity politics that was (and remains) so popular among college-educated first world radicals: not recognizing my own sense of gendered embodiment as something legible within the currently existing articulations of gender, I did not wish to "appropriate" another. Since then, my relationship to gender has shifted. I did not so much "come out" as transgender as "come into" a transgender subject position—one I felt had already been prearticulated.

Transgender people, in general, are placed in an impossible bind. On the one hand, the need to exert a stable gender identity in response to the violent hegemony and apparent naturalization of assigned-at-birth gender means that the transgender subject must produce an illusion of coherent gender. On the other hand, this is impossible, as gender is *always* a mimesis. Often exotified within queer theory and queer spaces as examples of the incoherence of heteronormative gender roles, we are frequently forced to speak out of both sides of our mouths when it comes to questions of gender essentialism: "yes, but . . . no." While it is the case that gender is always mimesis, the struggle for the transgender woman is to be a woman *ontologically, not referentially*—to say, "This is not drag; this is not a parody." The politicization of the transgender subject's present pain rather than future liberation forecloses the question: What does *transgender* exist in reference to? This foreclosure easily leads to liberal concepts of justice and equality. As Brown (1993) argues, claims to inclusion, which have origi-nated from far more liberatory intentions, are "tethered to a formulation of justice, which, ironically, reinscribes a bourgeois idea as its measure"; (394) the transgender woman seeks an "equal chance" at being included in the stable category of "woman," and transgender politics becomes deeply tied to a proliferation of precisely defined signifiers—as if we can some-how signify our way toward liberation. The tragic result of this contradic-tion, in combination with the renaturalization of capitalism within identity politics, is that the transgender subject must form a wounded attachment to the very terms of gender that oppress her in the first place. It is this fear of illegibility, the need to exist in spaces where one's relationship to gender is legible, even as one grapples with the intangibility of gender—the fic-tion of gender essentialism that trans people are forced to take on—that makes our need for intangible things such as "safety" and "security" so eas-ily co-optable. The incitement to vulnerability ("what *are* you?") serves to remind us of that.

The contradiction between *being* and *becoming* is one that we live inti-mately—how else can one explain the process of transition, of *becoming* what one already *is*—and yet we cannot, for fear of becoming a parody, identify it as such. Piled on top of that, the struggle for the nonbinary transgender woman is to establish the ontological foundation of her wom-anhood before she can find the space to afford a playfulness within that femininity—"No, this is not drag; . . . but yes, it is drag." In order to deal with this tension, I felt the need to produce an ever-increasing string of qualifiers in order to delicately navigate the world of first world "radical" queer politics. From genderqueer butch trans men who are bottoms, to binary-identified trans women who enjoy drag, there has been an endless and explosive proliferation of queer and transgender subject positions, held together by a matrix of (neo)liberal multiculturalism—sometimes in the guise of anticapitalism. What we have is an infinitely expanding fractal of politicized identities, each one produced in a state of resentment against another. Part of what motivates this process is that, within the logic of neo-liberal politicized identity, if one cannot name one's pain, then one's pain is not politicizable. This creates a further proliferation of subjectivities and resentments.

By now, the reader may have noticed that at certain moments, I unavoidably slip between signifiers such as "gay," "queer," and "trans" in discussing these discourses. This is somewhat unavoidable, since in many of these discourses—particularly pinkwashing discourses deployed by queerphobic Zionists—there is not just a conflation of "gay" and "trans" but also the assumption that the illegible "someone like me" ("what are you?") can be legible/"safe" only within the confines of a social formation called "LGBT" or "gay," located in the West/Israel. The heckles I have received, as with most transphobic attacks, do not fall neatly along the lines of self-identification. Transgender people, after all, are often singled out for violence simply for being the most visibly queer bodies, regardless of how we identify. But this fear of illegibility is also something internalized by transgender people—the notion that we can only really travel in spaces that have a certain a priori reading of gender. This wounded attachment to the gender binary, and the fiction of a transcendent (and trans-affirming) gender essentialism, lend themselves easily to imperialist cooptation. When the transgender subject reads (cisnormative) homonationalist narratives, even when we are not specifically hailed as *trans* subjects within them, the assumption is that it is *only* within those limited "gay friendly" spaces that we may find an even smaller subset of *trans-friendly* subspaces. I want to turn now toward a critical reading of three different texts that speak about gayness in transit—both the transit of gay migrants and the transit of gay signifiers—with the understanding that the transgender subject, although not always specifically referenced, is implicated within this. Although the three texts have very different politics—Marxist, homonationalist, and anticolonial—what they have in common is a certain *linguistic* attachment to gay signifiers.

Drawing from Foucault, Gay Marxist historian John D'Emilio, in his 1983 article "Capitalism and Gay Identity," correctly notes that "gay" and "lesbian," as identity formations, "are a product of history" whose "emergence is associated with the relations of capitalism" (102). This emergence is, of course, clustered around large cities. However, D'Emilio still essentializes gayness, equating gay liberation in a typical Marxist teleological fashion, with the rise of capitalism and the move toward a liberatory utopia. "Capitalism has created the material conditions for homosexual desire to express itself as a central component of some individuals' lives," he argues, and outlines his vision for a utopic gay socialist future: "Now, our political movements are . . . creating the ideological conditions that make it easier for people to make that choice" (109).

D'Emilio's historicism is useful, although his teleology is not. What we can take from a critical reading of this, however, is that holding on to an attachment to the subject position of "gay" or "lesbian" in the fashion that D'Emilio does (even while recognizing it as socially constructed), can be colonial. D'Emilio's gay socialist futurity has a temporality that marches to the same drum as manifest destiny. This settler futurity is the same practice as Marxist colonialism—for instance, consider the Soviet discourse around Chechens: "lumpen proletariats" who needed to go through all the proper stages of capitalist displacement and alienation in order to reach the telos of proletarian subjectivity necessary for socialism. Part of the problem here is that the subject of the proletariat contains within it the capitalist displacement that was necessary for the production of the proletariat—hence, a kind of jealous gaze is directed toward those who are seen as having not yet experienced this alienation, especially indigenous peoples who have not been fully assimilated into capitalism. I want to make a controversial claim here, in not viewing Marxism and late twentieth-century identity politics as dialectically antithetical, but rather reading certain dogmatic strains of Marxism as a form of proletarian identity politics. Within this universalized proletarian subject is another kind of wounded attachment. The proletariat subject position contains within it the very rupture of displacement that produced the proletariat class and the heteropatriarchy necessary to sustain capitalist production.

A similar kind of attachment to displacement is at play in liberal gay humanitarian narratives. In 2005, the tellingly named studio After Stonewall Productions released a film titled *Dangerous Living: Coming Out in the Developing World*. Featuring interviews with various LGBT activists from different countries outside the West, spliced up and lumped together haphazardly, the film delivers the following overarching messages: that it is not safe to be queer in the "developing world," that what queer spaces do exist in the "developing world" are to be found in certain metropolises— Cairo, Kuala Lumpur, Calcutta, Rio de Janeiro—and that these sites trace their genealogy to the Stonewall riots. Furthermore, according to the film, queerness/gayness and sometimes transness (when it is acknowledged) were invented in the West. Epistemic breaking points such as the Stonewall riots and canonized locales such as San Francisco and Greenwich Village are the originating points of this innovation against the backdrop of a timeless, pervasive heterosexism. This cosmopolitan gayness/queerness then "spreads" from the metropole to the periphery, forming a web from city to city. This coincides with Jack Halberstam's (excruciatingly white) analysis in his book *In a Queer Time and Place*: the idea of "metronormativity," that "the rural is made to function as a closet for urban sexualities in most accounts of rural queer migration" and that "the metronormative narrative maps a story of migration onto the coming-out narrative" (2005, 36–37). We can extend Halberstam's analysis further and see the ways that the closet/rural/(post)colony as well as out/urban/metropole get collapsed onto each other—the queer is always pulled closer to the heart of capital.

The overarching savior narrative occurs towards the end of the film, when each interviewee, in clips spliced together, tells his or her story of emigrating to the West. After a particularly heart-wrenching story of Ashraf Zanati's departure from Egypt, the narrator comments that "Ashraf Zanati left Egypt. Ashraf had become part of a planetary minority." Although the film purports to care about the status of queers in the "developing world," it actually forms a wounded attachment that fetishizes displacement and bifurcates the queer from his or her society. This narration of non-Western countries as inherently unsafe for queer subjects produces the very displacement it describes, in a manner similar to the ways nineteenth-century colonial archaeology laid the foundations for Zionism and the dispossession of Arab Jews. Writing about the European "discovery" and destruction of the Cairo Geniza—a building that had housed pieces of paper documenting centuries of Jewish Egyptian history—Shohat (2006) shows us that the discursive/ archival dislocation of Egyptian Jews by the forces of European/Ashkenazi colonialism anticipated the later dislocation of Egyptian Jews. This dislocation would form part of the backbone of Zionist historiography's production of a "morbidly selective 'tracing the dots' from pogrom to pogrom." The fetishization of queer displacement, as projected by *Dangerous Living*, performs a similar historical flip to the one Shohat documents: "If at the time of the 'Geniza discovery' Egyptian Jews were still seen as part of the colonized Arab world, with the partition of Palestine, Arab-Jews, in a historical shift, suddenly became simply 'Jews'" (Shohat 2006, 205). Through various colonial practices, there was a discursive bifurcation between the "Arab" and the "Jew"; in the case of

Dangerous Living there is a similar bifurcation between the "Egyptian" and the "Queer."

Joseph Massad (2002, 2007) coined the term "gay international" to refer to the colonial politics that are intrinsic to projects such as *Dangerous Living*. However, Massad falls into a similar trap, although for opposite reasons. Massad's writing is excellently critiqued in a blog post by Samir Taha (2013). Taha argues:

> Massad's whole thesis is premised on a vast and unbridgeable (except through an imperializing act) divide between the "West" and the "non-West," one in which the West is always positively defined as possessing certain epistemic categories, primary among them the category sexuality with everything that it contains from homophobia and heteronormativity to gay politics and queer resistance, while the non-West is also always contrastively and negatively defined as lacking both the categories and the need for the politics they contain and generate. The divide can be summed up in one statement: the West has sexuality, the non-West does not.

Massad even goes so far as to attack queer Arab activists for being inherently "complicit" in imperialism *by their very act of forming sexual identification.* He goes even further and blames their "complicity" for acts of queerphobic violence they later experienced! I would hate to see what Massad would have to say about transgender subjectivities—thankfully he has not yet seen fit to write about them/us. While *Dangerous Living*, consistent with the Zionist economy of gratitude and narratives of queer and trans Palestinians "fleeing" to Israel, posits queerness as a gift given by the West to the non-West, Massad actually makes a similar argument— just reversing the value judgment. The *signifier* "gay" still belongs to the West. The noble identification becomes an ignoble identification. This is the same kind of wounded attachment as transphobic second-wave feminism, which reified/reacted to the gender binary by reversing the value judgment without questioning the formation of the binary itself.

It is undeniably true that many queer, trans, and LGBT people from the third world migrate—for numerous reasons—closer to the heart of neocolonial capital (along with their straight/cisgender neighbors), just as it is undeniably true that signifiers such as "gay," "queer," and "trans," as English words, have histories that originate in the West. The problem here is not with the "truth" of these statements, but with their interpolation into discourse—the way these movements are narrated politically. In order to avoid the pitfalls of Massad, for instance, it is important to draw a distinction between the politics of *Dangerous Living* and the individual life narratives of the people interviewed in the film. What *Dangerous Living*, Joseph Massad, and John D'Emilio have in common is a certain *linguistic* attachment: they all fall for the deterministic trap of reading a signifier as attached to its point of origin. This is precisely what Foucault criticizes in "Nietzsche, Genealogy, History" (1977). Allow me to use one moment in *Dangerous Living* as an example of a different reading. Alyssa Sasot, a transgender woman from the Philippines, recounts the story of how she came to identify as transgender: "The term 'transgender' . . . well, thanks to the Internet. I learned it when I was in fourth year high school. I put like 'gays who look like women' [into the search engine] and, it says 'transgendered.' . . . *Oh!*" We must leave room for a kind of transcendence of subjectivities such as "transgender" if we are to avoid the reductionist pitfalls of Massad. There is, at least for an instant (the "*Oh!*" moment), a transcendence whereby the term "transgender" literally exists outside of geography or even history, within the intimate subjectivity of Sasot and others. "Transgender," at this moment, is neither a benevolent gift from the West nor an assimilation of Western cultural imperialism. And yet it is precisely the openness of this moment—the opposite of the unbridgableness of Massad's gap between West and non-West—that allows a vulnerability to imperialist co-optation, as the film attempts to credit the West for this subjectivity production.

Wendy Brown's words ring just as true today as they did twenty years ago when they were written. While Brown did not explore what, exactly, mobilizes wounded attachments, what we have seen since 1993 is an increase in the deployment of wounded attachments by neoliberalism and neocolonialism. The Zionist economy of gratitude, as part of a multibillion-dollar propaganda industry, is an economy in a very literal sense. Pinkwashing deploys preexisting tropes of Jewish victimization inherent to Zionism, in an attempt to hail the transgender subject into a debt of gratitude toward neoliberalism. This narrative deploys vulnerability as economic capital, and its historical rise coincides with a tactical and discursive shift by radical and progressive politics within the West. This shift has been a move toward hyperindividualized projects of semiotic and representational interventions into existing systems. This is encapsulated in the assumption that through better (media) representation, and precisely defined terminologies, transgender people and other oppressed people may find liberation.

The renaturalization of capitalism within late twentieth-century identity politics is both a product of and produced by the reframing of both temporality and the individual's relation to the collective within purportedly liberatory political projects. No longer part of a mass movement that aims toward liberation of the collective in historical time, we are instead relegated to a totality of atomized individuals, each struggling to survive. The struggles for survival are very much real, but the ways in which they have been politicized—even more, the ways in which survival within the existing system has become *the* political project—reflect an internalization of Margaret Thatcher's infamous quip "There is no alternative." We are often grappling with subjectivities that have been produced by disciplinary regimes in order not to survive. Liberation will mean the ceasing-to-be of many of these disciplined subjectivities. And there are few things more terrifying than calling for the death of one's own subject position.

But this may be the point where it makes sense to part from Brown, as Brown parts from Nietzsche. After all, Brown does not account for movements—such as, say, the Black Panther Party, to name one example—that politicized identity as part of a liberatory project, avoiding both liberal co-optation and crude Marxist reductionism. Rather than focus further on Brown's notion of wounds and traumas, it may be useful to reevaluate Fanon's notion of catharsis in the twenty-first century. What might we imagine a transgender catharsis could look like? To Fanon, catharsis happens as part of decolonial struggle, which is, in his words, "an agenda for total disorder. But it cannot be accomplished by the wave of a magic wand . . . or a gentleman's agreement." Fanon specifies that decolonial struggle "is an historical process" (1963, 2). Liberation, catharsis, and healing from trauma will not happen on the level of a matrix of individuals, or a more precise regime of signification, and no theoretical intervention (even on the part of this text) will bring it into being. Again, we cannot signify our way toward liberation as something that happens in historical time; we cannot make a priori promises of safety or security. There is unfortunately no predicting what, exactly, a historical unraveling of a violent system may bring about. But we can, at the very least, prepare ourselves, by critically examining what sort of political tropes we reproduce in attempting to name our pain. Demanding liberation in historical time, through a collective struggle that places more weight on the material than on the semiotic or symbolic, while simultaneously allowing geocultural cross-pollination of ideas and signifiers without a historically deterministic search for "origins" (Foucault 1977), may allow us to break out of cycles of debt and gratitude. But this change will not happen through theoretical intervention alone; it must happen through a structural and material transformation of the world we live in.

Acknowledgments

It is not without a sense of irony that, in an essay on economies of gratitude, I would like to acknowledge four friends, without whose love and support I would not have been able to write this essay. I would like to dedicate this essay to Skanda Kadirgamar, Amirah Mizrahi, Krys Méndez Ramirez, and Samir Taha. I will forever owe them a *debt of gratitude*.

Saffo Papantonopoulou is a transgender activist who has been involved in the BDS movement since 2009. She is pursuing a PhD in anthropology and Middle East studies at the University of Arizona, where her research is focused on Islamophobia, neoliberalism, queer resistance, and Ottoman historical memory in Greece.

Notes

1. As a point of clarification, contrary to how it is often construed, the use of the term "apartheid" is not to invoke a comparison with South Africa (although there are many similarities), but rather to apply a term with a legal definition (see Millard 2012).
2. I would call it "transnationalism," but that word is unfortunately already taken.

Works Cited

Althusser, Louis. 1971. *Lenin and Philosophy and Other Essays.* New York: Review Press.

Brown, Wendy. 1993. "Wounded Attachments." *Political Theory* 21(3): 390–410.

D'Emilio, John. 1983. "Capitalism and Gay Identity." In *Powers of Desire: The Politics of Sexuality,* ed. A. Snitow, C. Stansell, and S. Thompson. 100–113 New York: Monthly Review Press.

Fanon, Frantz. 1963. *The Wretched of the Earth.* New York: Grove Press.

Foucault, Michel. 1977. "Nietzsche, Genealogy, History." In *Language, Counter-*

memory, Practice: Selected Essays and Interviews, ed. D. F. Bouchard. 139–164 Ithaca: Cornell University Press.

Halberstam, Jack. 2005. *In a Queer Time and Place: Transgender Bodies, Subcultural Lives.* New York: New York University Press.

Hochschild, Arlie, and Anne Machung. 1989. *The Second Shift: Working Parents and the Revolution at Home.*

Klima, Alan. 2002. *The Funeral Casino: Meditation, Massacre, and Exchange with the Dead in Thailand.* Princeton: Princeton University Press.

Maikey, Haneen. 2013. Keynote speech at the "Homonationalism and Pinkwashing Conference," City University of New York. April 2013. http://videostreaming.gc.cuny.edu/videos/channel/37/recent/page1/.

Massad, Joseph. 2002. "Re-Orienting Desire: The Gay International and the Arab World." *Public Culture* 14(2):361–385.

———. 2007. *Desiring Arabs.* Chicago: University of Chicago Press.

Popper, Nathaniel. 2005. "Israel Aims to Improve Its Public Image." *Jewish Daily Forward,* October 14. http://forward.com/articles/2070/israel-aims-to-improve-its-public-image/.

Puar, Jasbir. 2007. *Terrorist Assemblages: Homonationalism in Queer Times.* Durham: Duke University Press.

ReMillard, Frances H. 2012. *Is Israel an Apartheid State? Do Israel's Practices in the West Bank, East Jerusalem, and Gaza Amount to Crimes of Apartheid under International Law? Summary of an International Legal Study Funded and Coordinated by the Government of South Africa.* Chapel Hill, NC: Israeli Committee Against House Demolitions-USA.

Scagliotti, John, Janeane Garofalo, and Don DiNicola. 2003. *Dangerous Living: Coming Out in the Developing World.* United States: After Stonewall.

Schulman, Sarah. 2011. "A Documentary Guide to 'Brand Israel' and the Art of Pinkwashing." *Mondoweiss,* November 30. http://mondoweiss.net/2011/11/a-documentary-guide-to-brand-israel-and-the-art-of-pinkwashing.html.

Shalit, Erel. 1994. "The Relationship Between Aggression and Fear of Annihilation in Israel." *Political Psychology* 15(3):415–434.

Shohat, Ella. 2006. "Columbus, Palestine, and Arab-Jews." In *Taboo Memories, Diasporic Voices.* 201–232. Durham: Duke University Press.

Taha, Samir. 2013. "Joseph Massad: An Occidentalist's Other Subjects/Victims." *Arab Leftist* (blog), April 21. http://arableftist.blogspot.com/2013/04/joseph-massad-occidentalists-other_21.html.

Trading Credit for Debt: Queer History-Making and Debt Culture

T. L. Cowan and Jasmine Rault

Once you start to see bad debt, you start to see it everywhere, hear it everywhere, feel it everywhere.

—*Stefano Harney and Fred Moten,* The Undercommons:
Fugitive Planning and Black Study

If you had gone to the opening of *Rare & Raw: Queer History Then and Now* at the Leslie-Lohman Museum of Gay and Lesbian History in New York City on February 15, 2013, you would have seen among the small selection of artworks "exploring the themes of queer history, visibility and notions of representation" ("Rare & Raw" 2013) twenty-seven framed photographs from Zoe Leonard's *The Fae Richards Photo Archive*, originally created for and coanimated by Cheryl Dunye's 1996 film, *The Watermelon Woman* (Fig. 1). Returning to the museum a few days later, you would have found the photos removed from the exhibit and in their place what looked like a foreclosure notice, or what we came to think of as the foreclosure installation: four documents taped to the wall, a record of the loan agreement between the museum and the Eileen Harris Norton Collection, which owns one of the three copies of *The Fae Richards Photo Archive* and which, on the day of the show's opening, "amended" the loan agreement such that there would be no loan at all (Fig. 2). With "regrets for the unfortunate timing and difficult circumstances," the loan was deemed too high risk and revoked, it seems, because of concerns about the material fragility and value of the photographs (Shim-Boyle, 2013).[1]

The story of this amended installation is compelling to us for a few rea-

 WSQ: Women's Studies Quarterly 42: 1 & 2 (Spring/Summer 2014) © 2014 by T. L. Cowan and Jasmine Rault. All rights reserved.

sons. Most immediately, as dykes of a certain age, we have an affective, aesthetic, and intellectual attachment to *The Fae Richards Photo Archive* and to *The Watermelon Woman*; in fact, both of us became committed to the kinds of recuperative and critical feminist and queer storytelling that Leonard, Dunye, and their many collaborators in the project were for(a)ging in the early 1990s. Furthermore, this transaction situates the Leslie-Lohman Museum and the *Rare & Raw* exhibit (and its project of queer history-making) as unreliable borrowers; that is, the foreclosure installation advertises bad credit and both the museum and the exhibit get thrown into the subject position reserved in U.S. history for African Americans and other minoritized groups figured as socioeconomically delinquent. Moreover, the capital (not) exchanged in this transaction—*The Fae Richards Photo Archive*—is a series of images signifying the forgotten or abandoned African American lesbian histories that Dunye and her collaborators work to repossess and revalue in *The Watermelon Woman*, a repossession that might be said to expose the violence of (cultural) capital itself, a system that has historically devalued the lives and work of African Americans and queers. And finally, this story is compelling for us because in the moment of encountering that familiar scene—cheap paper printed with legal text, contradictorily taped both haphazardly and with forceful, binding purpose across a prominent wall (usually the front door of a repossessed property)—we were reminded of the ways in which so much queer history-making negotiates the strained relationship between good credit and bad debt. That is, the eloquent shock of this foreclosure installation activated our thinking about queer history-making through debt as a mode of inquiry, as methodology, as "queer hermeneutics" and "black study" (Crosby et al. 2012, 130) that "runs in every direction, scatters, escapes" (Harney and Moten 2013, 61).

Here, we propose that the repossession of *The Fae Richards Photo Archive* effectively resituates *The Watermelon Woman* and *Rare & Raw* into the context of debt culture. As Paula Chakravartty and Denise Ferreira da Silva remind us, this is a culture "embedded in the colonial and racial matrix of capitalist accumulation of land (conquest and settlement), exploitation of labor (slavery, indentured labor, forced migration), appropriation of resources, and ultimately the very meaning of debt in what Walter Mignolo calls the 'modern/colonial world system'" (Chakravartty and da Silva 2012, 364). That is, we understand debt culture as a "totality of social relations" that describes the colonial, racial, and sexual conditions of not only economic/monetary subject positions and relations but also our social, political, intimate, and creative relations (Crosby et al. 2012, 130). We are interested in the ways that queer (art) history projects such as these grapple with the possibility of queering this debt culture, or being and relating to debt culture in such a way that puts us into contact with its excesses—debt as holistic, as capacious, as surplus, as crisis, as always owing and being owed, as proliferating, differentiating, and unifying. By approaching debt as a cultural condition and a mode of inquiry rather than as an individualized economic problem, we can recognize an uneasy and conflicted negotiation in these works: on the one hand we owe so much to the queers of the past, we must pay tribute, give credit where credit is due, take credit, make credit, become a credit; but on the other hand we are owed so much, an incalculable debt from generations of damages suffered, an unpayable, unsettleable, and unsettling debt that we can't possess and that dispossesses us.

Following Stefano Harney and Fred Moten's articulation of the black radical tradition of bad debt—"which is to say real debt, the debt that cannot be repaid, the debt at a distance, the debt without creditor, the black debt, the queer debt, the criminal debt" (2013, 61)—we attempt to make debt "a principle of elaboration" in the long contemporary moment of queer and feminist recovery efforts (150). For Harney and Moten bad debt figures as a "fugitive" structure of feeling running through "the undercommons" in which "the debtor seeks refuge among other debtors, acquires debt from them, offers debt to them. . . . This refuge, this place of bad debt, is what we call the fugitive public" (61). Harney and Moten allow us to think about the disciplinary function of debt, about the regulatory compulsion to turn debt into credit and profit, about which debts are counted and which forgotten, and about queer, black, criminal, fugitive living in the refuge of uncountable, incalculable, unregulated, and undisciplined debt. In this essay, we read *The Fae Richards Photo Archive*, *The Watermelon Woman*, and *Rare & Raw* for the ways that they elaborate the tensions of queer(ing) debt and indebtedness.

The Fae Richards Photo Archive

The Fae Richards Photo Archive is composed of staged and artificially aged photographs that function as archival traces of the African American lesbian history that Cheryl—Dunye's main character in *The Watermelon*

FIG. 1. Zoe Leonard, *The Fae Richards Photo Archive*, 1996. Installation view, *Rare & Raw*, Leslie-Lohman Gay and Lesbian Art Museum, New York, February 15, 2013. Courtesy of the Leslie-Lohman Gay and Lesbian Art Museum.

Woman—seeks to recover. Both the photos and the film can be seen as part of what has been called "the archival turn" in queer and feminist scholarship and art practices since the mid-1990s (Cvetkovich 2012), which continues in shows like *Rare & Raw*. As Ann Cvetkovich explains, this LGBTQ turn to archives is concerned as much with recovering, saving, and revaluing artifacts or things—especially the ephemera that might be discarded as junk or trash—as with preserving and valuing feelings, especially those bad affects that tend to be deemed unproductive or useless (Cvetkovich 2003). In *The Fae Richards Photo Archive*, these trashed lives and feelings take the form of "seventy-eight gelatin silver prints, four chromogenic prints and a notebook of seven pages of typescript on paper" (Whitney Museum of American Art). The photos—a collection of snapshots, film stills, and publicity photos—are over- and underexposed, grainy, dogeared, warped, and worn to look like they have just surfaced after years of dank dusty storage. The mottled effect of the captions creates the illusion of their having been typed out long ago. The back jacket of *The Fae Richards Photo Archive* picture book explains that "by experimenting with photographic conventions and borrowing from the lives of historical figures,

Leonard and Dunye challenge lines of race, class, and sexuality in history. Although Fae Richards never lived, she is drawn from the lives of many people. Her story, although fictional, is plausible. She stands as an homage to women whose lives are not recorded" (Leonard and Dunye 1996).[2] The photos chronicle the plausible fiction of Fae Richards's life (performed by Lisa Marie Bronson) from her adolescence and early career in the 1920s to her Hollywood acting work—in which she was primarily cast in the "Mammy" role—in the 1930s and then as a leading lady in black cast "race films" of the 1940s and 1950s. They also document Richards's relationship with the wealthy, white lesbian film director Martha Page (played by Alex Juhasz), Richards's career as a lesbian nightclub singer, and the intimate life Richards shared with her longtime partner, June Walker (played by Cheryl Clarke) in the 1950s, 1960s, and 1970s. Richards's story might be read as a satisfying narrative arc from good credit (within a white cultural-economic paradigm of the Southern melodrama, in which she plays the indentured and devoted servant) to a fugitive existence of bad debt in which ultimately she refuses this casting and seeks out not only roles in race films (certainly a fugitive public if ever there was one) but also black lesbian life. The tension and pressure exerted on this narrative arc comes from *The Watermelon Woman*'s parallel story of Cheryl as she struggles to reconcile her attachment to the photos and to Fae Richards's life with her own aspirations to achieve good credit by rejecting bad debt.

The irony of removing *The Fae Richards Photo Archive* from a show on queer art history (in a museum of gay and lesbian art history) because of concerns about the work's fragility is particularly poignant when we recall the story of these photographs' first exhibition in Dunye's film. The survival of these photographs—prematurely "distressed," introduced as time-worn and tattered, retrieved from basements, back rooms, and broken shoe boxes of an older generation of friends and fans of Fae Richards—and by extension black lesbian cultural history, is presented as the product of some very necessary mishandling. For example, Cheryl discovers a stash of photographs scattered among the piles of unsorted materials heaped in cardboard boxes at the Center for Lesbian Information and Technology (C.L.I.T.)—unsorted except by city and race. The earnest volunteer archivist (played by Sarah Schulman) tells Cheryl that the "black collection" is "very separate. . . . If we have any photographs that there are white people in, we just cross them out." At this point in the film, Cheryl learns that Fae Richards and the white movie director, Martha Page, were lovers just as Cheryl is starting a relationship with Diana, a classic model of blithe white privilege and cultural capital (played by Guinevere Turner, of *Go Fish* fame). The impossibility of imagining interracial lesbian histories is played for laughs in this scene, but the hilarious punch line turns out to be the effort to archive black lesbian histories at all (a point we'll return to). Cheryl is sternly informed that she most certainly may not reproduce the photographs "without the consensus-based approval of the board, which meets only every other month. Not content to wait [and despite being urged to 'respect your sisters'] she illegally documents the images with her video camera" (Cvetkovich 2002, 108). That is, Cheryl is compelled—by a disorganized, inefficient, and segregationist joke/parody of the Lesbian Herstory Archive—to disrespect her "sisters" and steal (a copy of) the photographs, repossessing these traces of history from obscurity and neglect by putting them back into a cultural economy of productive circulation (in Cheryl's life story, Dunye's film, and ultimately, queer feminist popular culture).

We meet more of these photographs through Fae Richards's dying lover, June Walker, who had collected treasures from their twenty-year relationship in a tattered paper folder, before passing it on to Cheryl, with a letter: "I was so mad that you mentioned the name of Martha Page. Why do you even want to include a white woman in a movie on Fae's life? . . . Please Cheryl, make our history before we are all dead and gone. But if you are really in 'the family,' you better understand that our family will always only have each other." But when Cheryl finally presents her documentary, played during the closing credits of Dunye's film, she does include Martha Page in Fae Richards's biography, explaining to us and to June, "I know she meant the world to you, but she also meant the world to me, and those worlds are different. . . . What she means to me, a twenty-five-year-old black woman, means something else. It means hope. It means inspiration. It means possibility. It means history. And most importantly what I understand is that I'm going to be the one who says, I am a black lesbian filmmaker, who's just beginning, but I'm going to say a lot more and have a lot more work to do." Cheryl builds an identity, "black lesbian filmmaker," and the conditions for its longevity and futurity—"who's just beginning"—through what Dunye figures as the deliberate mishandling of *The Fae Richards Archive*, against the wishes of June and the direction of the C.L.I.T.

The Watermelon Woman

As Kara Keeling argues, Cheryl's identity and its future are negotiated within the requirements of economic viability: "her professional aspirations demand that she articulate herself into the emergent market category of 'black lesbian filmmaker' in a way that will register within the terms of that market" (2005, 223). Cheryl's final documentary, along with the film's promotional materials, shows that this emergent-market category and economic subject depend on disarticulating "black lesbian filmmaker" from other black lesbians. Fae's relationship with Martha is foregrounded, while June's much longer relationship with Fae is "relegated via the voice-over narrative to the status of 'special friend'" (224). Similarly, the film's promotional materials feature Dunye and Turner as the film's "stars," excluding Valerie Walker, the black actor who plays Cheryl's best friend, Tamara, and who commands at least as much story line and screen time as Turner's character, Diana: "Fae's relationship with June, the way she sang for the [black] 'stone butches' in the bar, etc., do not appear to be part of the past that enables Cheryl to find 'hope,' 'inspiration,' or her 'history.' . . . It is via the logic of an interracial 'lesbian' relationship that the first 'black lesbian feature film' to be picked up for distribution appears" (224, 223). That is, the "black lesbian filmmaker" as an economically viable subject position, with history, longevity, futurity, and the possibility for distribution and circulation within systems of cultural and monetary capital, depends on both Cheryl's calculated mistreatment of *The Fae Richards Photo Archive* and her performance of distinction from other black lesbians in the film. Cheryl is trading debt for credit.

Despite Cheryl's performance of distinction, the subject position of economic viability that she embodies is never fully her own, and she is compelled to negotiate the ongoing legacies of state administered black dispossession and expropriation. In the scene directly following Diana's postcoital inventory of all her black boyfriends, Cheryl is misrecognized by the police as a young black man and gets arrested for being a "crackhead" and "on suspicion of stolen property"; the police officers (one white and one black), unable to conceive of a "black lesbian filmmaker," refuse to believe that a young black person of any gender or sexual orientation would have access to the capital or credit to legitimately purchase an expensive movie camera. Even with good credit, Cheryl is treated as a bad debtor. The carceral politics here, motivated by the generalized assumption of black poverty, reflect what Saidya Hartman has identified as black lives that are "still imperiled and devalued by a racial calculus and a political arithmetic that were entrenched centuries ago" (1997, 6). Indeed, as Hartman's work has shown, since the first efforts toward U.S. federally conferred "freedom," the right to personhood in the immediate postbellum period, free black subjecthood has been cast as indebted to the state: "the burden of debt, duty, and gratitude [was] foisted onto the newly emancipated in exchange or repayment for their freedom. . . . Thus, the transition from slavery to freedom introduced the free agent to the circuits of exchange through this construction of already accrued debt, an abstinent present, and a mortgaged future. In short, to be free was to be a debtor" (1997, 130–1). *The Watermelon Woman* suggests that the moral, legal, and affective structures of indebtedness continue to condition the possibilities for viable black subjectivities and, as Chakravartty and da Silva note, provide "a racial architecture in which postracial discourse and neoliberal practices combine to exact even more profit from the very penury resulting from the expropriation unleashed in previous moments and modalities of racial and colonial subjugation" (2012, 364). Indeed, in our contemporary stop-and-frisk, post-2008 moment of unequally distributed and racialized precarity and foreclosure, *The Watermelon Woman* seems importantly situated within our long moment of racial and colonial penury, in which the young black subject is always on the verge of, or in danger of, being called upon to "pay a debt to society" in the form of fines, imprisonment, and interest rates spiked for "high-risk borrowers."

When we look at Cheryl's performance of distinction through the lens of debt culture, of foreclosure and repossession, of market value and economic viability, and by allowing the *Rare & Raw* episode in the history of *The Fae Richards Photo Archive* to inform a new reading of the film, we see that debt logics function as the organizing principle, moral compass, and totalizing affect throughout. The film is framed by negotiations about payment, fairness, and questions about (black) queer temporalities. In the opening scene of *The Watermelon Woman*, Tamara and Cheryl are filming a fairly posh interracial wedding party. At the end of their shoot, the two friends are paid by a matronly white woman; Cheryl collects the envelope and then doles out Tamara's cut. The dialogue that follows establishes the film's debt logics:

TAMARA: Oooo, I love cash.

CHERYL: I don't like cash. I like checks. But this will have to do, okay? Can I use the equipment this weekend to work on my project?

TAMARA: You know, this is the third weekend in a row you want to use the equipment, but you've yet to shoot anything. Uh, my cut is fifty dollars short.

CHERYL: You remember what Rose and Guin said in the *Go Fish* book. If you want to make a film, you gotta make some sacrifices. Besides, we have to make money payments on the camera. Ticket to Hollywood, baby!

TAMARA: Uh, excuse you. I'm not into making sacrifices for some quote-unquote "future," all right? I want to take Stacey out this weekend for dinner and for that I need cash *today*. Okay? So just give me my money and cut the attitude.

CHERYL: I'll lend you some money.

TAMARA: Lend me some money? You gonna lend me my own damn money? You worse than white people in the bank.

CHERYL: Oh my god, it's raining.

TAMARA: I don't care if it's raining. Give me my damn money. What does one gotta do with the other? (Dunye 1996)

Here we see Cheryl as the financial administrator of her friendship/ small business with Tamara, but Tamara resists the terms that Cheryl sets. Tamara loves (untraceable, accessible) cash, while Cheryl prefers the more official scrip of a check. Tamara has no interest in savings or repayment plans, and she wants money for today, to take her girlfriend out, to spend on pleasure in the moment. Cheryl models good credit behavior by withholding a portion of Tamara's fee to cover the cost of their camera payments and, by offering to lend Tamara money, introduces a credit-debt relationality and moral evaluative framework into the friendship, which Tamara refuses. Unlike Cheryl, Tamara seems unfettered by the burden of indebtedness, duty, or obligation, embodying the bad debtor who refuses "to replace the love of leisure with the love of gain and supplant the bawdy pleasures with dispassionate acquisitiveness" (Hartman 1997, 127).

Indeed, rather than seeking out good credit as the condition for respectability, Tamara models Harney and Moten's bad queer black debt—portrayed here as a "means of socialisation" (2013, 61); that is, to live in/with bad debt is "not simply to be among his own; but to be among his own in dispossession, to be among the ones who cannot own, the ones who have nothing and who, in having nothing, have everything" (96). In her orientation to immanent pleasure, Tamara refuses what Hartman calls an "abstinent present and a mortgaged future" (Hartman 1997, 131) and moves toward the "fugitive public" of bad debtors, "debt at a distance to a global politics of blackness emerging out of slavery and colonialism, a black radical politics, a politics of debt without payment, without credit, without limit. . . . [This debt] is still shared, never credited and never abiding credit, a debt you play, a debt you walk, a debt you love" (Harney and Moten 2013, 64). Tamara takes no interest in sacrificing for "some quote-unquote 'future,'" refuses to subject her debt to credit, and throughout the film plays her debt as love (or sex).

The differing relationships with the duty of indebtedness are cast as the conflict through which Cheryl establishes economic subjecthood—with Tamara as a bad black debtor, June framing black queer history as shared debt, and Cheryl emerging as one who seeks abiding credit, situating her debt as the responsibility to profit from the past in order to secure her marketable future. However, as Keeling explains, Dunye's film "allows for a different possibility to be perceived. . . . That possibility might collect the 'stone butches,' the 'special friends,' 'the studs,' 'the femmes,' the 'woman-lovers,' and 'the queers' that were part of the working-class milieu to which Fae Richards herself belonged and make those ambivalent, destabilizing and unstable forces of desire and community cohere as a collective expression of a multifarious 'we' that complicates any innocent notion of 'the one' who says, 'I am a black lesbian filmmaker'" (2007, 224). This 'multifarious we' is the fugitive public of the undercommons, the refuge of bad debt that Cheryl resists, Tamara figures, and the film makes palpable even as its economic and cultural viability depend on betraying debt's "principle of social life" (Harney and Moten 2013, 153) and playing by the rules of credit. By enacting the tensions between the individual aspirational drive to credit and the pull of "bawdy pleasures" in common mutual debt, *The Watermelon Woman* raises the possibility of a destabilized, ambivalent, complicated, and queered debt culture.

Rare & Raw: Queer History Now and Then

The removal of *The Fae Richards Photo Archive* from the *Rare & Raw* exhibit, and its replacement with the foreclosure installation, prompted us to consider whether the gay and lesbian archival turn—the history-making impulse—is a symptom of the will to credit in debt culture, a will to respectability in a racist, homophobic culture. Up to this point, we have read *The Fae Richards Photo Archive* and its original exhibition in *The Watermelon Woman* through the interpretive framework of debt—the punitively racialized logics of credit and reclaimed bad debt as refuge—which allows us to recognize the disciplinary compulsion to betray, abandon, or escape the unmarketable or worthless. By bringing this elaborative interpretive framework to the *Rare & Raw* exhibition, we experience the contradictory impulses to pursue good credit and preserve bad debt as what Elizabeth Freeman calls a queer temporal "dialectics of feeling," that is, as an aestheticized "political unconscious consisting not only of repressed social conflict but also and crucially . . . effaced or foreclosed social bonds" (2010, 127). *Rare & Raw* curators Steph Rogerson and Kelly McCray pair contemporary pieces with artworks from an earlier generation to foreground the tensions between past and present, between the will to abandon, efface, or surpass our disreputable, irresponsible, useless, criminal histories and the present fact that we can't, haven't, and perhaps don't want to, a dialectics of feeling between the political unconscious of credit—let's call it the specter of respectability—and the foreclosed social bonds of bad debt.

These dialectics resonate throughout the exhibition. On the title wall, works by G. B. Jones and Tom of Finland are juxtaposed with Nina Levitt's life-sized diptych of Calamity Jane.[3] Paired sketches from G. B. Jones's *Prison Breakout* series (1991) and Tom of Finland's *Jailhouse* series (1987) depict queer sex between prison inmates and guards in a variety of configurations, bringing into focus the ways in which social, moral, and legal indebtedness are so often tied up with what Lauren Berlant and Michael Warner have famously called "criminal intimacies" (2000, 322). These intimacies "bear no necessary relation to domestic space, to kinship, to the couple form, to property, or to the nation" (322). In their plural configurations of threesomes, foursomes, and other orgy fantasies, these images of a proliferating vilified queer subject revel in erotic attachments to the bad debtor and encourage us to fantasize our way to their fugitive publics.

The works by G. B. Jones and Tom of Finland are small in comparison with Levitt's *Calamity* (1991), a photographic study of a subject who lived as much as possible outside the law. Levitt's portrait functions as a commentary on the selective project of queer history-making: three circular "portholes" (covering her gun, her knee, and her boot) are obscured by black exposed photographic paper in the image on the left; the image on the right is entirely black exposed photo paper with only the area of those three holes revealed. Levitt gives us a visual depiction of the exclusionary processes of our history-making, wherein some (white settler colonial) queer outlaws are remembered and cherished, while others are demonized, disowned, rendered invisible, or jailed. *Calamity* is in conversation with Kent Monkman's portraits of his Indian Princess drag persona, Miss Chief Eagle Testickle (from the 2006 series, *Emergence of a Legend*), another form of criminally indebted queer subjectivity, installed on the facing wall. Monkman's works "emulate nineteenth-century antique daguerreotypes [and] recall the history of early photographic portraiture, the Wild West, and colonization" (Rogerson and McCray 2013). These portraits remind us of our unpaid and unpayable settler colonial debts and of the acts of violence obscured by our selective celebrations of outlaws like Calamity Jane. Monkman's playful drag persona performs a sort of queer anticolonial Indigeneity, guiding us through the ways that Indigenous sexualities and cultures are both eroticized and demonized (Anderson 2004), regulated and disciplined through settler colonialism, and criminalized through enforced poverty and symbolic annihilation (Morgensen 2011). Furthermore, the femininities composed for these daguerreotypes gesture toward the ways that Indigenous and Métis women were forced to trade their land and culture for credit under Canada's "civilizing" process of applying for "scrip," a symbolic transfer through which the government gave them land "that had already been theirs from time immemorial" and in return, they "relinquished all future claims to [their] rights as . . . 'Treaty Indian'" (Adese 2011, 204). Monkman's delicate portraits of the feminized queerness of Cree-Métis subjectivities amend these histories of dispossession and, instead of being overshadowed by Levitt's large diptych of Calamity Jane's celebrated white Wild West butch criminality, materialize the racial logics of colonial exclusion that impel us to aggrandize certain figures, forms, and moments of queer history at the expense of others.

William E. Jones's *Tearoom* (1962/2007), a fifty-six-minute film screened on a loop and projected against the back wall of the middle installation space, uses edited footage of a 1962 police surveillance operation, which captures sex between men in a public restroom in Mansfield, Ohio. Filmed from behind a two-way mirror, the footage shows the sexual exchanges (money sometimes changed hands) and intimate, stolen moments before these men were arrested, and later incarcerated, for sodomy. Installed on the two facing walls of this middle space are Will Munro's mirrors from his *Blank Generation Series* (2005), silkscreened with hot-pink logos of "iconic underground club scenes [from the 1970s, 1980s, and 1990s] decimated by time and the catastrophic march of AIDS" (Rogerson and McCray 2013).

In the contemporary U.S. context of mass incarceration and the long moment of HIV/AIDS, these two pieces demand that we see ourselves in these painful and shimmering histories and consider the status of our intimacies in conditions of unequally distributed precariousness. This installation requires us to ask, whose queer fugitive intimacies are being policed today? In a history of "stolen moments," as queer histories tend to be, from whom or from what are these moments stolen? Who is configured today as owing a "debt to society" and what does it mean to be criminalized? As Michelle Alexander writes in *The New Jim Crow*, "In major cities [in the United States] as many as 80 per cent of young African American men now have criminal records and are thus subject to legalized discrimination for the rest of their lives" (2010, 7). In the racialized logics of criminalization today, aspirational white gays, lesbians, and trans* people "in committed relationships" (to each other, to the state, and to economic futurity) are now predominantly figured in the homonationalist imaginary as "law abiding" citizens and thus in the carceral economy as debt-free and creditworthy. But, as Dean Spade puts it, when we think of "the origins of contemporary gay and lesbian rights formation in anti-police activism in the 1960s and 70s," who would have predicted that the legacy of this activism would lead to "a neoliberal 'law and order' approach . . . that provides millions of dollars to enhance police and prosecutorial resources?" (2011, 88–89). As Spade suggests, and as Dunye's Cheryl demonstrates, the quest for respectability requires trading debt for credit and compromising the radical politics of bad, queer, black debt, and the fugitive publics from which their viability and marketablilty emerged in the first place. Rather than showcasing the triumph of debt-free queers, *Rare & Raw* offers viewfinder glimpses of our own belonging in the undercommons of inmates, decolonized Indian Princesses, and sodomites.

FIG. 2. The foreclosure installation, 2013. Documentation of the correspondence pertaining to the loan of *The Fae Richards Photo Archive* to the Leslie-Lohman Museum for *Rare & Raw*. Courtesy of the Leslie-Lohman Gay and Lesbian Art Museum.

Conclusion

In the opening scene of *The Watermelon Woman*, Tamara asks Cheryl (who has just changed the topic to weather, diverting attention away from her siphoning money out of Tamara's pay), "What does one thing gotta do with the other?" The question we ask here, What does debt culture have to do with queer history?, was generated by the unfortunate and yet strangely fortuitous repossession of *The Fae Richards Photo Archive*, which activated our recognition of debt as a proliferating structure of dialectical feelings that impels, saturates, and entangles "queer histories now and then." While the presence of *The Fae Richards Photo Archive* in the *Rare & Raw* exhibit might have initiated and staged a very different conversation—about the aesthetics of recovery and our fantasies for longevity, repayment plans, "making it right," and trading debt for good credit—its absence, we have argued here, informs a more conflicted engagement with the queer "archival turn," and what it means to queer debt as a creative, critical, interpretive project. The foreclosure installation scattered debt everywhere—backward in time to *The Watermelon Woman* and across the gallery to the rest of *Rare & Raw*. By following the capacious flight of debt beyond the incident of the amended loan, we start to see it everywhere, hear it everywhere, feel it everywhere. Queering debt requires tuning into the violent histories of credit's uneven distribution across the modern/colonial order of race and class and seeing, hearing, and feeling the refuge of owning nothing and owing everything.

Acknowledgments

We would like to thank Steph Rogerson, Hunter O'Hanian, and Zoe Leonard for the time they took to speak with us about the exhibit. We would also like to thank Alex Juhasz for sending us a working version of the script for *The Watermelon Woman* and for a helpful conversation about the film.

T. L. Cowan teaches performance studies and cultural studies at Eugene Lang College and the School of Media Studies at The New School University in New York City and is a Hemispheric Fellow at the Hemispheric Institute of Performance and Politics in the Americas at New York University.

Jasmine Rault is an assistant professor of cultural studies at Eugene Lang College at The New School University in New York City.

Notes

1. In conversations and correspondence with the curators of *Rare & Raw*, Steph Rogerson and Kelly McCray, the director of the Leslie-Lohman Museum, Hunter O'Hanian, and Zoe Leonard, we learned that there was some miscommunication about how *The Fae Richards Photo Archive* would be hung and exhibited for *Rare & Raw* and that despite efforts on all sides to care for the material fragility of the photographs, on the opening day of the exhibition the loan of the Archive was unilaterally renegotiated by the current owner of the work, the Eileen Harris Norton Collection. While the museum's standard contract asks whether the loaned works require directions for "special handling or installation," the museum provides no evidence that any such directions were received. The contract does show that the works were originally loaned to the museum from February 15 to March 17, 2013. However, the posted documents show that on February 15, the day of the exhibit opening, a letter was issued by Sean Shim-Boyle, collection manager for the Eileen Harris Norton Collection, "amending the loan," indicating that the

unframed components of the work would be repossessed immediately and that the framed photographs might be displayed until February 18, at which time they, too, would be removed from the exhibit. O'Hanian asserted that the Leslie-Lohman Museum would have "moved heaven and earth" to install the piece in accordance with the artist's wishes and found the entire situation "regrettable." And Leonard offered another work to be hung in the place of *The Fae Richards Photo Archive*. As of March 22, the artworks were still crated and awaiting shipment in the offices of the Leslie-Lohman Museum, presumably accumulating "interest."

2. After the film was released, the photos were collected in a small art book, *The Fae Richards Photo Archive*, produced by Dunye and Leonard (1996). The work was included in the 1997 Whitney Biennial in New York and was exhibited in a broad range of venues throughout its almost twenty-year history. There are only three sets of *The Fae Richards Photo Archive*, two in private collections and one in the Whitney's permanent collection.

3. Images of the artworks in *Rare & Raw* can be viewed at the Leslie-Lohman Museum website (http://www.leslielohman.org/exhibitions/2013/rare-and-raw.html).

Works Cited

Adese, Jennifer. 2011. "'R' Is for Métis: Contradictions in Scrip and Census in the Construction of a Colonial Métis Identity." *TOPIA: Canadian Journal of Cultural Studies* 25 (Spring): 203–12.

Alexander, Michelle. 2010. *The New Jim Crow: Mass Incarceration in the Age of Colorblindness*. New York: New Press.

Anderson, Kim. 2004. "The Construction of Negative Identity." In *Feminisms and Womanisms: A Women's Studies Reader*, ed. Prince Althea, Silva-Wayne Susan, and Christian Vernon, 229–238. Toronto, ON: Canadian Scholars' Press.

Berlant, Lauren, and Michael Warner. 2000. "Sex in Public." In *Intimacy*, ed. Lauren Berlant, 311–330. Chicago: University of Chicago Press Journals.

Chakravartty, Paula, and Denise Ferreira da Silva. 2012. "Accumulation, Dispossession, and Debt: The Racial Logic of Global Capitalism—an Introduction." *American Quarterly* 64(3): 361–85.

Crosby, Christina, Lisa Duggan, Roderick Ferguson, Kevin Floyd, Miranda Joseph, Heather Love, Robert McRuer, Fred Moten, Tavia Nyong'o, Lisa Rofel, Jordana Rosenberg, Gayle Salamon, Dean Spade, and Amy Villarejo. 2012. "Queer Studies, Materialism, and Crisis: A Roundtable Discussion." *GLQ: A Journal of Gay and Lesbian Studies* 18(1):127–47.

Cvetkovich, Ann. 2002. "In the Archives of Lesbian Feelings: Documentary and Popular Culture." *Camera Obscura* 17(1):1–147.

———. 2003. *An Archive of Feelings: Trauma, Sexuality, and Lesbian Public Cultures*. Durham: Duke University Press.

———. 2012. "Queer Archival Futures: Case Study Los Angeles." *E-misférica* (9.1–9.2).

Dunye, Cheryl. 1996. *The Watermelon Woman*. First-Run Features.

Freeman, Elizabeth. 2010. *Time Binds: Queer Temporalities, Queer Histories*. Durham: Duke University Press Books.

Hartman, Saidiya V. 1997. *Scenes of Subjection: Terror, Slavery, and Self-Making in Nineteenth-Century America*. New York: Oxford University Press.

Keeling, Kara. 2005. "'Joining the Lesbians': Cinematic Regimes of Black Lesbian Visibility," *Black Queer Studies: A Critical Anthology*, ed. E. Patrick Johnson, Mae G. Henderson, 213–227. Durham: Duke University Press.

Leonard, Zoe, and Cheryl Dunye. 1996. *The Fae Richards Photo Archive*. San Francisco: Artspace Books.

Morgensen, Scott Lauria. 2011. "Unsettling Queer Politics: What Can Non-Natives Learn from Two-Spirit Organizing?" In *Queer Indigenous Studies: Critical Interventions in Theory, Politics, and Literature*, ed. Qwo-li Driskill, Chris Finley, Brian Joseph Gilley, and Scott Lauria Morgensen, 132–52. Tucson: University of Arizona Press.

Harney, Stefano, and Fred Moten. 2013. *The Undercommons: Fugitive Planning and Black Study*. New York: Minor Compositions.

"Rare & Raw: The 2013 Queer Caucus Exhibition for the College Art Association." Press release. Leslie-Lohman Museum of Gay and Lesbian Art. http://leslielohman.org/about/press-release/2013/rare-and-raw-pr.html.

Rogerson, Steph, and Kelly McCray. 2013. Installation panels, *Rare & Raw: Queer History Then and Now*, Leslie-Lohman Museum of Gay and Lesbian Art, New York.

Shim-Boyle, Sean. "To Whom It May Concern" letter to the Leslie-Lohman Museum. February 15, 2013.

Spade, Dean. 2011. *Normal life: Administrative violence, critical trans politics, and the limits of law*. Cambridge: South End Press.

Whitney Museum of American Art. "Collection: Zoe Leonard; B. 1961; *The Fae Richards Photo Archive, 1993–96*." http://whitney.org/Collection/ZoeLeonard.

March 1969

Airea D. Matthews

Seated in the pews the best man whose arms draped the groom's shoulders
Passed a flask of hundred-proof grain from inside his tuxedo pocket

A mother fondled her fake pearls, walked the aisles trying to find a soloist
Asked the guests: *Who can sing His Eyes Are On the Sparrow? Amazing
Grace?*

Across town

On Hanover Street, in the YWCA's bathroom, a woman in lace
Huddled on the floor of an end stall; she heard the lobby phone

Ring incessantly; the receptionist on the intercom trumpeted her name
She balled up wads of Angel Soft around her hand, blew her nose;

Reapplied Maybelline every hour or so just in case the pressure of
Gowns, maids, her mother's second mortgage, florists, soloists

My sister's twitch
Forced her hand

At 3:15, three hours late

WSQ: Women's Studies Quarterly 42: 1 & 2 (Spring/Summer 2014) © 2014 by Airea D. Matthews. All
rights reserved.

She lifted her head off the toilet seat, called a yellow taxi to pick her up
While she waited one of the homeless women touched her shoulder:

It's better for the baby, honey

Once she arrived at church, she tripped walking down the altar
Busted her knee wide open, bled through her stockings, her garter

Her groom, many swigs in, balanced by his best men, hunched over
Her mother, at the ready, ran and lifted her daughter so odd voyeurs

Could witness a bride settle
Her lean dowry

Airea D. Matthews is a Cave Canem and Callaloo fellow as well as a Zéll Postgraduate Poetry Fellow at the University of Michigan. She was a 2013 Pushcart Prize nominee and was awarded the 2011 Michael R. Gutterman Prize in Poetry. She holds a BA in economics from the University of Pennsylvania, an MPA from the Ford School of Public Policy, and an MFA in poetry from the University of Michigan. Currently at work on her first full-length poetry collection, she lives in Detroit.

Hermeneutics

Amy Lawless

Employees gathered in the auditorium. They pulled notebooks and pens from briefcases and leather portfolios. Those satisfied with their year-end bonuses partook of the coffee service, which lined the rear wall. Eventually an elephant walked on stage behind a podium and took a giant dump. The size of the dump is not crucial. This prompted some people to help themselves to the pastries, but most just kept watching. One intern hotly fingered the corporate logo embroidered onto her leather folio. The elephant stood not moving and then crashed over and died. Some people stood up; some ran from the room. Some just had that *condom broke* look about their faces. Everyone looked around for someone to take control of the situation. Some thought the elephant just needed a doctor. Others were certain of its death. My father stood up and addressed the crowd: *No. This recently happened at Hermeneutics Corporation. Sure, it's shocking, but this was the expected outcome. Everyone will be fine. Just fine.*

Amy Lawless is the author of two collections of poetry, most recently *My Dead* (Octopus Books, 2013). Her collaborations with Angela Veronica Wong appeared in *Pinwheel* and *Best American Poetry 2013*. In 2011 she was a New York Foundation for the Arts fellow. She lives in New York City.

PART VII. **ALERTS AND PROVOCATIONS**

The Discreet Transient

Janet Yoon

Janet Yoon is an architect based in Los Angeles, co-founder of the design research collective Local Provisions Studio, and currently teaches as an adjunct faculty at Woodbury University. Her work examines the socio-economic-political fringe to remotely sense the durability of contemporary urban space-making. She is also interested in the role of real-time in architecture as a potential platform for calibrating inequities in the American power structure. Her current research is situated in remote locations in the American West as well as the economically recalibrated landscape of contemporary suburbia.

The Formerly Middle Class[1] (FMC) nomenclature is used to describe a subset of the population once operating within a middle-class lifestyle, driven from that economic milieu during the financial and housing foreclosure crisis beginning in the late 2000s. Often living in cars or in temporary housing, this subset does not identify with the traditional definition of "homeless," and strives to recreate their domestic landscape within the suburban places they are familiar with, or aspire to belong to. The FMC struggle to retain the appearances of their social status, counting on the temporariness of this difficult economic conjuncture.

The FMC's way of inhabiting the middle class suburban environment is rooted in an expertise that allows for inconspicuousness. They avoid shelters and other amenities that would identify them as homeless and spend already thinly spread resources on avoiding detection and blending in within the middle-class milieu. The FMC constantly roam and evaluate the fitness of a space or a schedule for use. They maximize the possibility of spaces that are taken for granted and are considered unexceptional and uncomplex.

1. David Brooks, "The Formerly Middle Class," *The New York Times* (November 2008), accessed February 28, 2013, http://www.nytimes.com/2008/11/18/opinion/18brooks.html?_r=0.

A day in the life of the FMC: Sleep in car – 24 Hour Fitness/YMCA for workout/shower – work if employed or library with free wifi if unemployed – UPS, Fedex, or post-office mailbox to collect bills/correspondence – Hospital parking lot or Walmart parking lot. Motel on weekly rate if income is sufficient. Other places: Laundromat/dry cleaners, coffee shop, fast food restaurant, college/university campus. Daily tasks include shower and charging mobile phone.

The FMC's understanding of the city is situational, and takes full advantage
of slack spaces that may go unnoticed, at least for a while. They demonstrate
a paradigm shift in defining the boundaries of shared communal and public
spaces. No longer limited to outdoor spaces and public amenities, the
expanded definition of communal space now includes zones of operational
slack in suburban infrastructure, online communities, and shared real-time

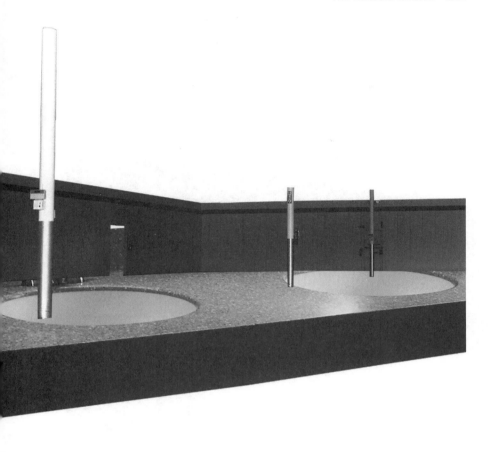

information. The FMC are constantly on the move to find ideal locations that allow them to avoid identification. Hospital parking lots afford relatively safe rest, with the FMC slipping in under the pretense that they are waiting on a sick family member inside. Streets with no sidewalks, no overlooking windows, or adjacent woods reduce foot traffic and provide opportunities to enter and exit the car without detection. This brings up the issue of schedule – knowing when to be where and how long one can reside in a slack space, undisturbed and undetected. College campuses and facilities may be accessed if the individual has a good understanding of how a college campus is staffed and maintained – or is the kind of person that would have information about how to use these spaces. Big retailer parking lots allow

vehicles to park overnight. Often times, residue from their previous lives keep the FMC afloat, like pre-paid gym memberships, mailboxes, and knowledge of facilities with public access. Hygiene is important, and it inserts an everyday-life structure into the uncertainties and constant movement of individuals – the shower becomes a hub. The FMC loiter not around street corners, but around gyms and free wifi. And the use of technology to communicate, anonymously, with others and to obtain information allows the FMC to control the degree of isolation that they may experience.